Best KeyWords for Resumes, Cover Letters, and Interviews

By Wendy S. Enelow

100 Winning Cover Letters for $100,000+ Jobs

100 Winning Resumes for $100,000+ Jobs

101 Ways to Recession-Proof Your Career

1500+ Keywords for $100,000+ Jobs

Best KeyWords for Resumes, Covers Letters, and Interviews

Best Cover Letters for $100,000+ Jobs

Best Resumes and CVs for International Jobs

Best Resumes for $100,000+ Jobs

Best Resumes for People Without a Four-Year Degree

Cover Letter Magic

Expert Resumes for Computer and Web Jobs

Expert Resumes for Managers and Executives

Expert Resumes for Manufacturing Careers

Expert Resumes for People Returning to Work

Expert Resumes for Teachers and Educators

Resume Winners From the Pros

Winning Interviews for $100,000+ Jobs

THE AUTHOR: Wendy S. Enelow is a recognized leader in the executive job search, career coaching and resume writing industries. In private practice for 20 years, she has assisted thousands of job search candidates through successful career transitions. She is now the Founder and President of the Career Masters Institute, an exclusive training and development association for career professionals worldwide. A graduate of the University of Maryland, Wendy has earned several distinguished professional credentials – Certified Professional Resume Writer (CPRW), Job and Career Transition Coach (JCTC), and Credentialed Career Master (CCM). Wendy can be contacted at wendyenelow@cminstitute.com.

Best *KeyWords*
For **Resumes,**
Cover Letters,
and **Interviews**

POWERFUL COMMUNICATION TOOLS FOR SUCCESS

Wendy S. Enelow, CPRW, JCTC, CCM

IMPACT PUBLICATIONS
Manassas Park, Virginia

ISBN: 1-57023-195-8

Library of Congress: 2002115034

Publisher: For information on Impact Publications, including current and forthcoming publications, authors, press kits, online bookstore, and submission requirements, visit our website: www.impactpublications.com.

Publicity/Rights: For information on publicity, author interviews, and subsidiary rights, contact the Media Relations Department: Tel. 703-361-7300, Fax 703-335-9486, or email: info@impactpublications.com.

Sales/Distribution: All bookstore sales are handled through Impact's trade distributor: National Book Network, 15200 NBN Way, Blue Ridge Summit, PA 17214, Tel. 1-800-462-6420. All other sales and distribution inquiries should be directed to the publisher: Sales Department, IMPACT PUBLICATIONS, 9104 Manassas Drive, Suite N, Manassas Park, VA 20111-5211, Tel. 703-361-7300, Fax 703-335-9486, or email: info@impactpublications.com.

Contents

Best KeyWords for Resumes, Cover Letters, and Interviews

1

Introduction

KeyWord: The "hot" words associated with a specific industry, profession, or job function ... generally a noun, short phrase, abbreviation, or acronym. When used effectively, a KeyWord or KeyWord phrase can communicate an entire message with just a simple word or two.

FIVE YEARS AGO no one had ever heard of KeyWords, let alone KeyWord scanning. The concept of KeyWords and the technology to support their use had just begun to penetrate the employment and job search market. At its onset, KeyWord scanning really only impacted those individuals in the technology and related industries.

KeyWords Are Everywhere

Today, however, KeyWords are everywhere – in every industry and every profession – and must be a vital component of each and every job seeker's campaign. Consider these frequent observations:

- You talk to a resume writer, recruiter, career coach, career counselor, outplacement consultant, or human resources professional, and each of them stresses the importance of KeyWords in today's competitive job search market.

1

- You read an article on the latest employment trends, and the focus of the article is on the Internet and KeyWord Scanning.

- You attend a job search training seminar, and the facilitator stresses how critical KeyWords are when writing a great resume and "nailing" your interviews.

- You listen to a CNN news broadcast about the latest employment trends, and the reporter highlights the importance of KeyWords in today's electronic job search market.

- You purchase a book on resume writing, cover letter writing, job searching or interviewing, and the focus of each book is on KeyWords and how vital they are to your successful job search campaign.

- You search the Internet for job leads and postings, and virtually every ad instructs you to include the appropriate KeyWords in your resume, cover letter, and other job search communications.

Answers to KeyWord Questions

Ask yourself these questions as you prepare your resume and letters and prep for the job interview:

- What are KeyWords and where did they come from?

- Where do I put KeyWords in my resume?

- Where do I put KeyWords in my cover letter?

- How do I use KeyWords in my job search interviews?

- What is all the talk about KeyWords and resume scanning?

- Which KeyWords are right for me, my profession, and my industry?

Best KeyWords for Resumes, Cover Letters, and Interviews provides answers to these and many more questions about KeyWords in today's job market. It is the first comprehensive guide on the subject of

KeyWords and their use throughout the entire job search process. Designed for all types of job seekers, regardless of age, occupation, or experience level, this book will teach you how to use KeyWords to create a focused, repetitive, and employer-centered communication process throughout your entire job search campaign.

Coming Up

The following chapters are organized into three distinct sections:

1. Introduction (Chapter 1)

Addresses the importance of KeyWords and how to use them throughout all phases of your job search – resume writing, cover letter writing, and job interviews. Chapter 1 also includes information that is critical to KeyWord scanning and how to optimize its results for you and your job search.

2. KeyWords by Industry & Profession (Chapters 2-24)

These chapters are the heart of this book, giving you a comprehensive listing of more than 1,000 KeyWords for all major industries and professions. Each KeyWord and KeyWord phrase is presented in a sentence to demonstrate its use and the message it conveys to your reader.

3. Action Verbs, High-Impact Phrases & Personality Descriptors (Chapter 25)

This chapter includes more than 500 Action Verbs, High-Impact Phrases, and Personality Descriptors for use in developing your resume and cover letter content, and for all of your interviews. Review these lists carefully, select the words and phrases that accurately reflect your career, qualifications, and experience, and then incorporate them into all aspects of your search campaign.

KeyWords and Their Origins

KeyWords are nothing new. In fact, you've probably used many of them throughout your entire working life. They are buzz words – the "hot" words associated with a specific industry, profession, or job function – that clearly communicate a specific message about a specific job function, qualification, accomplishment, or responsibility. KeyWords are best defined as nouns, noun phrases, abbreviations, or acronyms ... words such as "benefits plan design" (for Human Resources), "market share ratings" (for Marketing), "new business development" (for Sales), "logistics management" (for Transportation), "SAP" (for Manufacturing), and "platform architecture" (for Information Technology).

Today, trends in resume writing, interviewing, hiring, and employment in general have changed, greatly influenced by the tremendous competition in the job search market and the recent difficult economic times. To be effective in your job search and catch an employer's interest, your resumes and cover letters must be action-driven and clearly demonstrate the value you bring to a company. And, there is no better manner in which to accomplish this than with the use of powerful KeyWords and KeyWord phrases that showcase your qualifications, capabilities, and skills. KeyWords get you noticed, not passed over.

To further help you understand the concept of KeyWords and their powerful use, here is a sample listing of KeyWords for the primary industries and professions outlined in this book:

Industry/Profession	KeyWord/KeyWord Phrase
Administration	Office Management
Association Management	Member Retention
Banking	Debt & Equity Financing
Customer Service	Customer Loyalty
Engineering	Project Management
Finance	Treasury Administration
General Management	P&L Management
Health Care	Acute Care
Hospitality	F&B Outlets
Human Resources	Compensation
Human Services	Client Advocacy
Information Technology	Webcasting
International Business	Emerging Markets
Law & Legal Affairs	Intellectual Property
Manufacturing	Process Automation
Marketing	Competitive Intelligence
Public Relations	Crisis Communications
Purchasing	Vendor Sourcing
Real Estate	Industrial Development
Retail	Merchandising
Sales	New Product Introduction

Security	VIP Protection
Senior Management	World-Class Organization
Teaching & Education	Curriculum Development
Transportation	Traffic Management

In addition to KeyWords for specific industries and professions, more general, "professional" KeyWords should also be key components of your resume, cover letters, thank-you letters, interviews, and other job search activities. For example, your "professional" KeyWords might include:

Business Planning	Performance & Productivity Improvement
Customer Service	Business Process Design & Optimization
P&L Management	Team Building & Team Leadership
Project Management	Oral & Written Communications
Change Management	Problem Solving & Decision Making
PC Technology	Presentations & Negotiations
Consensus Building	Organization & Administration
International Business	PC & Internet Technology
Efficiency Improvement	Cost Reduction & Avoidance
Revenue Growth	Bottom-Line Profit Improvement

The potential list of your "professional" KeyWords goes on and on. See how many more you can think of, and use them to create strong sentences and phrases that will give your resumes, cover letters, and interviews an energy and power of their own.

After you've assembled a complete listing of your "professional" KeyWords, go to the chapter that most closely matches your experience and select the KeyWords that are applicable to your specific skills and background. Then, use those words to create resumes and cover letters that briefly, yet comprehensively, communicate your qualifications and capture an employer's interest in you. And, be sure to use those same KeyWords in your interviews, thank-you letters, and all other job search activities.

Another excellent use of the KeyWords in this book is to educate yourself about the skills, qualifications, and knowledge required by industries and professions other than your own. If your entire career has been in the manufacturing industry and you're now interested in pursuing opportunities in sales and marketing, carefully review the KeyWords for those professions to better familiarize yourself with what is required of a qualified candidate. Examine your background and see what experiences you have that required those same skills. Then, incorporate those Key-Words into your job search materials and demonstrate to a prospective employer that you have the "right" stuff.

One final concept to consider is that a minor change to a KeyWord can significantly alter its meaning. For example:

KeyWord:	Sales Negotiations
Message:	Negotiate customer sales contracts, pricing, Terms, and conditions.
KeyWord:	Executive Negotiations
Message:	Negotiate directly with top-level decision makers.
KeyWord:	International Negotiations
Message:	Negotiate with international customers, vendors, and suppliers.

Just as KeyWords are an essential component of your job search, so are Action Verbs, words used to present your qualifications, achievements, and results (your KeyWords) in an action-driven style. Action Verbs are common verbs such as organized, delivered, led, negotiated, administered, transacted, designed, conceived, created, reengineered, and directed. These are the words that will give your resume energy, power, and punch.

For example, suppose you want to use the KeyWord phrase "customer service." In essence, you have two options:

KeyWords without Action Verbs:

Responsible for the daily operations of the customer service center.

KeyWords with Action Verbs:

Planned, staffed, and managed the daily operations of a 45-employee customer service center.

It's obvious that the sentence using the Action Verbs comes across more powerfully and is a much better reflection of the quality and caliber of experience you might bring to a prospective employer. Refer to Chapter 25 for a listing of Action Verbs, High-Impact Phrases, and Personality Descriptors that you can use in all of your job search communications.

Using KeyWords in Your Resume

Your choices for how and where to include KeyWords in your resume are virtually unlimited. You can integrate them into the summary section at the top of your resume, incorporate them into your job descriptions, use them to highlight your accomplishments, or include them in a separate section titled Professional Skills and Qualifications. My recommendation is to use them in all the different sections of your resume, working to fit your KeyWords comfortably into your resume so that they become a part thereof and not just an afterthought.

The following brief resume excerpts demonstrate how best to integrate KeyWords into your resume. Note that all the KeyWords below are highlighted in bold so that you can quickly spot them. It is NOT necessary to do so on your resume, although some job seekers do to draw visual attention to them. I generally prefer NOT to highlight them in a resume, fearing that if I put too much information in bold type, it will be unattractive and nothing in particular will stand out.

Example #1
Integrating KeyWords Into Your Career Summary

CAREER SUMMARY:

Highly experienced, client-oriented **Software Development** and **Programming Manager**. Accomplished **leader**, capable of building **motivated and productive teams**. Significant **software design** and **engineering** expertise. **Project management** responsibility for both **government and industry projects**, including **RFP preparation**, **subcontractor negotiations**, **budgeting**, and **technical documentation**. **P&L** management experience. **MBA** degree.

Example #2
Incorporating KeyWords Into Your Job Descriptions

Controller (1999 to 2002)
AMES DISTRIBUTION, Detroit, MI

Recruited to join the **accounting** and **financial management** team of a professional services corporation. Challenged to strengthen **accounting practices**, streamline **financial reporting** processes and improve the quality of **financial data**. Concurrently, managed corporate **legal**, **tax**, and **administrative** affairs. Led **investor presentations**, negotiated **corporate credit transactions**, and coordinated all **regulatory filings**.

Example #3
Using KeyWords to Highlight Your Achievements

Health Care Administrator (1998 to Present)
UNION HEALTH CARE ASSOCIATES, Pittsburgh, PA

Project Highlights & Career Achievements:

- Led **health care practice** through successful transition to thrive in a **managed-care** environment.
- Designed new market-driven, community-oriented **patient care model**.
- Consultant for start-up **home pain management therapy program** that grew to $2.8 million in first-year **revenues**.
- **Mentored new physicians**, helping to grow practice 30%.
- Researched and implemented **computerized digital technology** for in-house **medical testing** and **results reporting**.
- Spearheaded introduction of leading-edge **quality care models** and systems.

Example #4
Integrating KeyWords Into a Separate Resume Section

PROFESSIONAL SKILLS & QUALIFICATIONS:

Executive Secretary / Office Manager with 12 years' experience in the **Retail** and **Distribution** industries. Qualifications include:

- **Executive & Board Relations**
- **Regulatory Reporting**
- **Confidential Correspondence**
- **Special Events Planning & Management**

- **Executive Office Management**
- **Staff Training & Development**
- **Federal Property Acquisition**
- **Relationship Management**

Using KeyWords in Your Cover Letter

KeyWords also are remarkably effective tools for use in developing your cover letters, broadcast letters (letters sent without a resume; generally longer than the more typical cover letter), and other job search correspondence. They strengthen the presentation of your skills, qualifications, and experience, as well as demonstrating your competencies, achievements, and successes. What's more, you can, and should, customize your cover letters to use the KeyWords that relate directly to the position for which you are applying. If an advertisement asks for a candidate with experience in supply chain management, be sure to include those specific words in your cover letter, along with purchasing, logistics, materials management, storeroom management, and any other related skills you offer.

As with your resume, KeyWords can be used in various cover letter sections, styles, and formats. Following are brief cover letter excerpts to demonstrate how best to integrate KeyWords into your letters.

Example #1
Integrating KeyWords Into Cover Letter Text

My career is best summarized as follows: Years of **senior management** experience with two **global** corporations – Excelsior Bank and Voice of America – and now my current position as **President/CEO** of a **start-up technology venture**. The breadth of my experience is remarkably broad, from managing VOA's entire **Latin American operation** to the more finite functions of building an **operating architecture** and **business infrastructure** for a new and highly specialized enterprise.

Example #2
Putting KeyWords Into a Separate Skills Section

Highlights of my professional skills that may be of particular interest to you include the following:

- **Strategic Sales & Market Planning**
- **Competitive Sales Negotiations**
- **Key Account Development**
- **Competitive Market Intelligence**
- **New Product Introduction**
- **Sales Training & Leadership**
- **Client Retention & Loyalty**
- **U.S. & International Sales**

Example #3
Incorporating KeyWords as Career Highlights

Highlights of my career that may be of particular interest to you include the following:

- Ten years' experience as **Managing Director, Senior VP, Executive VP, COO,** and now **President/CEO.**

- Success in **start-ups, acquisitions, turnarounds, high-growth** companies, and **multinational** organizations.

- Innovative performance in **business development** through **internal growth, mergers, acquisitions, joint ventures,** and **strategic alliances.**

- Outstanding **P&L** performance measured via **revenue and profit growth, cost reduction, market penetration,** and other key indices.

- Expertise in **sales, marketing,** and the entire **customer development/ management** process.

Example #4
Using KeyWords in a Double-Column Format

Your Qualifications	My Experience
MBA Degree	MBA Degree from **Harvard Business School**
Human Resource Management	10 years' experience in **HRM** and **OD**
HRIS Technology	Implementation of $2.8 million **HRIS technology**
Benefits & Compensation	Design of IBM's **compensation plans**
Management Recruitment	**Recruitment** of IBM's newest executive team

Please note that **KeyWords** are also powerful tools to incorporate into your other job search materials (e.g., thank-you letters, leadership profiles, career biographies, Internet postings, networking letters). In fact, you can also use them in general business correspondence, proposals, reports, capital financing requests, advertisements, marketing communications, publicity, publications, and public speaking presentations. Their use in professional documents is limited only by your imagination.

Using KeyWords in Your Job Interviews

KeyWords are an essential component of any successful job interview. Whether used in a written document or spoken during conversation, KeyWords can communicate volumes of information by just using a few words and phrases specific to your industry and/or your profession.

Consider the difference in interview responses to the question, *"Are you PC proficient?"* when KeyWords are used versus when they're not.

When KeyWords are NOT used:

"Yes, I have a great deal of PC experience from both of my last jobs and can learn to use new software very quickly."

When KeyWords are used:

"Yes, I'm proficient with **Microsoft Word, Access, Excel, PowerPoint,** and **Lotus.** In addition, I have some hands-on experience working with **PhotoShop, QuarkXpress,** and **Word-Perfect.** Most recently, I've been appointed to the **PC Training Team** at my current company where I'm responsible for one-on-one and group training on new PC software."

It's quite obvious the tremendous difference in impact that the use of KeyWords will make in all of your job search interviews. Be sure that you take the time to read as much as you can about a company prior to your interview so that you can determine what KeyWords you should use during the interview ... KeyWords that you know are important to them and their operations.

KeyWords and Resume Scanning

KeyWords are the standard by which tens of thousands of companies and recruiters screen applicants' resumes to identify core skills and qualifications. Using advanced KeyWord scanning technology, resumes are electronically reviewed to identify the KeyWords that match the specific hiring criteria. As such, it is critical that you include those KeyWords in your resume, cover letters, and all other job search communications. Whether this strategy and electronic mechanism for evaluating a candidate's qualifications is an appropriate tool or not, the fact remains that KeyWord scanning has become an increasingly dominant tool in today's hiring market.

It is important to note that KeyWords do NOT have to be in any particular section, or even in a separate section, on your resume or cover letter to get noticed. Scanning technology is evolving as quickly as other technologies and can easily identify a KeyWord no matter where it is positioned in a document.

Do not allow yourself to be passed over because you do not have the "right" words in your resume. Integrate the KeyWords from this book into your resume as they accurately reflect your experience. Not only will you meet the technological requirements for KeyWord scanning, you will also create powerful career marketing tools. And, we all know that the winners in job search are those that can "sell" their qualifications, highlight their achievements, and distinguish themselves from the competition. Let the KeyWords in this book help you do just that.

Choosing the Right KeyWords

As you review the KeyWords in this book that are specific to your career, you'll see that many represent the functions you perform on a daily basis. Others may be new words to you, but I'm sure you're familiar with their underlying concepts. In fact, I'm sure most of these KeyWords reflect the skills and experience you've gained throughout your career.

As you explore the various chapters of this book, examine the Key-Words and use them to:

- Create powerful resumes, cover letter, thank-you letters, career profiles, and other job search communications. Let a prospective employer know that you've got the "right" skills and qualifications to meet their needs.

- Communicate your skills, qualifications, and achievements during all of your job interviews. Demonstrate that you have the "right" skills and you'll be well on your way to great job offers and wonderful new opportunities.

Add Your Own KeyWords

No KeyWord list is comprehensive. Words, language and communication are fluid and dynamic processes that cannot be boiled down into something that is finite and limited. With that said, know that this book was written to provide you with a vast selection of KeyWords that you can use in your job search. However, just as important, you'll want to add other KeyWords that reflect additional skills and qualifications you offer.

2

Administration

Sample Job Titles

Administrative Assistant

Administrative Director

Administrator

Corporate Administrative Officer (CAO)

Corporate Secretary

Departmental Administrator

Executive Assistant

Executive Secretary

Manager of Administrative Services

Office Administrator

Office Assistant

Office Manager

Office Services Manager

Secretary

Secretary to the President

Vice President of Administration

KeyWords and KeyWord Phrases

Administration: Appointed Senior **Administration** Director responsible for office affairs, messenger services, equipment acquisition and allocation, records management, courier services, and headquarters facilities operations.

Administrative Infrastructure: Streamlined **administrative infrastructure**, integrated similar functions, reduced staffing requirements, and saved over $200,000 annually.

Administrative Processes: Redesigned **administrative processes** to streamline functions, eliminate redundancy, and expedite workflow.

Administrative Support: Provided high-level **administrative support** and managed organizational liaison affairs for the President, CEO, and CFO.

Back Office Operations: Reorganized **back office operations** for a 22-branch banking network, reduced daily settlement time by one hour and redesigned to branch reporting system.

Budget Administration: Retained accountability for all administrative and office management operations while assuming additional responsibility for **budget administration** for 16 individual cost centers throughout the corporation.

Client Communications: Designed, wrote, and directed production of advertisements, promotions, marketing collaterals, sales materials, and other **client communications**.

Confidential Correspondence: Prepared **confidential correspondence** for CEO's signature.

Contract Administration: Directed **contract administration** affairs for over $22 million in contractual and legal agreements with business associates nationwide.

Corporate Recordkeeping: Responsible for **corporate recordkeeping** of all Board meeting minutes and agendas.

Corporate Secretary: Appointed **Corporate Secretary** to the Board of Directors.

Customer Liaison: Served as the direct **customer liaison** to $1 + million accounts.

Document Management: Designed recordkeeping, reporting, and **document management** systems to streamline workflow and enhance accountability.

Efficiency Improvement: Spearheaded a series of reorganization initiatives for **efficiency improvement**, productivity gain, and quality improvement.

Executive Liaison Affairs: Managed **executive liaison affairs** on behalf of the senior executive team.

Executive Officer Support: Coordinated meeting planning, conference scheduling, travel and transportation arrangements to **support executive officers**.

Facilities Management: Directed **facilities management**, use and resource allocation for six manufacturing plants throughout Kentucky and Tennessee.

Front Office Operations: Trained and supervised a team of 16 secretaries, clerks, and support personnel managing **front office operations** at Xerox headquarters.

Government Affairs: Prepared reports, correspondence, and documentation for company-wide **government affairs** and reporting functions.

Liaison Affairs: Coordinated high-level staffing functions to improve **liaison affairs** with the top 10 customers worldwide.

Mail and Messenger Services: Outsourced **mail and messenger services** to third-party contractor, saving the company over $250,000 in annual operating costs.

Meeting Planning: Directed **meeting planning** for two major conferences, including conference agendas, guest speakers, logistics, travel, transportation, meals, and special events.

Office Management: Promoted to **office management** position leading a staff of 14 and controlling a $300,000 annual operating budget.

Office Services: Streamlined and consolidated **office services** for 16 branches throughout the state of Maryland.

Policy and Procedure: Authored **policies and procedures** for all administrative, office services, purchasing, inventory, and facilities maintenance programs.

Product Support: Worked in cooperation with Sales and Marketing teams to design improved product support and customer **support programs**.

Productivity Improvement: Introduced time and territory management processes that drove a better than 10% gain in **productivity**, quality, and efficiency.

Project Management: Coordinated **project management**, personnel, and resources for development of emerging multimedia technologies.

Records Management: Streamlined document flow and enhanced **records management**.

Regulatory Reporting: Managed **regulatory reporting** with local, state, and government agencies.

Resource Management: Evaluated organizational needs, designed flowcharts, and directed **resource management** and allocation.

Technical Support: Provided **technical support** for specific PC applications to administrative staff worldwide.

Time Management: Created innovative **time management** systems for manufacturing, sales, marketing, order processing, and administrative staffs.

Workflow Planning/Prioritization: Designed innovative **workflow planning and prioritization** strategies, resulting in a better than 25% improvement in productivity and efficiency ratings.

KeyWord Answers to Interview Questions

Tell me about yourself.

"Let me begin by telling you that I have more than eight years' experience in **office administration** with two very interesting organizations – a large mining and construction company and a small, privately owned real estate investment firm. In both positions, I was directly responsible for all **administrative affairs**, including the design of **administrative systems and processes,** all **general correspondence and recordkeeping, contract administration, meeting planning, customer service,** and a variety of **daily business management** functions. In addition, I independently planned and managed a host of **special projects,** from selecting a new **telecommunications** system to coordinating **annual executive meetings and conferences.**"

What is the most valuable skill you bring to our company?

"What I do best is **plan, organize, and execute**. No matter the assignment, I am able to quickly determine what needs to be done, when, and how. Every supervisor I've ever had has continually commented on my ability to quickly take control of what needs to be done and get it done. Those skills, combined with a **strong work ethic** and **commitment to my employer,** are what has accounted for the **rapid promotion** during my career."

What do you consider to be your most significant achievement or contribution?

"In my current position, I was asked to take over responsibility for **regulatory reporting** functions. For a number of reasons, the company was six months behind in both **state and federal reporting,** files were in total disarray, and several agencies were threatening legal action. The entire project was dumped in my lap. With the help of two assistants, I was able to regain control, complete all delinquent filings, and bring the company up-to-date in less than 60 days. Even the agencies to which we are accountable were impressed!"

GLORIA J. McMEYERSON
2992 East End Avenue
Frederick, Maryland 20789
(410) 888-8392

April 15, 2003

John Macy, Jr.
Human Resources Director
The ASAP Administration Company
212 Glenn Valley Drive
Hagerstown, MD 20990

Dear Mr. Macy:

I am writing to express my interest in employment opportunities with your
organization and have enclosed my resume for your review.

As you will note, I have a strong blend of administrative/clerical and
"people-to-people" skills. I am well-organized, efficient, and work well
either independently or as part of a team. I thrive in situations where I
interact with people – co-workers, supervisors, clients, and the general public.
What's more, I can manage numerous projects simultaneously and have
consistently met all my performance goals and objectives.

With major changes having occurred in my life, I am now ready to tackle new
challenges and meet new opportunities. I am enthusiastic, dedicated, and determined to launch and sustain a successful career.

I would welcome the opportunity for a personal interview at your convenience
and thank you for your consideration.

Sincerely,

Gloria J. McMeyerson

Gloria J. McMeyerson

Enclosure

ROSLYN M. CHAMBERS

2395 Fair Oaks Court   Home (301) 339-4132
Silver Spring, Maryland 22591   Office (202) 695-4208

AREA ADMINISTRATIVE MANAGER

High-Performance Administrator with 15+ years experience supporting multi-site regional
sales, marketing, sales training, and customer operations. Expert organizational, leadership,
team building and communication skills. Recognized for professionalism, creativity,
resourcefulness, and competence in managing administrative affairs and supporting
organizational goals.

CORE COMPETENCIES:

- Sales & Marketing Support
- Senior Staff Relations & Communications
- Vendor & Customer Communications
- Policy & Procedure Compliance
- Productivity & Performance Management

- Project Planning & Management
- Special Events & Meetings Management
- Problem Solving & Decision Making
- Workload Planning & Prioritization
- Staff Training & Development

PROFESSIONAL EXPERIENCE:

RAYBURN MICROSYSTEMS, INC., Washington, D.C.   1985 to Present

Area Administrative Supervisor

Promoted through a series of increasingly responsible administrative positions supporting large-scale regional sales and customer management programs. Currently work in
cooperation with Area Vice President and other senior management to plan and direct
administrative affairs for the Southern Area (12 states with 125 field sales representatives). Lead a team of 12-15 field administrators. Work independently with little or no
direct supervision.

Process Design & Performance Improvement

- Design and implement enhanced administrative processes, procedures, and systems to
  support rapid regional growth ($450 million in 1994 to $830 million projected for
  1997). Anticipate organizational needs and initiate appropriate actions to obtain
  resources, technologies, and personnel to meet peak workload demands.

Operating Support

- Consult with Vice President, Human Resources Director, Controller, and other senior
  staff to plan workload, allocate personnel, coordinate special projects, and facilitate
  the entire administrative function. Work in cooperation with management teams to
  resolve problems impacting efficiency and productivity of the organization.

Management Support

- Independently direct administrative affairs on behalf of Vice President. Draft correspondence and other communications, coordinate meetings and calendar requests,
  prioritize incoming projects, process travel arrangements, and prepare expense
  reports. Represent Vice President with other departments and divisions.

ROSLYN M. CHAMBERS - *Page Two*

Special Events Management

- Plan, staff, budget, and manage sales meetings, conferences, leadership programs, and special events. Coordinate communications with hotels, caterers, transportation companies, meeting planners, exhibitors, suppliers, and speakers. Most notable event was the 1995 Southern Area Kick-Off Meeting with 300 + in attendance.

Human Resource Affairs

- Hire, train, schedule, supervise, and evaluate the work performance of administrative, clerical and support personnel. Define long-term staffing requirements, coordinate staff training and development programs, and initiate disciplinary action as appropriate. Participate in annual performance reviews and long-range career planning/direction.

Facilities Management

- Coordinate office relocations, consolidations, and renovation projects to accommo-date growth and new hires. Redesign existing space layouts to enhance efficiency and ensure optimum utilization of all physical resources. Manage telecommunications, security, and other systems installations. Saved $6,300 on proposed $7,000 fire systems upgrade project through strategic negotiations and vendor management.

Purchasing Management

- Plan and direct purchasing programs for office equipment, services, supplies, and furnishings. Source new vendors, negotiate pricing and discounts, coordinate logistics, and maintain inventory levels. Currently manage purchasing operations through corporate headquarters.

Financial Affairs

- Maintain $11,000 checking account, reconcile petty cash accounts, and prepare informal financial statements for review by senior management. Justify increased spending to meet operating, staffing, facilities, and administrative requirements.

RRT DEVELOPMENT CORPORATION, Alexandria, Virginia   1972 to 1985

Fast-track promotion from Receptionist to Order Operations Clerk to Administrative Assistant to Director of DoD Sales to **Executive Assistant to Vice President of Federal Sales Systems Group**. Managed all administrative support functions for a 200 + person field sales organization. Trained/supervised less experienced administrative staff.

- Participated in a series of internal change and process redesign initiatives to improve the efficiency of order processing, data entry, proposal preparation, sales administra-tion, and customer service/support.

EDUCATION & CAREER TRAINING:

- Frontline Leadership
- Business As Usual Seminar
- Career Architect Planning
- Managing Field Compensation
- Sexual Harassment & Performance Management
- Time Management & Conflict Management

3

Association and Not-For-Profit Management

Sample Job Titles

Agency Director

Association Director

Board Director

Certified Association Executive (CAE)

Chairperson/Chairman

Chief Administrative Officer (CAO)

Chief Executive Officer (CEO)

Chief Financial Officer (CFO)

Chief Operating Officer (COO)

Committee Chairperson/Chairman

Committee Member

Executive Director

Executive Vice President

Foundation Chairperson/Chairman

Fundraiser

Legislative Affairs Officer

Marketing Director
Media Relations Officer
Membership Development Manager
Political Affairs Officer
President
Public Policy Officer
Research Director
Special Events Director
Vice President

KeyWords and KeyWord Phrases

Advocacy: Orchestrated a large member **advocacy** program designed to reduce regulatory oversight over industry-specific operations.

Affiliate Members: Expanded membership to include **affiliate members** of primary vendors, contractors, and subcontractors to the association.

Board Relations: Managed high-profile **board relations** and presentations, with an emphasis on increasing corporate giving and annual funding.

Budget Allocation: Directed **budget allocation** and reporting functions for the association and its 210 nationwide chapter organizations.

Budget Oversight: Led management team responsible for **budget oversight** and administration of over $50 million in annual funding.

Chapter: Established **chapter** network to expand member services and increase the sale of member products, training, seminars, and other revenue-generating programs.

Community Outreach: Spearheaded design and development of advertising and promotional materials to expand **community outreach** and support continued operation of community centers and recreational programs.

Corporate Development: Guided executive management team in the conceptualization, design, and execution of targeted **corporate development** campaigns.

Corporate Giving: Expanded **corporate giving** campaigns throughout regional and national communities.

Corporate Sponsorship: Negotiated $2 million **corporate sponsorship** with Johnson & Johnson to fund industry training and educational opportunities.

Education Foundation: Formed an **education foundation** and funded with grant dollars from NIH, the Centers for Disease Control, and several private organizations.

Educational Programming: Directed 9-person training team responsible for **educational programming**, curriculum development, classroom instruction, and program certification.

Endowment Funds: Administered over $200 million in annual **endowment funds** from public and private supporters.

Foundation Management: Senior Executive with full operational responsibility for **foundation management**, funding, staffing, technology, and long-range development strategy.

Fundraising: Led teams of up to 200 volunteers for the American Red Cross annual **fundraising** campaign.

Grassroots Campaign: Utilized successful **grassroots campaign** to support legislative passage of favorable family leave law.

Industry Association: Established new **industry association** to represent the interests, issues, and financial needs of key players in the downsizing aerospace industry.

Industry Relations: Drove forward a high-profile **industry relations** initiative to advocate for the passage of favorable trade legislation.

Leadership Training: Designed high-performance **leadership training** programs for top-level association management nationwide.

Marketing Communications: Led creative team in the design and production of multimedia **marketing communications** for both member development and fundraising programs.

Media Relations: Appointed Association Spokesperson responsible for **media relations**, broadcast interviews, and crisis communications.

Member Communications: Wrote monthly newsletters, weekly Internet memos, and other **member communications** to improve member retention.

Member Development: Increased annual revenues from product sales by 34% through implementation of innovative **member development** programs and promotions.

Member-Driven Organization: Transitioned from hierarchical organization into **member-driven organization** responsive to the needs of 2,000+ members and 500+ affiliate members.

Member Retention: Improved **member retention** rates 15% by expanding regular communications and increasing number of services.

Member Services: Expanded **member services** to include training programs, legislative and regulatory support, compensation models, loan financings, and a group buying consortium.

Mission Planning: Assembled and facilitated 6-person industry team to guide **mission planning** and define organizational vision.

Not-For-Profit: Senior Operating Executive of **not-for-profit** industry association formed to provide marketing, financial, technological, and educational support to human services organizations throughout the state of Massachusetts.

Organization(al) Leadership: Challenged to provide strong and decisive **organizational leadership** through a period of change, transition, and revitalization.

Organization(al) Mission: Redefined **organizational mission** in response to changing economic and service delivery requirements.

Organization(al) Vision: Charted a clear **organizational vision** to lead the association into the year 2000.

Policy Development: Guided **policy development** in cooperation with the Board of Trustees and major corporate sponsors.

Political Affairs (Political Action Committee - PAC): Formed and led the organization's first-ever **PAC** to meet increasingly complex legislative and regulatory requirements impacting member companies worldwide.

Press Relations: Managed high-profile **press relations** with print and broadcast media.

Public Policy Development: Led congressional staff responsible for **public policy development** and dissemination.

Public Relations: Spearheaded a winning **public relations** program targeted to corporate and industrial business partners, increasing annual funding by more than $20 million.

Public/Private Partnerships: Forged **public/private partnerships** with MIT, the University of Pittsburgh, Virginia Polytechnic, and the University of Texas to manage cooperative research programs.

Regulatory Affairs: Directed all **regulatory affairs**, compliance, and reporting functions to meet local, state, and federal requirements for not-for-profit status.

Research Foundation: Established a joint public/private funded **research foundation** leading the nation in oncological research and drug development.

Speakers Bureau: Successfully marketed the association's **speakers bureau** to affiliate member organizations nationwide.

Special Events Management: Directed **special events management** teams responsible for production and execution of seminars, conferences, social meetings, and other events throughout the year.

Volunteer Recruitment: Spearheaded a successful **volunteer recruitment** program in support of annual fundraising campaign.

Volunteer Training: Designed and led **volunteer training** in communications, recordkeeping, data entry, and fundraising.

KeyWord Answers to Interview Questions

Tell me about yourself.

"Since beginning my career in **association management** 12 years ago, I've had a great run! Starting as a **Membership Development Associate**, I earned six promotions, each time retaining all of my previous responsibilities while meeting the challenges of each new assignment. As such, I have a wealth of experience in all facets of **association operations** – budgeting, educational programming, member services, public relations, media services, board relations, policy development, and **regulatory affairs**. Whether designing a **marketing** piece, planning a **special event**, negotiating with **industry trade groups**, or establishing a **new member program**, I've done it all and done it well."

What is the most valuable skill you bring to our company?

"Undoubtedly, my greatest skill and value to any organization is my ability to **build camaraderie** across diverse **interest groups**. This is best exemplified by a recent environmental project requiring the full cooperation of our association, both **state and federal regulatory agencies**, local **politicians**, our **membership**, and the **general public**. Each group had its own entirely different agenda which had put the project in a very tenuous situation. By opening channels of **communication** with each group, we were able to identify the core issues impeding the project's progress, and I was able to facilitate their prompt and efficient resolution. As such, the project was brought to closure, achieving everyone's goals and meeting our association's objectives."

What do you consider to be your most significant achievement or contribution?

"There is no doubt that my greatest achievement has been my success in **membership development** and **retention**. When I joined my current employer, our membership was stagnant and retention was a constant problem. Today, our membership is increasing an average of 22% annually and our retention rates are the highest they've ever been. In fact, my team and I are currently consulting with a sister organization to share our insights into **member services** and **member outreach**."

JACK ARTHUR

10415 Republican Lane
Topeka, Kansas 66673

Phone: (601) 469-5753   Fax: (601) 469-3826   Email: jarthur2393@aol.com

March 24, 2003

John D. Valenti
Chairman of the Board
International Association of Painters
2938 Main Street
Reading, MA 02837

Dear Mr. Valenti:

As one of the top three executives in a national nonprofit organization, I am recognized for my expertise in building strong, efficient, cost-effective, and productive operations responsive to our members' needs. My efforts, and those of the two other members of the executive management team, were the foundation for the tremendous financial and operational success of NARP.

When we started years ago, the organization was an unknown entity. Through our efforts in building a strong business culture, developing sound financial policies, introducing advanced technology, and driving member development, we now boast of a national reputation and strong bottom line. My contributions to that organization and the value I bring to IAP are best summarized as follows:

Financial Leadership

I built NARP's entire financial, accounting, internal auditing, and budgeting infrastructure from the ground floor. This included developing a progressive cash management program, managing payroll and related tax affairs, negotiating lines of credit, and managing investments valued in excess of $3 million. Further, I launched a series of aggressive cost reduction initiatives that reduced overhead costs within specific categories by as much as 40%. Through my efforts, NARP ended 1998 with a projected investment reserve of one year's operating expense.

Organizational & Administrative Leadership

My contributions to the Board of Directors, Executive Committee, and Finance Committee were strong and active. Perhaps most notable were my efforts in relationship development – with legal counsel, bankers, investors, insurance managers, government officials, and others – all critical to the long-term development and viability of the association. I am a strong communicator with keen negotiation and interpersonal relationship management skills.

John D. Valenti – Page Two
March 24, 2003

Human Resources Leadership

When I joined NARP there was no HR function. Under my leadership, we developed a complete HR function, recruitment and benefit programs, retirement plans, training programs, job descriptions, employee manuals and more. Today, NARP has a fully integrated HR organization able to support the association as it continues to grow, expand, and strengthen its operations.

Office Technology

In an attempt to keep pace with the rapid emergence of new technologies, I spearheaded the acquisition and implementation of a host of computer systems designed specifically for association management. Further, I led the acquisition of several generations of telephone/ telecommunication systems. As such, I bring to IAP a good working knowledge of the technology and telecommunication tools available to meet industry needs and enhance productivity.

Program & Convention Management

My contributions to programming, conventions, and meetings have focused on the planning and logistical "side of the house." Over the years, I coordinated efforts for up to 10 events per year which hosted up to 20,000 total participants. In addition, I have been active in providing content development concepts to better service our national membership.

As you can see, the strength of my experience in Association Management is broad and has always been devoted to forward action to achieve member support and strong financial performance. Please also note that I have an MBA in Finance and a BS in Business, both from Long Island University.

My goal is to continue within Association Management; however, my direction has changed. Throughout my entire career, I have been quite interested in the Building, Construction & Housing industry and, in fact, worked for a $200 million REIT early in my career. Through this experience, I developed a strong foundation and understanding of the industry, its partners, its financial demands, and its operating requirements. Years later, I earned my real estate license, just to keep my "fingers in the pot." Now, I am ready to make a full transition to an association whose mission is to service that industry. I'm sure you will agree that my experience places me in a well qualified position for such an opportunity.

I would welcome a personal interview to discuss your current executive staffing requirements and would be pleased to provide any additional information you require. Thank you.

Sincerely,

Jack Arthur

Jack Arthur

Enclosure

PHILLIP W. MORRISON

3204 Edgemont Place
Chevy Chase, Maryland 22351
Home: (410) 669-4352   Email: pwm2299@aol.com   Office: (410) 182-2343

NOT-FOR-PROFIT ASSOCIATION EXECUTIVE

Dynamic 10-year executive management career leading large-scale, not-for-profit organizations worldwide. Expert in evaluating organizational needs and creating proactive development, relief, service, and outreach programs that have consistently achieved/ surpassed operating goals.

CORE COMPETENCIES:

- Development Issues - Theory & Practice
- Fundraising & Marketing
- Multi-Site Management
- Strategic Planning & Policy Development
- Humanitarian Relief
- Public & Private Partnerships
- Board Relations & Donor Negotiations
- Health Care & Education Services

Extensive international experience with excellent knowledge of the political and social cultures, trends, and operating environments in both Africa and Latin America. Fluent Spanish and French.

PROFESSIONAL EXPERIENCE:

HUMAN RELIEF SERVICES - HRS, Landover, Maryland   1973 to Present

Distinguished management career with one of the world's largest and most diversified private voluntary organizations sponsoring sustainable self-help programs in the areas of agriculture, primary health care, education, micro-credit lending, and human rights. HRS is also one of the world's leaders in emergency relief assistance.

Throughout majority of tenure, served as Senior Executive of regional operations worldwide with full responsibility for strategic planning, programming, financial management, human resources, administration, marketing, resource acquisition, and daily operations management. Demonstrated expertise in fundraising, cross-cultural relations, team building, and leadership.

Special Assistant to the Deputy Executive Director - World Headquarters (1995 to Present)

Promoted to newly created position and challenged to leverage resources from affiliate European organizations to expand international programming. Currently directing the development of an innovative international support program combining monetary and in-kind fundraising in cooperation with U.S. farmers and the U.S. government.

Coordinator - Domestic Outreach & Education - World Headquarters (1994 to 1995)

Created new strategy to expand cooperative efforts with the organization's 196 affiliates nationwide. Launched a portfolio of marketing, educational, and communication programs to increase awareness, expand partnerships, and increase program funding. Held collateral responsibility for a number of annual special events and fundraising initiatives to support worldwide operations. Planned strategies and directed efforts that raised $14 million in funding.

PHILLIP W. MORRISON - *Page Two*

Home: (410) 669-4352   Email: pwm2299@aol.com   Office: (410) 182-2343

Regional Director - Central America & Caribbean, Nicaragua (1992 to 1994)

Senior Operating Executive directing all HRS operations in six countries and large-scale special projects in three other countries. Directed the allocation of over $25 million in annual funds to expand agricultural, primary health care, sanitation, micro-credit lending, and other cutting-edge development programs in a highly charged political environment.

* Defined programming requirements, acquired resources, and assembled management team to resettle ex-combatants from both sides of the conflict following 10-year civil war in El Salvador.
* Introduced quality-driven program management and audit review processes, and unique project approval/management process to transition program "ownership" to local nationals.
* Structured, negotiated, and obtained $1.3 million grant from USAID to improve water and sanitation services.

Regional Director - East Africa & the Indian Ocean, Kenya (1987 to 1992)

Senior Operating Executive leading the successful introduction of new development strategy designed in previous position. Challenged to transition strategy from concept into action, building what was the single largest field operation in HRS. High-profile position included direct responsibility for permanent operations in seven countries and major relief programs in three others. Managed $80 to $100 million in annual funding and 250+ paid staff.

* Led the largest and most sophisticated program in the 53-year history of the organization, delivering relief services to over 2.6 million displaced Ethiopians each month.
* Spearheaded development of the first-ever cross border relief programs in Somalia.
* Restructured management hierarchy throughout the nine-country region, implemented decentralized management system, and created a local ownership philosophy to strengthen program commitment of both HRS and local national teams.
* Launched the successful introduction of the new Africa Development Strategy and created model for worldwide implementation over the next 10 years.

Deputy Director - Africa Region / Director - African Development Group (1985 to 1987)

Spearheaded a massive effort to redirect the focus of development programming throughout the region and build strategic partnerships with other major donor agencies worldwide. Focused new strategy on local program ownership, popular participation, and institution building. Dedicated $20 million to finance implementation of new strategy in Africa.

Program Director (1977 to 1984) with assignments in Southern Africa, East Africa, and Central America. Managed development and emergency relief programs for 100,000+ people.

Program Assistant (1973 to 1977) in Guatemala, Nicaragua, and Ecuador.

EDUCATION: **MBA - Finance/International Business,** Columbia University
Graduate School of Business
BS - Economics, Boston College

4

Banking

Sample Job Titles

Assistant Branch Manager
Assistant Cashier
Assistant Vice President
Bank Manager
Branch Manager
Cashier
Chief Executive Officer (CEO)
Commercial Credit Officer
Consumer Credit Officer
Customer Service Representative (CSR)
Credit Analyst
Credit Officer
Director of Commercial Banking
Director of Consumer Banking
Director of Credit Administration
Director of Depository Services
Division Director
Executive Vice President

First Vice President

Lending Officer

President

Regional Vice President

Risk Manager

Second Vice President

Teller

Underwriter

Vice President

KeyWords and KeyWord Phrases

Asset-Based Lending: Controlled over $6 billion in **asset-based lending** programs allocated for capital investments, acquisitions, and joint venture programs of major corporate clients.

Asset Management: Administered NationsBank's **asset management** function, including direct control of a $2.8 billion portfolio.

Audit Examination: Managed **audit examination** of all GE Credit operations nationwide.

Branch Operations: Senior Manager with full responsibility for staffing, service, and administration of **branch operations** throughout the Ohio Delta Region.

Cash Management: Directed corporate **cash management**, treasury, foreign exchange, and currency hedging programs.

Commercial Banking: Transitioned Central Fidelity from a small community bank into a major **commercial banking** center with the introduction of lending, commercial paper, and credit operations.

Commercial Credit: Structured, negotiated, and executed over $200 million in **commercial credit** transactions in FY95.

Consumer Banking: Expanded **consumer banking** programs to include 24-hour ATM services and 24-hour credit authorization.

Consumer Credit: Controlled a $450 million **consumer credit** portfolio, all loan authorizations, and all loan recovery procedures.

Correspondent Banking: Negotiated **correspondent banking** relationships with major financial institutions throughout the Pacific Rim.

Credit Administration: Directed **credit administration** for all personal loans exceeding $50 million.

Credit Analysis: Designed bank-wide models for **credit analysis** and credit valuation.

De Novo Banking: Established **de novo banking** operations to support Mellon's expansion throughout emerging Latin American markets.

Debt Financing: Structured and negotiated over $350 million in **debt financing** to ensure continued operation of GE's Appliance Sales Division.

Deposit Base: Built **deposit base** by 25% over two years, exceeding all objectives for fee income, new customers, and penetration of new commercial markets.

Depository Services: Administered **depository services** for all commercial clients, real estate investment partnerships, and major construction programs.

Equity Financing: Negotiated $1.2 billion in **equity financing** to fund LBO.

Fee Income: Accelerated regional expansion and increased **fee income** by 18%.

Foreign Exchange (FX): Managed Commercial Federal's global **foreign exchange** program.

Global Banking: Senior Operating Executive with full responsibility for the strategic planning, staffing, and start-up of **global banking** operations to transition First National from a domestic institution into a worldwide player in the financial arena.

Investment Management: Directed **investment management**, allocation, and reporting of all general and limited partnership programs for American Saving's Real Estate Division.

Investor Relations: Authored and published monthly communications to strengthen **investor relations** and support the bank's long-range expansion objectives.

Lease Administration: Designed and directed **lease administration** programs for advanced information, electronics, and telecommunications equipment.

Letters of Credit: Negotiated $800 million in **letters of credit** to fund international commodities trading.

Liability Exposure: Reduced **liability exposure** with the introduction of more stringent lending and credit authorization procedures.

Loan Administration: Managed **loan administration**, documentation, and regulatory reporting functions in support of headquarters and branch operations.

Loan Processing: Directed 12-person professional and administrative support staff responsible for **loan processing** and documentation.

Loan Quality: Introduced improved internal controls, credit analysis, and credit administration procedures to enhance **loan quality** and performance.

Loan Recovery: Directed **loan recovery** of more than $300 million in outstanding credits.

Loan Underwriting: Managed department responsible for **loan underwriting** and analysis of customer creditworthiness.

Lockbox Processing: Managed night shift **lockbox processing** and funds transfer operations.

Merchant Banking: Direct liaison between MNB, VISA, MasterCard, American Express, and Discover to coordinate all **merchant banking** and reporting functions.

Non-Performing Assets: Restored the institution's liquidity with the recovery of over $480 million in **non-performing assets**.

Portfolio Management: Directed **portfolio management** for venture capital and investor lending programs.

Receivership: Appointed CEO to manage the institution through **receivership** and projected turnaround/asset workout.

Regulatory Affairs: Facilitated all **regulatory affairs**, reporting, and compliance programs for a multi-site banking operation.

Relationship Management: Focused service staffs on building and strengthening the institution's **relationship management** programs with large retail and commercial customers.

Retail Banking: Built and managed the region's #1 ranked **retail banking** firm (based on quality of service, ease in lending/credit, and staff performance).

Retail Lending: Expanded **retail lending** into non-traditional customer markets and increased loan portfolio by $120 million in first year.

Return-On-Assets (ROA): Structured and negotiated divestiture of all bank operations in Southern Texas and delivered 34% **ROA**.

Return-On-Equity (ROE): Designed loan administration and recovery programs that increased the bank's **ROE** performance by an average of 12% annually.

Return-On-Investment (ROI): Acquired a small community bank, expanded services and programs, and divested in 1994 for a 23% **ROI** to principal investor group.

Risk Management: Spearheaded design and implementation of an aggressive **risk management** program that, over the next 10 years, reduced bad debt portfolio by over $2 billion.

Secondary Markets: Directed loan sales throughout **secondary markets** in the U.S. and Canada.

Secured Lending: Restructured **secured lending** programs to reduce exposure and improve recovery.

Securities Management: Recruited to ASB America to build and direct their first **securities management** operation.

Transaction Banking: Senior Officer specializing in **transaction banking** for major corporate loans and credits.

Trust Services: Administered the bank's **trust services** program and over $750 million in trust funds.

Unsecured Lending: Expanded loan programs to include **unsecured lending** for preferred customer base.

Wholesale Banking: Introduced **wholesale banking** services to accelerate growth and diversification.

Workout: Directed an aggressive loan **workout** department that restructured and recovered 89% of outstanding debt.

KeyWord Answers to Interview Questions

Tell me about yourself.

"Banking is in my blood! My father and two of my uncles were bankers, both of my grandfathers were bankers, and so are three of my brothers. It's the "family business" so to speak. With that said, let me tell you that I have eight years' experience in **banking**, mostly concentrated in **commercial lending** and **commercial credit** operations. Although my experience does include some **retail banking**, my primary functions have involved **structuring and negotiating high-dollar credit transactions** for **Fortune 500 corporate clients**. In addition, I have a great deal of experience in **loan packaging and syndication, equity and debt financing, real estate investment trusts**, and **loan workout and recovery**. In total, I've participated in more than $2.8 billion in **transactions** over the past five years."

What is the most valuable skill you bring to our company?

"My **negotiating skills** are by far my greatest talent. When others have thought that deals would be impossible to close, I've been able to negotiate the contracts and close the **transactions**. When terms of specific **contracts** were unacceptable, I've been able to successfully renegotiate despite conflicting interests. And, when managing **debt recovery** projects, I've been able to negotiate realistic **workouts** in often poor **economic conditions**."

What do you consider to be your most significant achievement or contribution?

"In June of 2000, I was asked to evaluate a **loan package** for one of the nation's largest telecommunication companies. Despite the company's strong **financial position** and overall positive **market indicators** for the industry, the overall volatility within the entire technology market concerned me. As such, despite initial **loan committee approval**, I was able to demonstrate the potential risks of the transaction to the senior members of the **Board of Directors**, and we withdrew our bank from consideration. Today, that company is bankrupt."

NEAL DOUGLAS
13458 S.W. 62nd Street
Portland, Oregon 96542
(801) 386-7991
douglasneal@aol.com

January 18, 2003

Allison Hentges
Director of Human Resources
National Bank of America, Inc.
9349 Fifth Avenue, 34th Floor
New York, NY 10031

Dear Ms. Hentges:

I am a well-qualified Banking Professional recognized for my expertise in solving operating problems, improving customer relations, accelerating fee income and asset growth, and strengthening personnel performance. Despite the competitive challenges, I have consistently delivered results.

- **If your goal is to increase lending volume,** I originated over $1 million in mortgages within less than two years.

- **If your goal is to increase deposit growth,** I captured $8.8 million in net deposits in 1995.

- **If your goal is to strengthen your market position and customer image,** I led a number of marketing, business development, and outreach programs which dominated local markets and outperformed our competition.

- **If your goal is to enhance customer service,** I spearheaded a number of successful programs that not only increased customer satisfaction, but improved staff's focus on service, retention, and performance.

My goal is to secure a management position with a leading financial institution seeking qualified, career-oriented professionals looking for long-term opportunities for employment and promotion. I appreciate your consideration and look forward to what I anticipate will be the first of many positive communications. Thank you.

Sincerely,

Neal Douglas

Neal Douglas

Enclosure

RICHARD W. JACKSON

4014 Davidson Lane
St. Louis, Missouri 60604

Home   (358) 208-9256
Office   (358) 488-3478
E-Mail   RWJ@netlink.com

COMMUNITY BANKING EXECUTIVE

Strategic Planning/Banking Services & Products/Sales & Marketing/Deposit Growth Commercial & Consumer Lending/Mortgage Lending/Credit Administration/Workout & Recovery MIS Technology/Finance & Budgeting/Human Resources/Multi-Site Operations Management

Dynamic professional career leading banking institutions through start-up, turnaround, merger, acquisition, and growth. Delivered strong and sustainable gains in revenue, fee income, and asset value within highly competitive and volatile markets. Excellent planning, organizational development, and leadership qualifications. Expert negotiator, spokesperson, and change agent. Able to effectively communicate high-level technical and financial information to nontechnical audiences.

PROFESSIONAL EXPERIENCE:

President – WESTERN GLOBE CORPORATION   1993 to 1995

Transitioned career out of banking and into a commercial enterprise to accelerate growth of this natural gas marketing company following deregulation and entry into a competitive business market. Given full autonomy for identifying and capitalizing upon opportunities to recreate Western Globe as diversified energy provider to industrial and commercial customers.

- Nurtured relationships with previous business colleagues and associates to launch Western Globe's successful entry into the commercial energy markets. Delivered 100% revenue growth within less than two years.
- Spearheaded selection and implementation of fully integrated MIS technology to automate all core business functions.

President & CEO – FINANCIAL FEDERAL   1988 to 1993

Appointed President & CEO following the merger of Myers Bank, State Bank, and Tress Federal to create Financial Federal. Challenged to lead the new organization through an aggressive reorganization, turnaround, and return to profitability. Held P&L responsibility for the institution and all business units (e.g., Lending, Mortgage Banking, Funds Acquisition, Sales/Marketing, HR, MIS, Operations, Finance and Budgeting, Strategic Planning, Customer Service).

- Met/exceeded all turnaround objectives for this $750 million savings and loan. Consolidated 660 employees in 59 locations in 7 states to 420 employees in 23 locations throughout Missouri. Transitioned from 1987 loss of $21 million to 1990 earnings of $8+ million.
- Orchestrated the workout and recovery of over $60 million in non-performing assets.
- Created, launched, and marketed a series of consumer, mortgage, and small commercial lending programs to reestablish the institution and rebuild solvent portfolio.
- Repositioned the new institution within the marketplace, restored confidence within the consumer and commercial communities, and launched a well-targeted marketing and public relations campaign to rebuild market image.

NOTE: *Appointed Co-Director to facilitate two-year transition and integration of operations following Prairie Bancorp's acquisition of Financial Federal in 1991.*

RICHARD W. JACKSON – *Page Two*

Vice President of Administration – MYERS BANK F.S.B.   1982 to 1988

Member of five-person executive management team leading the transition of Federal Savings & Loan Association into a publicly owned federal savings bank (Myers). Redesigned organizational infrastructure, reengineered operations, and guided the institution through a period of rapid growth and diversification. Led strategic planning and market repositioning.

Directed the Administration Division (MIS, Human Resources, General Services) with 30 employees and a $5 million annual budget. Created dynamic business processes, operations, policies, and procedures to meet changing organizational needs.

- Recreated Federal through an aggressive merger and acquisition program with six other institutions to create newly formed Myers Bank.
- Instrumental in building assets from $140 million to $680 million, expanding locations from 7 to 47 and increasing employee base from 100 to 500.

Vice President of Management Systems – FEDERAL SAVINGS & LOAN
1977 to 1982

Promoted from Management Systems Specialist to Vice President within two years. Evaluated organizational needs and facilitated design/implementation of improved operating and administrative processes impacting all key business units. Concurrent responsibility for spearheading a number of new programs and services to diversify the bank's portfolio.

- Invested over $2 million in technology upgrades to automate and upgrade operating processes. Led conversion from service bureau to in-house information systems.
- Guided the development of operating, administrative, and back office procedures for the start-up of the first retail banking network in the state of Missouri.
- Orchestrated development, staffing, budgeting and start-up of property management company to expand statewide real estate practice.
- Introduced new cash management program, space management systems, security training program, and a portfolio of other internal processes.
- Directed construction of four retail deposit facilities. Brought project in on time and within budget despite construction overrides and accelerating costs.

Director of Claims Processing – MISSOURI WORKER'S COMPANY   1974 to 1977

Member of five-person management team challenged to reengineer and modernize the operations, processes, and technologies of $54 million fund (80,000+ claims annually). Led implementation of automated claims processing systems, redesigned core business systems, developed training programs, and supervised 100+ personnel through seven direct management reports.

MIS Consultant – CMB, INC.   1973 to 1974

Teaching / Research Assistant - NATIONAL SCIENCE FOUNDATION   1972

EDUCATION: MISSOURI STATE UNIVERSITY
                        MS Degree (Industrial Engineering), 1974
                        BS Degree (Industrial Engineering), 1972

5

Customer Service

Sample Job Titles

Account Administrator
Account Manager
Account Representative
Account Services Coordinator
Customer Acceptance Representative
Customer Account Manager
Customer Loyalty Manager
Customer Relationship Manager
Customer Service Associate
Customer Service Manager
Director of Account Relations
Director of Customer Service
Key Account Manager
Key Account Service Manager
Sales Administrator
Sales Support Administrator
Telemarketing Manager
Telemarketing Representative
Vice President of Customer Service

KeyWords and KeyWord Phrases

Account Relationship Management: Directed all customer service functions for major **account relationship management** and development projects.

Customer Communications: Created a complete portfolio of print, broadcast, and video **customer communications** in cooperation with Sales, Marketing, Product Development, and Operations.

Customer Development: Member of cross-functional team responsible for strategy, operations, and service planning for new **customer development** initiatives.

Customer Focus Groups: Facilitated **customer focus groups** with large consumer groups to expand Levi's penetration into emerging seniors' market.

Customer Loyalty: Championed development and global market launch of IBM's first-ever **customer loyalty** programs to retain competitive market lead.

Customer Management: Drove forward innovative **customer management** initiatives to expand level, scope, and caliber of both in-house and field service organizations.

Customer Needs Assessment: Facilitated cross-functional teams responsible for **customer needs assessment** and service delivery.

Customer Retention: Pioneered innovative, incentive-based **customer retention** initiatives that contributed to a better than 20% gain in long-term client relationships.

Customer Satisfaction: Measured **customer satisfaction** through mail and telephone surveys, customer focus groups and email communications.

Customer Service: Credited with building a world class **customer service** organization supporting field sales and product distribution programs through 22 states in the Eastern U.S.

Customer Surveys: Designed and administered **customer surveys** to further clarify customer expectations, product and service requirements, cost objectives, and competitive partnerships.

Field Service Operation: Managed a 62-person regional **field service operation** supporting IBM PC and peripherals installations.

Inbound Service Operation: Staffed a 24/7 **inbound service operation** supporting surgical implants and devices at leading healthcare research and medical centers nationwide.

Key Account Management: Supported **key account management** team with complete service, support, and administration.

Order Fulfillment: Expanded **order fulfillment** operations to include off-site contractors to meet increased demand while controlling escalating costs.

Order Processing: Led a 62-person **order processing** operation to the highest levels of productivity in the 42-year history of the company.

Outbound Service Operation: Revitalized **outbound service operation**, expanded technical and training staff, introduced PCs and email communications, and restored customer credibility.

Process Simplification: Orchestrated a company-wide **process simplification** program to streamline order entry, processing, fulfillment, billing, collection, and service operations.

Records Management: Redesigned and automated customer **records management** system to more accurately track historical data, product requirements, and pricing.

Relationship Management: Designed service-based **relationship management** programs to strengthen customer retention and loyalty.

Sales Administration: Directed the entire **sales administration**, budgeting, and reporting function for the $5.8 million Central LA sales and service region.

Service Benchmarks: Created the industry's first-ever **service benchmarks** for Internet customer support.

Service Delivery: Redesigned **service delivery** processes, increased staff field time by 30%, and improved customer satisfaction ratings 89%.

Service Measures - Introduced quantifiable **service measures** to track individual technician performance.

Service Quality: Spearheaded design and implementation of measurable **service quality** parameters to support company-wide continuous quality improvement initiative.

Telemarketing Operations: Recruited to direct the start-up of nation-wide **telemarketing operations** to complement direct and distributor sales programs.

Telesales Operations: Pioneered **telesales operations** to introduce IBM's new consumer-based technology.

Virtual Administration: Opened new business providing **virtual administrative** services through the use of state-of-the-art information, Internet, and telecommunications technologies.

KeyWord Answers to Interview Questions

Tell me about yourself.

"Building **positive customer relationships** is what I do best. Whether working to service an existing **customer account**, resolve a **customer service problem**, or develop systems to streamline and enhance **customer service operations**, I have consistently exceeded all **service and retention objectives**. Equally important is my success in **training** other **customer service professionals** in **communications, project management, customer relationship management**, and **customer retention**. To date, I have earned three **commendations** from Sprint for 'excellence in customer service management' and a **corporate award** for 'employee training and development.' In addition, I was featured in Sprint's quarterly employee magazine as one of the 'Top 10 **Customer Service Associates**' in the corporation."

What is the most valuable skill you bring to our company?

"**Communications** and **interpersonal relations** are my strongest skills and the foundation for my success in **customer service management**. I really do enjoy people and find that I'm able to quickly **build rapport** and **establish relationships**. I value my customers and I want them to know that. When I tell them I'll call back, I do. When I tell them I'll research a problem and resolve it, I do. When I tell them I'll email them information, I do. I execute, I follow through, and my customers always appreciate the effort."

What do you consider to be your most significant achievement or contribution?

"Over the past three years, I've trained more than 50 newly hired **customer service representatives** for Sprint's Regional Operations Center. I'm most proud of the fact that 47 of them are still with the company and that 12 of them have been promoted to **supervisory** positions. This clearly demonstrates that not only can I manage **customer service operations** with excellent results, I can also train others to perform equally well in challenging, fast-paced situations."

JODY STEVENSON
12 Warren Avenue
Miami, Florida 33389

Phone: (305) 845-2837   Email: jodys@prodigy.net

February 21, 2003

John Garber
Holiday Inn Express
5600 Seminole Avenue
Miami, FL 33827

Dear Mr. Garber:

Please accept this letter and enclosed resume as an application for the position of Assistant Manager. I bring to the position a unique combination of professional experience and personal qualifications, including:

- Two years of progressively responsible account management experience with Pepsi.

- Experience coordinating cross-functional customer service and support teams.

- Outstanding performance in building and managing customer relationships.

- Outgoing personality with strong communication, problem-solving, and decision-making skills.

- Ability to independently manage time, client commitments, and resources.

- PC proficient with Microsoft Word, email, the Internet, and several proprietary software programs.

- Four-year college degree with solid academic performance and outstanding athletic achievements.

I would welcome the opportunity for a personal interview and thank you in advance for your consideration. My resume is enclosed for your review.

Sincerely,

Jody Stevenson

Jody Stevenson

Enclosure

NOREEN COLLINS
noreen.r.collins@customer.net

899 South Pacific Grove   Residence (415) 548-9721
Valley Vista, California 90898   Office   (415) 684-3145

CUSTOMER SERVICE / CONSUMER AFFAIRS / RESPONSE CENTER MANAGEMENT
Building & Directing High-Profile Customer Management Organizations

- Strategic Business Planning
- Technology Acquisition
- Vendor Sourcing / Negotiations
- Contract Development / Compliance
- Market Research / Analysis

- Customer / Client Service Management
- Multi-Site Call Center Management
- Human Resource Allocation
- Professional Training & Development
- Process / Procedure Standardization

Built two high-profile customer response/customer management organizations that consistently exceeded productivity, quality, and customer satisfaction objectives.

PROFESSIONAL EXPERIENCE:

SIMPSON FOODS, San Francisco, California   1984 to Present

Fast-track promotion through a series of increasingly responsible management positions leading nationwide customer service/customer response operations of one of the largest food manufacturers in the U.S. Received several distinguished corporate performance awards including:

- Award For Above And Beyond The Call Of Duty (1996)
- TQM Team of the Quarter (1993 and 1994)
- Consumer Affairs Award for Continued Excellent Performance (1990 and 1992)
- Consumer Affairs Award of Excellence (1986 and 1989)

Operations Manager — Customer Response Information Services (1993 to Present)

One of only three professionals retained by the company following complete downsizing of the in-house customer response organization and start-up of outsourced operation. Retained responsibilities as Operations Manager (since 1989) while shifting focus to a nine-site organization (two large contracted centers and seven remote, in-house centers).

Currently direct a team of 150 vendor-based contractors and 15 managers nationwide handling over 2.5 million calls annually. Manage an $8 million annual operating budget. Negotiate vendor contracts and monitor vendor compliance with operating standard and objectives (e.g., call volume, call duration, productivity, documentation, customer satisfaction).

- Led the successful transition from in-house to outsourced operation. Met 100% of all target dates and milestones. New operation has reduced cost per contact by 25% in two years with long-term projections indicating further reductions in both call and mail response costs.

- Wrote a complete business plan to standardize all policies and procedures (e.g., coupon refunds, claims processing, nutritional information, shipping) and provide contractors with a single operational reference manual.

- Designed/directed a 13,000-hour training program at vendor site. Educated personnel in Simpson standards, quality objectives, customer satisfaction, and 3,000+ products.

NOREEN COLLINS
Page Two

Operations Manager — Customer Response Information Center (1989 to 1993)

Promoted to direct the start-up and management of an integrated, full-service customer response and fulfillment center. Established strategic plans and operating goals, designed departmental infrastructure, determined staffing and technology requirements, and created policies/procedures for all facets of service management. Administered a $4.8 million budget and directed a staff of 80. Managed crisis communications and national product recalls.

- Built internal customer response organization from ground floor into a nationwide operation servicing more than one million customers annually.

- Transitioned customer response from a function that had been scattered throughout the corporation into a cohesive and accountable work group. Reduced costs per contract by 60% and mail turnaround time from 21+ days to three.

- Wrote business plan and led introduction of voice response technology. Co-directed project from initial feasibility/cost analysis through vendor sourcing and final implementation.

- Devised an employee hotline to obtain recommendations for productivity and quality improvements. Reduced operating costs by more than $500,000.

- Led internal training programs to enhance staff capabilities (e.g., communications, customer management, problem resolution, documentation). Created a forum for the ongoing exchange of information between all core operating functions.

Working in cooperation with executive management team, developed reengineering strategy to transition to outsourced consumer response operations. Effectively directed the complete downsizing of internal department and accepted new assignment directing the contracted response operation.

Customer Information Analyst (1987 to 1989)

Direct liaison between the Customer Response Information Center and Marketing, Quality Assurance, Legal, and Manufacturing. Translated information regarding consumer issues, trends, and market opportunities to support diverse product development, design, packaging, distribution, and promotional efforts. Conducted detailed analyses of consumer data, identified and research complaints, and resolved issues impacting consumer purchasing/satisfaction.

Senior Home Economist / Chef (1985 to 1987)
Development Technologist (1984 to 1985)

Promoted within six months to product development position providing critical technical, culinary, and consumer expertise to lead expansion of Simpson's product portfolio.

EDUCATION: MBA, Ohio State University, 1985
MS, Institutional Management, University of Illinois, 1983
BS, Food & Nutrition, Florida A&M University, 1981

PROFESSIONAL ACTIVITIES:

Member   Society of Consumer Affairs Professionals, Incoming Call Center Management
Presenter   "Training & Hiring," Customer Service Organization National Conference, 1993

6

Engineering

Sample Job Titles

Associate Engineer

Chemical Engineer

Chief Engineer

Chief Scientist

Design Engineer

Development Engineer

Director of Engineering

Director of Quality Assurance

Director of R&D

Electrical Engineer

Electronics Engineer

Engineering Associate

Engineering Manager

Environmental Engineer

Facilities Engineer

Hardware Engineer

Industrial Engineer

Laboratory Manager

Laboratory Researcher

Lead Engineer
Maintenance Engineer
Manufacturing Engineer
Mechanical Engineer
Nuclear Engineer
Optics Engineer
Plant Engineer
Process Engineer
Professional Engineer
Project Director
Project Engineer
Project Manager
Quality Engineer
Quality Manager
R&D Engineer
Research Scientist
Scientist
Senior Engineer
Software Engineer
Systems Engineer
Team Leader
Test Engineer
Vice President of Development
Vice President of Engineering
Vice President of Technical Operations
Vice President of Technical Services

KeyWords and KeyWord Phrases

Benchmark: **Benchmarked** best practices for systems, electronics, and communications engineering.

Capital Project: Managed $4 million **capital project** for the development of facilities engineering, renovation, and new construction projects.

Chemical Engineering: Advanced **chemical engineering** processes through introduction of leading edge prototyping, testing, and quality management protocols.

Commissioning: Directed **commissioning** of over $10 million in new industrial facilities.

Computer-Aided Design (CAD): Outsourced **CAD** engineering to better utilize resources of internal staff for advanced systems design.

Computer-Aided Engineering (CAE): Introduced **CAE** methodologies into GE's in-house R&D department.

Computer-Aided Manufacturing (CAM): Delivered a 22% gain in production yields following implementation of **CAM** processes.

Cross-Functional Team: Led a 200-person **cross-functional team** challenged to enhance systems performance through improved engineering capabilities.

Customer Management: Coordinated headquarters and field engineering personnel responsible for **customer management**, loyalty, and retention.

Development Engineering: Managed a $4 million budget for **development engineering** and prototype design projects.

Efficiency: Delivered a 23% gain in departmental **efficiency** through introduction of advanced engineering, technical support, and documentation procedures.

Electrical Engineering: Selected from a competitive group of more than 200 candidates for admission to USC's **Electrical Engineering** School.

Electronics Engineering: Graduated #1 in class of 420 with a M.S. Degree in **Electronics Engineering**.

Engineering Change Order (ECO): Issued **ECOs** as mandated by U.S. Department of Energy for $12 million systems development project.

Engineering Documentation: Standardized **engineering documentation** and facilitated an immediate increase in field productivity.

Environmental Engineering: Recruited by CEO to direct the start-up and subsequent management of Dow's first in-house **Environmental Engineering** Department.

Ergonomic Techniques: Pioneered advanced **ergonomic techniques**, reduced employee absences 40%+ and lowered workers' compensation costs $2+ million annually.

Experimental Design: Accelerated **experimental design** with the recruitment of two Ph.D. scientists.

Experimental Methods: Redesigned **experimental methods** to eliminate non-essential tasks and expedite project completion.

Facilities Engineering: Managed a 32-person, $15 million **Facilities Engineering** Department responsible for 18 manufacturing, distribution, and public warehousing sites.

Fault Analysis: Introduced advanced **fault analysis** and isolation procedures that increased systems availability by 45%.

Field Performance: Measured **field performance** based on systems operability and user functionality.

Final Customer Acceptance: Managed **final customer acceptance** and systems testing for all new technology installations.

Hardware Engineering: Directed **hardware engineering** and testing for new systems deployment.

Industrial Engineering: Created the corporation's first-ever **Industrial Engineering** Department to enhance ergonomic design of manufacturing and distribution facilities.

Industrial Hygiene: Trained staff responsible for field training and information dissemination regarding **industrial hygiene** and safety requirements.

Maintenance Engineering: Managed 100-person department responsible for **maintenance engineering** and systems documentation at Xerox's flagship manufacturing plant.

Manufacturing Engineering: Senior Executive leading a 200-person **manufacturing engineering** group supporting facilities throughout North America, Latin America, Europe and the Pacific Rim.

Manufacturing Integration: Facilitated **manufacturing integration** of newly acquired technology resources.

Mechanical Engineering: Delivered over $20 million in **mechanical engineering** projects on time and within budget despite difficult field conditions.

Methods Design: Supervised **methods design** for chemical, mechanical, HVAC and electronics engineering.

Nuclear Engineering: Challenged to revitalize the corporation's **Nuclear Engineering** Division and facilitate development/delivery of new product and systems technology.

Occupational Safety & Health Administration (OSHA): Administered the corporation's **OSHA** compliance and training program.

Operating & Maintenance (O&M): Authored **O&M** manuals for all facilities.

Optics Engineering: Innovated advanced **optics engineering** methods and processes to accelerate product development and global market launch.

Plant Engineering: Managed a 45-person **plant engineering** team responsible for new facilities construction and large-scale renovation.

Process Development: Re-invented the corporation's **process development** programs to link engineering with operations and support long-term performance/productivity gains.

Process Engineering: Led team responsible for **process engineering**, design, and implementation.

Process Standardization: Orchestrated **process standardization** of all activities involving electrical and electronics engineering teams.

Product Design: Credited with **product design** of advanced chemical compounds critical to continued AIDS research and protocol development.

Product Development Cycle: Directed a two-year **product development cycle** for the introduction of advanced navigation systems and technologies.

Product Functionality: Challenged to enhance **product functionality** with the introduction of new electronics technologies.

Product Innovation: Guided **product innovation** across multiple engineering disciplines, contributing to a better than 45% gain in sales, profits, and market share ratings.

Product Lifecycle Management: Chaired in-house committee responsible for **product lifecycle management**, from initial design and engineering through commercialization.

Product Manufacturability: Enhanced **product manufacturability** with the introduction of an in-house systems engineering and design group.

Product Reliability: Enhanced **product reliability** to the strongest in the electronics industry with the introduction of scheduled preventive maintenance and testing programs.

Productivity Improvement: Delivered 34% **productivity improvement** following implementation of advanced robotics technology into large-scale manufacturing operations.

Project Costing: Guided **project costing** for all major R&D and engineering projects to ensure optimum profit margins and protect company assets.

Project Planning: Orchestrated interdisciplinary team responsible for **project planning**, scheduling, budgeting, costing, and staffing.

Project Management: Senior Executive responsible for all field **project management** programs incorporating latest electronics and avionics technologies.

Prototype: Spearheaded **prototype** development of next generation products.

Quality Assurance: Created and managed a comprehensive **quality assurance**, quality review, and regulatory compliance function.

Quality Engineering: Promoted as first-ever **quality engineering** professional in the entire Ericsson organization.

Regulatory Compliance: Achieved/surpassed all **regulatory compliance** standards despite issues negatively impacting product performance.

Research & Development (R&D): Led a 12-person **R&D** team challenged to advance systems technologies into emerging new media markets.

Resource Management: Directed **resource management** function for all R&D facilities, technologies, and data center operations worldwide.

Root Cause: Identified and eliminated **root cause** of non-performing electronic and electrical systems.

Scale-Up: Managed plant **scale-up** operations for all newly commissioned environmental engineering and remediation facilities.

Software Engineering: Led 15-person **software engineering** team credited with the development and profitable commercialization of next generation product line.

Specifications: Authored **specifications** for all facilities development, technology development, and manufacturing operations.

Statistical Analysis: Developed **statistical analysis** models to monitor field performance of advanced navigation systems.

Systems Engineering: Launched **systems engineering** group to manage predictive failure analysis, root cause analysis, and remediation projects.

Systems Integration: Forged partnership with major hardware vendor to pioneer industry-leading **systems integration** projects.

Technical Briefings: Led **technical briefings** to state and federal government agency officials regarding the progress of the $45 million Des Moines Incineration Facility.

Technical Liaison Affairs: Managed **technical liaison affairs** between the corporation, vendors, customers, and business partners worldwide.

Technology Development: Recognized for unprecedented performance in the leadership of advanced **technology development** programs.

Test Engineering: Revitalized **test engineering** operations and improved systems reliability by 19%.

Turnkey: Planned, staffed, and directed field operations for over $200 million in **turnkey** design and engineering projects.

Work Methods Analysis: Conducted large-scale **work method analysis** project to identify strategies to enhance productivity, quality, and performance.

KeyWord Answers to Interview Questions

Tell me about yourself.

"My most distinguishing characteristic is that I have **master's degrees** in both **Mechanical Engineering** and **Electrical Engineering**. This places me in a uniquely qualified position as a **Senior Facilities Engineer**, able to manage large-scale **plant design, construction, scale-up,** and **production operations**. I've held dual roles, responsible for both **facilities design and engineering** as well as **new product development,** preparing me to pursue future career interests in either discipline. In addition, I have a wealth of experience in **technical documentation, tech-**

nical communications, project management, methods design, process development, and OSHA reporting."

What is the most valuable skill you bring to our company?

"My most valuable skill is the breadth of my engineering experience, including my expertise in both **mechanical and electrical engineering**, as well as my work experience in **systems engineering, process engineering, HVAC**, and **systems integration**. Because of this broad experience, I can quickly and accurately evaluate the requirements for complete projects, determining what **personnel, technologies, engineering systems, finances**, and other **resources** will be required to achieve **project milestones**. In addition, and again because of the wide range of my experience, I am able to effectively **communicate** with personnel from every **engineering discipline**."

What do you consider to be your most significant achievement or contribution?

"Last year, our plant experienced a major fire that devastated the production floor while doing significant damage to the warehouse and loading docks. In cooperation with five other engineers, I was given lead responsibility for getting the plant back up and running. With more than 100 workers on the site each day, we **rebuilt the production area, designed and installed all new electrical and HVAC systems**, and **renovated** all damaged areas. Most significant, the project was completed in 120 days and we achieved all **customer delivery objectives**."

CHRISTIAN LAMBERT
9348 Mississippi Street
Minneapolis, Minnesota 55321
606-535-6533

March 21, 2003

Abbott Laboratories
1401 Sheridan Road
Dept. 39Y, A-1
North Chicago, IL 60064

RE: Environmental Coordinator

Dear Sir/Madam:

With 13 years of professional experience in Environmental Engineering, I bring to Abbott Laboratories an in-depth knowledge of environmental issues, regulations, and compliance impacting chemical and industrial manufacturing. The scope of my responsibility has varied widely, from environmental review and analysis of proposed site acquisitions to comprehensive assessment of the waste by-products generated in large manufacturing operations. Highlights of my career include:

- Expertise in resource recovery and conservation.
- Completion of 100+ Superfund projects.
- Extensive knowledge of soil, air, and groundwater remediation systems and technologies.
- Design of environmental systems for hazardous waste, hazardous materials, air emissions, and wastewater discharges.

Most significant has been my success in resolving long-standing environmental issues, achieving compliance with state and federal regulations, and reducing the costs associated with environmental engineering and remediation. Further, I have worked closely with senior management to guide acquisition, divestiture, and product development efforts.

Although currently employed, I am anxious to return to a manufacturing environment and would be delighted to have the opportunity to interview with Abbott Laboratories. I appreciate your confidentiality and look forward to speaking with you. Thank you.

Sincerely,

Christian Lambert

Christian Lambert

Enclosure

WALTER N. BUSEY

buseywaltern@engineeringtest.com

9340 Balmont Avenue
Mesa, Arizona 86333

Home (615) 321-6547
Office (615) 987-2312

DESIGN, ENGINEERING, & MANUFACTURING
Advanced Information, Telecommunications, Electronic Packaging Technologies
Expertise in Team Building, Productivity/Efficiency Gain, Quality & Resource Maximization

CORE COMPETENCIES:

- Product Design & Mechanical Engineering
- Project Planning & Management
- Environmental Testing
- Reliability & Performance Analysis
- Automated Design Technologies
- Concurrent Design & Engineering

- Production & Assembly Operations
- Product Cost & Production Scheduling
- Subcontractor Negotiations
- Materials Planning & Management
- Product Testing & Prototyping
- Customer Presentations & Negotiations

PROFESSIONAL EXPERIENCE:

Engineering Manager (Section Supervisor)   1988 to Present
Space Inc., Mesa, Arizona

Senior Engineering Manager with full responsibility for strategic planning, staffing, budgeting, and technical performance of all power control electronic system design projects. Lead team of 15 professional engineers throughout entire project cycle, from initial design through prototype, test, quality, and transition to full-scale production.

- Manage $4 million in annual project budgets. Completed 10+ projects over eight years with total cost of over $30 million.
- Coordinate production planning and scheduling, purchasing, and subcontracting. Provide engineering expertise to internal and outsourced manufacturing teams involved in supply/material management programs.
- Lead technical presentations to major customers nationwide for both new contracts and renewals. Instrumental in winning over $1.2 billion in contract awards.
- Spearhead project teams responsible for the redesign and improved manufacturability of existing products and technologies.
- Coordinate the selection and integration of advanced technologies for project design, vibration and thermal analysis, scheduling, systems integration, and other core functions.

RESULTS:

- Built a talented and technically proficient mechanical engineering team successful in delivering cost-effective, high-performance designs, products, and technologies.
- Spearheaded the redesign of assembly processes for a major systems component and delivered $500,000 in annual cost savings.
- Implemented custom hybrid circuits/surface mount components, reducing volume 70%.
- Directed team in the standardization and documentation of all mechanical engineering processes and methods for electronic box design.

WALTER N. BUSEY – *Page Two*
buseywaltern@engineeringtest.com

Engineering Manager   1985 to 1988
Greinert Systems, Palo Alto, California

Recruited back to previous employer as Manager of Mast Engineering, a sophisticated mechanical engineering group designing mobile, collapsible antenna systems for deployment worldwide. Transferred to Mechanical Design Project Manager on a multi-million dollar project. Responsible for managing cost, schedule, and technical performance of reconfigured rack-mounted ESM equipment. Led a team of seven professional engineers and up to $1 million in annual project budgets.

- Appointed to design team facilitating the concept development of electronic support measures equipment for unique customer applications.
- Actively involved in the implementation of an advanced noise testing simulation facility.

Engineering Specialist   1981 to 1985
Litton-Applied Technology, Sunnyvale, California

Lead Engineer for more than $250,000 annually in systems design projects, ranging from computer components to advanced digital and RF electronics. Concurrent responsibility for the design evaluation and oversight of power supply and microwave device subcontractors.

- Facilitated the selection, acquisition and integration of workstation technology into the Mechanical Engineering Group to enhance finite element analysis capabilities.

Senior Engineer   1977 to 1981
Greinert Systems, Needham, Massachusetts

Only mechanical engineer in the entire design facility. Produced mechanical and environmentally resistant designs for sophisticated, high-vibration applications. Assisted in project budgeting, scheduling, task definition, and team supervision/technical support.

- Appointed Cost Proposal Manager for large RFP.
- Doubled yield of high voltage magnetics in production through product/process redesign.

EDUCATION:

M.S., Engineering Management, University of California - Los Angeles, 1991
M.S., Mechanical Engineering, University of California - Santa Cruz, 1986
B.S., Mechanical Engineering, *Magna Cum Laude*, Boston University, 1977

PERSONAL PROFILE:

Two-year tour of duty with the U.S. Army. Vietnam era veteran. Honorably discharged.
Design and assemble personalized golf clubs as a small, independent venture.
NCGA Golf Tournament Player. Member of Arizona Golf Association.

7

Finance, Accounting, and Auditing

Sample Job Titles

Accountant

Accounting Manager

Actuary

Assistant Bookkeeper

Assistant Controller

Audit Manager

Auditor

Bookkeeper

Broker

Certified Financial Planner (CFP)

Certified Public Accountant (CPA)

Chief Administrative Officer (CAO)

Chief Financial Officer (CFO)

Chief Operating Officer (COO)

Comptroller

Controller

Deputy Director

Finance Manager

Financial Consultant

Funds Manager

Investment Representative

Junior Accountant

Leasing Administrator

Mutual Fund Manager

Portfolio Manager

Registered Representative

Senior Accountant

Senior Auditor

Staff Accountant

Tax Manager

Trading Manager

Treasurer

Vice President of Corporate Development

Vice President of Finance

Vice President of Finance and Administration

Vice President of Leasing

KeyWords and KeyWord Phrases

Accounts Payable: Streamlined **accounts payable** functions, established common vendor files, eliminated duplication and reduced monthly processing time by 20%.

Accounts Receivable: Introduced improved **accounts receivable** and collection policies that decreased outstanding receivables by an average of 40% monthly.

Asset Disposition: Determined proper **asset disposition**, sale, and leasing options following plant divestiture.

Asset Management: Established **Asset Management** Division to control $55 million in capital equipment and technology.

Asset Purchase: Structured and executed **asset purchase** of Zylog Corporation in Canada.

Audit Controls: Implemented a stringent program of **audit controls** to reverse previous findings during Coopers & Lybrand external audit review.

Audit Management: Directed financial and operational **audit management** programs of 89 sales, manufacturing, and distribution businesses worldwide.

Capital Budgets: Formulated, justified, and managed $8 million in **capital budgets** annually.

Cash Management: Redesigned **cash management** processes, renegotiated banking relationships, and created the corporation's first comprehensive corporate treasury function.

Commercial Paper: Structured and negotiated over $125 million in **commercial paper** transactions with Chase Manhattan Bank.

Corporate Development: Provided strategic, financial, legal, and negotiations expertise for **corporate development** initiatives, including mergers, acquisitions, joint ventures, and technology licenses.

Corporate Tax: Led a team of eight responsible for **corporate tax** filings in more than 1,000 local, state, and federal jurisdictions.

Cost Accounting: Implemented automated **cost accounting** systems to analyze all labor, material, technology, process, quality, testing, and manufacturing costs for each product line.

Cost Avoidance: Introduced proactive management techniques to strengthen focus on **cost avoidance** and elimination within each manufacturing process.

Cost Reduction: Delivered over $2.8 million in first year labor, inventory, and delivery **cost reductions**.

Cost/Benefit Analysis: Conducted large-scale **cost/benefit analysis** studies to capitalize upon long-term growth and profit improvement opportunities.

Credit & Collections: Reduced DSO by 28% through improved **credit and collection** processes.

Debt Financing: Negotiated $2.5 million in **debt financing** with a major banking institution and a regionally-based venture capital firm.

Divestiture: Planned and executed profitable **divestiture** of the $1.5 million emerging electronic commerce product line.

Due Diligence: Orchestrated complex **due diligence** reviews in cooperation with outside financial advisors, accountants, and legal counsel.

E-Commerce: Launched the company's entrance into **e-commerce** to capitalize upon Internet marketing and partnership alliance opportunities.

E-Trade: Designed and implemented client-server based **e-trading** system to allow the instantaneous processing of stock and bond transactions.

Employee Stock Ownership Plan (ESOP): Led Weinhold Winers through successful LBO and **ESOP** transactions, creating a corporation that is now ranked #1 in nationwide market share.

Equity Financing: Structured a three-way partnership between 3M, Telecom, and IBM for $160 million in **equity financing** for new technology venture.

Feasibility Analysis: Led 22-person finance team managing complex **feasibility analysis** and developing projections for TLC's global market expansion.

Financial Analysis: Created team-based **financial analysis** models integrating financial data for all 52 operating locations worldwide.

Financial Audits: Planned and managed more than 50 **financial audits** throughout all Xerox sales and service operations.

Financial Controls: Designed and implemented a comprehensive program of **financial controls** and accountability to reverse previous years' losses.

Financial Models: Developed **financial models** for cost/benefit analysis, joint venture analysis, staffing analysis, and compensation design.

Financial Planning: Directed **financial planning** functions for both U.S. and European operations, and presented final results to the Board of Directors.

Financial Reporting: Eliminated unnecessary **financial reporting** and created a comprehensive PC-based program to integrate financial data from all operating divisions.

Foreign Exchange (FX): Implemented **foreign exchange** and currency hedging programs to protect IBM's Asian assets.

Initial Public Offering (IPO): Raised $54 million in public and private investment to fund **IPO**.

Internal Controls: Designed and implemented a comprehensive program of **internal controls** governing finance, accounting, capital assets, and technology acquisitions.

International Finance: Resigned core domestic financial systems and processes to create a new **international finance** function to support business expansion and product line diversification.

Investment Management: Assigned concurrent executive responsibility for administration of $50 million in **investment management**.

Investor Accounting: Personally managed **investor accounting**, reporting, and presentations.

Investor Relations: Created a sophisticated **investor relations** program, restoring credibility throughout the financial community.

Job Costing: Restructured **job costing** standards to eliminate excess expenses and strengthen bottom-line profitability of all key projects.

Letters of Credit: Issued $10 million in **letters of credit** to fund the acquisition of gold, silver, and other precious commodities.

Leveraged Buy-Out (LBO): Led management team in successful **LBO** of ABC Transportation, formed new executive team, and re-launched national sales programs.

Liability Management: Created a formal **liability management** program to control major losses resulting from downward trend in the aerospace industry.

Make/Buy Analysis: Designed PC-based templates to support **make/buy analysis** for the Construction and Real Estate Investment divisions.

Margin Improvement: Restructured corporate pricing on all major product lines and delivered a 12% **margin improvement**.

Merger: Identified opportunity, negotiated and executed transaction for the 1999 Xerox and IBM **merger**.

Operating Budgets: Managed $2 million in annual **operating budgets** allocated for personnel, facilities, and administrative expenses.

Operational Audits: Planned and directed **operational audits** of all Red Cross blood banking facilities to ensure compliance with Red Cross policy and federal regulations.

Partnership Accounting: Designed multi-tiered **partnership accounting** systems for 25 limited and general partnership real estate development projects.

Profit Gains: Accelerated **profit gains** through an aggressive program of facilities consolidation, staff reduction, and asset divestiture.

Profit/Loss (P&L) Analysis: Reviewed historical data to prepare complex **P&L analysis** as part of acquisition due diligence plan.

Project Accounting: Managed **project accounting** function for the $3.6 million Bayside Tunnel Development Project in New Orleans.

Project Financing: Negotiated $2.5 million in World Bank **project financing** for economic development programs in Ghana.

Regulatory Compliance Auditing: Established a structured process to expedite **regulatory compliance auditing**, reporting, and defense.

Return on Assets (ROA): Increased **ROA** on real estate investments by 26%.

Return on Equity (ROE): Invested $10 million in start-up industrial products company and, over six years, achieved an average 22% **ROE**.

Return on Investment (ROI): Purchased failing company, revitalized sales and distribution, and delivered a 48% **ROI** to investor group.

Revenue Gain: Negotiated distribution contracts throughout the Pacific Rim, delivering a 12% **revenue gain** in first year.

Risk Management: Strategized and implemented TouchTone's first-ever corporate **risk management**, insurance, and pension plan administration function.

Shareholder Relations: Restored corporate credibility through a combined **shareholder relations** and shareholder communications initiative.

Stock Purchase: Identified opportunity for market expansion and negotiated transaction for $837 million **stock purchase** of the Telephone Group, Inc.

Strategic Planning: Facilitated cross-functional executive team through a complex, multi-year **strategic planning** process.

Treasury: Redefined the vision, mission, and objectives of the Corporate **Treasury** Department to align financial targets with operational goals.

Trust Accounting: Developed and implemented formal **trust accounting** and pension plan reporting functions to replace reliance on third-party administrator.

Workpapers: Streamlined accounting processes to reduce **workpapers** and documentation requirements.

KeyWord Answers to Interview Questions

Tell me about yourself.

"For the past four years, I've worked as a **Senior Accountant** with one of the top public accounting firms in Seattle. Beginning as a **Junior Accountant**, I advanced rapidly through several increasingly responsible positions to my current assignment. In this capacity, I am responsible for managing a host of **corporate accounting** functions including, but not limited to, **payables, receivables, cost accounting, project accounting, cash management, departmental budgeting, corporate budgeting, capital expenditures, internal auditing, asset reporting,** and **monthly financial reporting.** Further, I have been a driving force in the introduction of several critical **cost containment** programs that have improved our **bottom-line net earnings** by an average of 12%."

What is the most valuable skill you bring to our company?

"Throughout my professional career, and even in my earlier days while still a college student, I have consistently demonstrated superb **analytical, problem-solving,** and **reasoning skills.** Never daunted by a challenge, I have accepted several **special projects** with my current employer – projects that no one else wanted because of the depth of **analytical review** required to identify the underlying problems and determine the proper resolution. To me, **analysis** is second nature. I thoroughly enjoy the intense **research** and review that it requires, the often complex **mathematical calculations,** and, most importantly, the ability to impact positive change."

What do you consider to be your most significant achievement or contribution?

"My most recent notable accomplishment was a $200,000 **cost savings** I delivered by renegotiating all of our **telecommunications** and **technology service contracts.** After a **strategic review** of all existing contracts, I **sourced new vendors, negotiated several new contracts, renegotiated existing contracts,** and improved the responsiveness of our service providers. **Projections** for next year **forecast** another $75,000 in **savings** to be realized year-after-year."

BERNARD PFEIFER

832 Westend Street
Watertown, New York 16452

Home 818.438.7971
Office 818.867.2010

September 1, 2003

Michael Caufield
Bayside Manufacturing, Inc.
1900 Commercial Way
Bayside, NY 11387

Dear Mr. Caufield:

Corporate finance is no longer just a "numbers" game. As the Senior Financial Manager with Merlena, my responsibilities have extended far beyond finance to include strategic and tactical business planning, marketing, new product development, MIS, sales administration, manufacturing, and general operating management within several of the corporation's emerging and high-growth business units. Results have been significant:

- Financial leadership for development and market launch of three major product lines, subsequently generating over $30 million in new revenues to the corporation.
- Reorganization of core business function, delivering a 25% staff reduction with no loss in performance.
- Financial and operating oversight for PC system installations and upgrades to automate field sales and marketing organizations.
- Management of a dynamic $20+ million budgeting process impacting all major operating units throughout the corporation.
- Coordination of large-scale business operating plans with particular emphasis on financial, capital, marketing, and organizational development components.

My management style is direct and decisive, yet flexible in responding to the constantly changing demands of my staff, management teams, and the marketplace. Most significant is my ability to work across diverse divisions (e.g., sales, marketing, contracts, MIS, product development), linking finance with operations to facilitate expansion, reorganization, and operating improvements.

Never satisfied with the "status quo," I earned a reputation throughout Merlena for not only the strength of my financial expertise, but for my ability to communicate and coordinate cooperative efforts through cross-functional business teams. I look forward to speaking with you to further highlight my qualifications and explore your specific financial needs and operating objectives. Thank you.

Sincerely,

Bernard Pfeifer

Bernard Pfeifer

Enclosure

DAVID M. WILLIAMS, CMA
23564 Mountain View Court
Portland, Oregon 98326
Home Office: (503) 335-9832 / Email: david.williams@navigator.com

SENIOR OPERATING & FINANCE EXECUTIVE

Corporate Planning / Financial Analysis / Financial Reporting / Treasury / Credit Management
Mergers & Acquisitions / Joint Ventures / Strategic Marketing Partnerships / Creative Leadership

Top-flight professional career as a member of the senior management team of several high-growth, high-tech corporations. Contributed millions of dollars in revenues and profits through achievements in debt and equity management, operating cost reduction, market development, contract negotiations, and general business management.

1982	**Certified Management Accountant (CMA)**
1979	**MBA**, University of Washington
1976	**BS / Business & Finance**, Seattle Pacific University

PROFESSIONAL EXPERIENCE:

Principal   1995 to Present
FINANCIAL SERVICES NETWORK, Portland, Oregon

Founded executive consulting practice specializing in strategic business planning, finance, investment acquisition, marketing, technology development, and organizational change. Major projects:

Acting CFO with Greene Video (media post production company) to represent their interests in their complex and high-profile acquisition by MultiMedia Company (multimedia entertainment group which had just completed $50+ million IPO). Introduced the parties and negotiated key elements of acquisition agreement between owners, attorneys, and financial counsel. Devoted nine months to managing an aggressive financial and operations reorganization prior to acquisition.

- Restored credibility throughout the banking, credit, and vendor communities.
- Restructured over $8 million in corporate debt as part of buyout by MultiMedia Company.
- Negotiated and resolved complex IRS issues, saving over $300,000 in principal and penalty liabilities.

Senior Finance & Marketing Manager, U.S. Capital, a premier provider of capital equipment acquisition and leasing services and business partner of my previous employer. Retained to launch the start-up of sales, marketing, and business development programs throughout the Western U.S.

- Delivered significant financial contracts and sales transactions. Closed $5 million in one year.
- Structured, negotiated, and closed leasing transactions between technology providers (e.g., Philips Symons, Sony, Discreet Logic) and financial institutions.

Director of Finance & Administration   1992 to 1995
SYMONS TELEVISION SYSTEMS, INC., San Francisco, California
($100 million manufacturer of electronic broadcast equipment for networks and cable systems worldwide.)

Recruited as **Manager of Credit & Financial Services** for the corporation's marketing, sales, and field service organization supporting operations in North America, South America, and the Pacific Rim. Promoted to **Director of Finance & Administration** for the group within first year and given full responsibility for Accounting, MIS, Sales Administration, Human Resources, and Operations (e.g., logistics, inventory, shipping, purchasing). Staff accountability for 20-person professional staff.

SYMONS TELEVISION SYSTEMS, INC. *(Continued):*

- Established new operating division to fund customer acquisitions. Negotiated strategic partnerships with lending institution and third-party agent for funding, finance administration, and collection. Business unit has now grown to $44 million in annual sales revenues.

- Rewrote corporate credit policy, centralized collections on a regional basis, and improved receivables by 20 days. Consulted with corporate legal staff in Venezuela to develop strategic and tactical plans for recovery of $1+ million in past due receivables.

Chief Financial Officer / Executive Vice President   1987 to 1992
LINTEK, INC., Cadwell, Oregon
(High-growth manufacturer of high-tech underwater electrical systems.)

Senior Finance Executive directing corporate finance, accounting, credit, treasury, tax, shareholder relations, venture capital negotiations, and lease/contract negotiations. Concurrent executive management responsibility for business development, marketing, and operations.

- Restructured corporate debt and increased company net worth by more than 100%.
- Negotiated financial, legal, and contractual terms for 10-year international license with U.K. company for technology marketing and distribution. Generated immediate cash and market share.
- Featured in Wall Street Journal Network Business News Small Business Report for negotiation of export financing from the state of California and EXIM Bank to fund Lintek's international business operations. Repaid $1+ million in funds within two years.
- Led U.S. and foreign patent acquisition program to protect applications under development.

Chief Operating Officer / Executive Vice President / Board Director   1982 to 1987
MOUNTAIN REGIONAL BANK, North Peak, California

Senior Operating Executive leading an aggressive reorganization and restructuring of multi-branch banking system to position company for sale. Directed a staff of 90 in corporate finance and administration, legal, accounting, budgeting, human resources, sales/marketing, banking services, lending/credit, customer service, and regulatory affairs.

- Reengineered all core processes and delivered long-term gains in profitability and productivity.
- Delivered 25%+ average rate of return on commercial properties.
- Successfully penetrated new market niches and expanded professional clientele.

Administration & Corporate Planning Executive   1979 to 1982
COASTAL BANK, Los Angeles, California

PROFESSIONAL ACTIVITIES:

Teaching	Guest Lecturer in Finance, Washington State University
	Guest Lecturer in Finance, Certified Management Accountants Workshop
Affiliations	Broadcast Cable Financial Managers Association (Chair, Membership Committee)
Honors/Awards	Outstanding Young Men of American Award, U.S. Jaycees, 1981 and 1984
	Toastmaster of the Year (local chapter), Toastmasters International, 1974

8

General Management, Executive Management, and Consulting

Sample Job Titles

Acting Director

Acting President

Assistant Vice President

Associate Director

Board Director

Business Manager

Business Unit Leader

Chairperson/Chairman

Chief Administrative Officer (CAO)

Chief Executive Officer (CEO)

Chief Operating Officer (COO)

Consultant

Corporate Director

Corporate Vice President

Director

Division Director

Division Vice President

Executive Consultant

Executive Director

Executive Vice President (EVP)

First Vice President

Founder

General Manager

General Partner

Interim Director

Interim Executive

Interim President

Management Consultant

Manager

Managing Director

Managing Partner

Officer

Operations Manager

Owner

Partner

President

Principal

Second Vice President

Senior Manager

Senior Vice President

Superintendent

Vice President

KeyWords and KeyWord Phrases

<u>Accelerated Growth</u>: Led RDL through a period of <u>**accelerated growth**</u> and international market expansion, resulting in a 200% gain in revenues and 300% improvement in EBIT.

Acting Executive: Appointed **Acting Executive** with full responsibility for strategic planning and business leadership during year-long nationwide search for new CEO.

Advanced Technology: Pioneered the design, development, and market launch of **advanced technology** for both information and telecommunications applications.

Benchmarking: Led **benchmarking** project to develop best-in-class manufacturing practices.

Business Development: Guided marketing and **business development** programs throughout the U.S., Canada, Latin America, and Europe.

Business Reengineering: Spearheaded the most successful **business reengineering** project in IBM's history, delivering a 25% reduction in annual operating costs while driving revenue improvement by more than 50% across all major product categories.

Capital Projects: Directed over $18 million in **capital projects** and technology acquisitions to upgrade manufacturing complex.

Competitive Market Position: Conducted worldwide competitor intelligence surveys to determine Smith's most aggressive **competitive market position** for long-term revenue and profit growth.

Consensus Building: Demonstrated proficiency in **consensus building**, team building, and executive liaison affairs.

Continuous Process Improvement: Pioneered innovative technologies and work systems to drive **continuous process improvement** across all four manufacturing and distribution facilities.

Corporate Administration: Appointed to the Board of Directors with responsibility for all **corporate administration**, recordkeeping, and stockholder reporting functions.

Corporate Communications: Expanded **corporate communications** programs to include monthly direct response campaigns to the top 250 customers nationwide.

Corporate Culture Change: Credited as the Lead Executive directing IBM's successful **corporate culture change** throughout all 300+ strategic business units worldwide.

Corporate Development: Personally structured, negotiated, and executed 25 mergers, acquisitions, joint ventures, strategic alliances, technology licenses, and other **corporate development** projects with business partners worldwide.

Corporate Image: Created a new, high-impact **corporate image** introduced through major print and broadcast media channels nationwide.

Corporate Legal Affairs: Recruited to revitalize **corporate legal affairs** and introduce improved strategies to protect corporate intelligence, technologies, and markets.

Corporate Mission: Defined **corporate mission** in response to rapidly changing market demographics.

Corporate Vision: Created a common **corporate vision** across all major product lines and strategic business units.

Cost Avoidance: Introduced best practice work processes to extend the life cycle of capital manufacturing equipment and promote **cost avoidance** over the next five years.

Cost Reduction: Pioneered innovative process improvements that **reduced costs** by $450,000 in first six months.

Crisis Communications: Directed high-profile **crisis communications** arising from major product recall.

Cross-Cultural Communications: Demonstrated proficiency in **cross-cultural communications** with business partners throughout the Pacific Rim and Far East regions.

Cross-Functional Team Leadership: Selected by the CEO to direct a **cross-functional team** evaluating potential reengineering, change management, and technology acquisitions.

Customer-Driven Management: Challenged to refocus organization and introduce a **customer-driven management** philosophy to regain competitive lead.

Customer Loyalty: Recognized as a pioneer in **customer loyalty** and retention within the highly competitive consumer products industry.

Customer Retention: Introduced interim customer communications programs, a series of special promotions and a one-on-one service program that improved **customer retention** rates by 78%.

Decision-Making Authority: Held full **decision-making authority** for all expenditures for the Aerospace & Engineering Divisions of QDL.

E-Commerce: Recognized market opportunity, hired technology team, and implemented sophisticated **e-commerce** systems to allow customers access to Grant's entire product catalog (with secure ordering capabilities).

Efficiency Improvement: Drove an organization-wide **efficiency improvement** project, integrated similar functions into core operations, and reduced costs by 12% in first year.

Emerging Business Venture: Identified opportunity, structured partnership, and captured **emerging business ventures** throughout Eastern Europe.

Entrepreneurial Leadership: Provided decisive, action-driven, **entrepreneurial leadership**.

European Economic Community (EEC): Guided corporate expansion throughout emerging and mature markets within the **EEC**.

Executive Management: Member of 6-person **Executive Management** Team credited with transitioning Apex from multi-year losses to sustained profitability.

Executive Presentations: Designed and led **executive presentations** to Board of Directors, shareholders, Wall Street analysts, and financial auditors.

Financial Management: Member of 6-person Senior Management Team and the most Senior Financial Executive responsible for all financial planning, **financial management**, and long-range business development functions.

Financial Restructuring: Orchestrated an aggressive **financial restructuring** of all technology support operations, reducing annual costs by $2.8 million and strengthening competitive lead.

Global Market Expansion: Guided Johnson Controls's expansion throughout the **global market**.

High-Growth Organization: Delivered strong revenue and profit results in start-up, turnaround, and **high-growth organizations**.

Infrastructure: Redesigned and streamlined organizational **infrastructure** to capitalize upon human resource, operational, and financial competencies.

Interim Executive: Appointed **Interim Executive** with full P&L responsibility for $8 million corporation.

Leadership Development: Designed **leadership development** programs for all mid-level and senior management personnel throughout the organization.

Long-Range Planning: Guided **long-range planning** for operations, sales, marketing, and customer service.

Management Development: Introduced leadership training, technology training, communication skills training, and other **management development** programs.

Margin Improvement: Realigned product mix and captured a 12% **margin improvement**.

Market Development: Identified opportunity to expand customer reach and led targeted **market development** programs throughout Central and South America.

Market-Driven Management: Revitalized corporation and introduced **market-driven management** systems to accelerate revenue growth against competition.

Marketing Management: Senior Executive leading strategic planning, product development, and **marketing management** programs across all seven major business units.

Matrix Management: Operated within a **matrix management** environment transcending all core business, operating, financial, marketing, and human resource functions.

Multi-Function Experience: Promoted rapidly through a series of increasingly responsible management positions, gaining broad-based, **multi-function experience** across corporate finance, marketing, strategic planning, and product management.

Multi-Industry Experience: Gained broad **multi-industry experience** within the plastics, metals, and ceramics manufacturing industries.

Multi-Site Operations Management: Senior Executive with full P&L responsibility for **multi-site operations management** of production facilities in Frankfurt, Rome, and Salzburg.

New Business Development: Challenged to identify and capture opportunities for **new business development**, market growth, and revenue improvement throughout the Northeastern U.S.

Operating Infrastructure: Streamlined corporate **operating infrastructure**, consolidated administrative functions from six offices into headquarters, replaced non-performing staff, and introduced a performance incentive program.

Operating Leadership: Provided decisive, proactive, and market-driven **operating leadership** within a politically volatile business market.

Organization(al) Culture: Redefined corporate vision, rewrote mission statement, and revitalized **organizational culture**.

Organization(al) Development: Pioneered innovative **organizational development** initiatives including pay for performance, diversity management, process redesign, and change management.

Participative Management: Fostered employee empowerment and **participative management** practices throughout the manufacturing organization.

Performance Improvement: Led 6-person task force in the design and implementation of **performance improvement** initiatives throughout all 22 branch operations.

Policy Development: Directed **policy development** for all sales, service, and support functions nationwide.

Proactive Leadership: Credited with providing the corporation with **proactive leadership** despite four changes in ownership over a two-year period.

Process Ownership: Introduced **process ownership** into the quality function, eliminating the need for physical inspection and improving product quality ratings to a consistent 98%.

Process Reengineering: Spearheaded **process reengineering** and redesign of all core production planning, scheduling, and manufacturing management systems.

Productivity Improvement: Delivered measurable **productivity improvements** across the field organization.

Profit & Loss (P&L) Management: Promoted to General Manager with full operating and **P&L management** responsibility for $8.2 million distribution facility.

Profit Growth: Implemented new selling strategies designed to accelerate **profit growth** and expansion into high-growth mass merchant markets.

Project Management: Appointed Leader of 22-person **project management** team leading technology introductions and enhancements throughout RDL's nationwide logistics organization.

Quality Improvement: Recruited to provide strategic and tactical leadership for quality improvement and **quality management** functions.

Reengineering: Led corporate-wide **reengineering** and revitalization program, reducing losses by $2.8 million and improving market share ratings by 29%.

Relationship Management: Directed key account **relationship management** functions for 25 of the corporation's largest customer accounts.

Reorganization: Challenged to lead the corporation through an aggressive **reorganization** and divestiture of non-performing business units, products, and technologies.

Return-On-Assets (ROA): Restructured corporate assets and improved **ROA** by 36%.

Return-On-Equity (ROE): Invested over $10 million in emerging technology ventures with goal of a better than 52% **ROE**.

Return-On-Investment (ROI): Replaced in-house benefits professional with third-party administrator and improved **ROI** by 18% within first year.

Revenue Growth: Drove 27% **revenue growth** against stiff market competition in the New England region.

Sales Management: Led a 62-person, multinational **sales management** team supporting 1,000+ distributors worldwide.

Service Design/Delivery: Delivered 22% improvement in customer retention through improved **service design/delivery** systems.

Signatory Authority: Held $2 million contract **signatory authority** for the corporation.

Start-Up Venture: Challenged to identify and capitalize upon opportunities to develop and direct **start-up ventures** in the former Soviet Union markets.

Strategic Development: Evaluated new product opportunities and directed **strategic development** of business plans, financial projections, marketing plans, and field sales teams.

Strategic Partnership: Structured and negotiated a **strategic partnership** with Mobil Oil to manage joint exploration projects in the Middle East.

Tactical Planning/Leadership: Transitioned strategy into **tactical plans** to drive market growth and diversification.

Team Building: Introduced performance-driven **team building** processes into the materials management and engineering organizations.

Team Leadership: Provided decisive **team leadership** and direction to a 2,000-person manufacturing organization.

Total Quality Management (TQM) - Championed the development and implementation of **TQM** programs and achieved ISO 9002 within six months.

Transition Management: Effectively guided Apollo Systems through six changes in operating executives and the resulting **transition management** functions.

Turnaround Management: Recognized by the Board of Directors for expertise in **turnaround management** and return to profitability of 3M's newest product marketing group.

World Class Organization: Transitioned NEBS from a family-owned start-up venture into a **world class manufacturing and service organization**.

KeyWord Answers to Interview Questions

Tell me about yourself.

"I am the consummate **Management Executive** with more than 20 years of **senior-level operating management** experience. Beginning my career in outside **sales** and **customer relationship management**, I was promoted rapidly through a series of increasingly responsible positions – from sales to **sales management** to **regional operations management** to my current position as the COO of a million-dollar technology services company. Most notably, I've taken this company from a **privately held venture** generating $25 million a year to our current status as one of the top five companies in the national market. Much of the company's growth and profitability can be attributed to my **strong leadership** in providing a sound **strategic plan**, negotiating **critical strategic alliances**, leading **road shows** to obtain **financing,** and building an **operating infrastructure** to support accelerated **expansion**."

What is the most valuable skill you bring to our company?

"Defining a company's **mission**, creating a clear **vision statement**, recruiting **top management talent**, and providing day-to-day **operating leadership** are the greatest talents I bring to your organization. Throughout my career, I have been the one responsible for defining each company's **model for growth and expansion**, their **resource requirements**, **financial** needs, **personnel** needs, and action plan to achieve **revenue and profit objectives**. And, I have succeeded! As you read my resume, you'll see that in each position I delivered **double-digit growth** despite **intense market competition**."

What do you consider to be your most significant achievement or contribution?

"When I joined the Axis Company, sales were $25 million a year. Within just five years, my team and I have increased annual sales to more than $300 million with **bottom-line profits** averaging 22%. In fact, based on our **successful and profitable growth**, many of our processes have been **benchmarked** and incorporated by several of our top competitors."

BRYCE R. BURTON

2500 Santa Monica Blvd. #222   Phone: (310) 681-3829
Santa Monica, California 93872   Fax: (310) 681-3726

December 30, 2003

Phillip Carson
Roweson Manufacturing
900 Oleson Boulevard
Montgomery, AL 39283

Dear Mr. Carson:

Building corporate value is my expertise. Whether challenged to launch a start-up, orchestrate an aggressive turnaround, or accelerate growth, I have consistently delivered strong financial results. The value I bring Roweson can best be summarized as follows:

- More than 10 years of direct P&L responsibility across diverse industries and market sectors.
- Strong, decisive, and profitable leadership of global sales and marketing organizations.
- Keen financial, negotiating, and strategic planning performance.
- Consistent and measurable gains in operations, quality, and efficiency productivity.
- Outstanding record of leadership in the consumer products and management consulting industries.

To each organization, my teams and I have delivered strong and sustainable operating, market, and financial advantages critical to long-term growth, profitability, and competitive performance. Most notably, I:

- Increased sales 9.6%, reduced headcount 45%, shortened leadtimes 60% and improved quality performance 300% for a $120 million company.
- Orchestrated successful turnaround and return to profitability of Stockton Fabrics. Cost reductions surpassed $2 million, account base increased 15%, and annualized cash flow improved $1.2 million, while launching the most successful new product introduction in the company's history.
- Accelerated market growth of The Miller Group of Companies in a highly competitive and volatile market, increasing revenues 45% within the first year and delivering equally significant reductions in operating costs and corporate debt.

My goal is a top-level management position with an organization seeking to achieve market dominance as well as aggressive revenue and profit projections. I am most interested in interviewing for the position of Vice President of Operations where I will provide the strategic and tactical leadership critical to success in today's fast-moving environment. I look forward to meeting with you and the other principals.

Sincerely,

Bryce R. Burton

Bryce R. Burton

Enclosure

EDWARD T. PATTERSON
3985 Dunhill Drive
San Ramon, California 90631

Residence: (315) 359-7873   Business: (315) 359-8742
Email: ETP@aol.com   Fax: (315) 359-2676

SENIOR OPERATING & MANAGEMENT EXECUTIVE

Senior Executive with a long and successful career building start-up, turnaround, and high-growth organizations. Delivered strong and sustainable financial gains in challenging markets nationwide through decisive leadership, influence, and action. MBA Degree. Expertise includes:

General Business & Operations Management

- Distinguished performance on the executive management teams of four corporations, providing strategic leadership, vision, and tactical action to deliver improved financial, performance, and profit results. Successful in identifying and capitalizing upon new business opportunities through integration of technical, personnel, financial, and operating resources to dominate markets and drive long-term asset and revenue gains. Accomplished in customer relationship management and high-quality customer service.

Corporate Finance & Deal Making

- Ten years experience structuring and negotiating complex corporate financing transactions with Wall Street bankers and brokers, venture capital firms, private investors, and others to fund new ventures, market expansion initiatives, new product and service offerings, and cash flow. Participated and/or led over $2 billion in total financial transactions throughout career. Expert in investor relations and investor reporting. Experienced Board Director.

Advanced Technology

- Spearheaded development of proposed investment in client/server technology to develop innovative applications for consumer financial services. Led year-long project feasibility analysis and nationwide market research/market survey, developed complex risk analysis process, and identified optimum strategies for technology development, documentation, prototyping, and full-scale market launch.

Technical / Non-Technical Communications

- Bridged the gap between executives and technology development teams to ensure that projects were financially viable, technically appropriate, and capable of meeting long-term organizational, productivity, and performance goals. Able to communicate highly technical information to non-technical personnel.

Marketing Management

- Conceived, developed and executed top-producing marketing campaigns across diverse customer sectors nationwide. Delivered unprecedented performance results through innovation in campaign design, production, and marketing leadership. Strong qualifications in new product development and launch.

Team Building & Organizational Leadership

- Track record of success in building and leading top-producing professional, technical, support, and management teams meeting the challenges of start-up, turnaround, and high-growth organizations. Extensive background in management training and development, organizational design, business process design, budgeting, and project leadership.

EDWARD T. PATTERSON - Page Two

PROFESSIONAL EMPLOYMENT HISTORY

Director   1996 to 1997
Pioneer Financial Services, San Ramon, California

Directed high-profile technology feasibility project for development of client/server PC network. Project was initiated to enhance competitive position, increase cross-sell performance, reduce staffing requirements, and automate the entire credit decisioning and documentation process. Managed a complex cost/risk analysis to evaluate "buy versus build." Authored recommendations for development, beta testing, and deployment.

President / Chief Executive Officer / Director   1993 to 1995
Lewis Federal Bank, F.S.B., Lewis, California

Senior Operating Executive with full P&L responsibility for the turnaround, internal reorganization and market repositioning of this $125 million corporation. Directed operations at eight facilities and with a total workforce of 150. Developed successful strategy to divest under- and non-performing assets, restructured liabilities, renegotiated funding, and increased market penetration in all sectors. Provided long-term vision and created multi-year action plan. Achieved/surpassed all turnaround objectives.

National Director of Marketing & Business Development   1990 to 1993
Federal Housing Authority, Washington, D.C.

Joined the senior management team to spearhead an aggressive market expansion to position Federal Housing Authority as a diversified financial services institution. Developed business strategies to diversify customer base, established internal business systems and processes to accommodate increased workload, and pioneered innovative marketing programs. Directed development of award-winning "Community Banks - Main Street to Wall Street."

Vice President - Capital Markets   1988 to 1989
Resources, Inc., Provo, Utah

Recruited to plan and orchestrate the start-up of a new business venture, building new business infrastructure, designing internal operating processes, implementing new technology, and driving new venture to profitability. Transitioned concept into full-scale operation and developed $200 million senior LBO debt portfolio.

Credit Manager   1980 to 1988
Citicorp / Citibank, New York, New York

Fast-track promotion through a series of increasingly responsible management positions leading high-profile start-up ventures, marketing organizations, and new business development initiatives nationwide. Delivered strong and sustainable performance results in each position through success in team building and leadership.

Active duty with U.S. Army (1970 to 1974). Retired as Lt. Colonel in U.S. Army Reserve in 1995.

EDUCATION

MBA (Banking & Finance), Golden Gate University, 1979

BA (Sociology), University of California, 1977

9

Health Care

Sample Job Titles

Administrator

Assistant Administrator

Budget Director

Chief Executive Officer (CEO)

Chief Financial Officer (CFO)

Chief Nursing Officer (CNO)

Chief Operating Officer (COO)

Clinical Marketing Director

Clinical Services Director

Controller

Director of Administration

Director of Billing

Director of Finance

Director of Inservice Education

Director of Patient Accounting

Director of Reimbursement

Doctor

Executive Director

Executive Vice President (EVP)

Finance Manager

General Manager

Health Care Administrator

Hospital Administrator

Inpatient Services Director

Laboratory Technician

Laboratory Manager

Managed Care Director

Medical Affairs Officer

Medical Director

Nurse

Nursing Administrator

Nursing Director

Nursing Home Administrator

Outpatient Services Director

Physician

Physician's Assistant

Quality Assurance Director

Registered Nurse

Risk Manager

Senior Nursing Executive

Surgeon

Vice President

KeyWords and KeyWord Phrases

<u>Acute Care Facility</u>: Chief Executive Officer of a 434-bed **<u>acute care facility</u>**, six free-standing community clinics, and a large health care research complex.

<u>Ambulatory Care</u>: Structured three-year contractual agreement with Ryder for the delivery of on-site **<u>ambulatory care</u>** services at corporate headquarters.

Assisted Living: Established the region's first-ever **assisted living** center within the Monticello Retirement Village.

Capital Giving Campaign: Spearheaded multimedia communications, advertising, and direct mail programs for a successful $10 million **capital giving campaign**.

Case Management: Created a multi-discipline **case management** protocol for the evaluation, diagnosis, and treatment planning of all incoming HIV-positive patients.

Certificate of Need (CON): Authored **Certificate of Need** requesting $2 billion in funding for development of 1,000-bed research facility.

Chronic Care Facility: Recruited to plan and direct the financial turnaround of a 250-bed **chronic care facility** with affiliated hospice.

Clinical Services: Restructured health care delivery procedures to expand **clinical services** throughout the metropolitan region.

Community Hospital: Led 2-year construction project for the development of a 500-bed **community hospital** targeted to indigenous populations throughout Central Arkansas.

Community Outreach: Won Board funding for the development and execution of an aggressive **community outreach** and health care education program.

Continuity of Care: Implemented processes to enhance the **continuity of care** among surgeons, attending physicians, nursing staff, and administration.

Cost Center: Transitioned **cost center** into profit-producing venture with the introduction of corporate contracts for on-site health examinations.

Electronic Claims Processing: Introduced **electronic claims processing** into group medical practice and improved collections by 34% annually.

Emergency Medical Systems (EMS): Joined the start-up management team developing the University of Maryland **Emergency Medical Systems** organization.

Employee Assistance Program (EAP): Launched the start-up, staffing, budgeting, and service delivery of Westinghouse's first-ever **EAP**.

Fee Billing: Streamlined documentation processes and accelerated **fee billing** for private pay and Medicare patients.

Full Time Equivalent (FTE): Staffed new health care facility with 120 **FTEs** and 60 on-call nursing personnel.

Grant Administration: Full management responsibility for **grant administration** of more than $200 million in annual research funds from Carnegie Mellon University, USC, and Brigham Young.

Health Care Administrator: Senior **Health Care Administrator** with full operating, staffing, clinical, technical, and P&L responsibility for the entire health care complex.

Health Care Delivery Systems: Devoted 10 years to the research and design of integrated **health care delivery systems**, models, and protocols.

Health Maintenance Organization (HMO): Led presentations and won support of Board of Directors for the start-up of a new **HMO** focused on comprehensive, preventive health care.

Home Health Care: Managed a large **home health care** agency offering in-home respiratory, physical, and chemotherapy services.

Hospital Foundation: Established DC General's not-for-profit **hospital foundation** to support long-range funding, facilities expansion, and pioneering research.

Industrial Medicine: Recruited as Raytheon's first-ever in-house physician to guide the development of a complete **industrial medicine** and occupational medicine facility.

Inpatient Care: Expanded **inpatient care** programs to include 24-hour nursing services for acutely ill patients diagnosed with Legionnaire's Disease.

Long-Term Care: Negotiated partnership with the USC Medical Center to establish a new **long-term care** facility for communicable diseases.

Managed Care: Forged innovative **managed care** partnerships with leading health care providers and administrators throughout Detroit.

Management Service Organization (MSO): Integrated best practices from HMO and PPO practices throughout the region to create a comprehensive **MSO** network.

Multi-Hospital Network: Structured and negotiated the integration of Los Angeles's six primary care facilities to create a **multi-hospital network** offering comprehensive acute and long-term hospice care.

Occupational Health: Introduced an **occupational health** program with required preventive health care teaching and reduced on-the-job accidents by 45% in first year.

Outpatient Care: Expanded service offerings in a large **outpatient care** facility and increased number of annual patient visits by 18%.

Patient Accounting: Restructured the hospital's **patient accounting** operations and accelerated collections to the best in the region.

Patient Relations: Designed print and video communications to strengthen **patient relations** and the credibility of newly renovated, inner-city hospital complex.

Peer Review: Managed **peer review** issues resulting from alleged malpractice incidents.

Physician Credentialing: Established and administered **physician credentialing** program for all new doctors entering the MSO network.

Physician Relations: Developed a formal **physician relations** program to attract and retain renowned cardiologists to the practice.

Practice Management: Created innovative **practice management** models and methodologies to strengthen quality of care.

Preferred Provider Organization (PPO): Forged relationships with leading health care specialists throughout the region to create a unique **PPO** network offering comprehensive diagnostic and clinical services.

Preventive Medicine: Advocated for establishment of a comprehensive **preventive medicine** program throughout all public school and day care facilities in Denver.

Primary Care: Transitioned from specialty neurology practice into **primary care** in response to changing patient demographics.

Provider Relations: Partnered clinical services with marketing programs to create a unique **provider relations** and provider support program.

Public Health Administration: Revitalized West Virginia's **Public Health Administration** services and policy.

Quality of Care: Introduced **quality of care** standards, protocols and reporting requirements to meet JCAHO standards.

Regulatory Standards (JCAHO): Resolved long-standing non-compliance issues and achieved 100% compliance with all regulatory standards mandated by **JCAHO** and state agencies.

Rehabilitation Services: Negotiated public and private funding for the start-up of **rehabilitation services** for paraplegics, quadriplegics, and other long-term rehab patients.

Reimbursement Program: Managed a multi-million dollar third-party **reimbursement program**, implemented new collection procedures, and recovered over $90,000 in outstanding receivables.

Risk Management: Authored a formal **risk management** policy for the entire medical facility, all affiliated health care clinics, and the region's largest healthcare research facility.

Service Delivery: Improved **service delivery** through restaffing and implementation of stringent quality of care standards.

<u>Skilled Nursing Facility</u>: Held full P&L, operating, staffing, regulatory, and clinical service delivery responsibility for a 180-bed **skilled nursing facility**.

<u>Third-Party Administrator</u>: Introduced new patient filing and documentation processes to meet changing requirements of **third-party administrator**.

<u>Utilization Review</u>: Designed and administered **utilization review**, peer review, and other internal quality management processes.

<u>Wellness Programs</u>: Forged the development of corporate **wellness programs** impacting all 3,000+ employees of the RayChem Corporation.

KeyWord Answers to Interview Questions

Tell me about yourself.

"In defining 'who' I am, there are really two aspects of my professional career that are critical. First and foremost, I'm a **physician** with more than 15 years' experience in the delivery of **patient care**, working primarily in the **medical disciplines** of **neurology** and **neurophysiology**. Just as significant, I am an experienced **hospital administrator** with current responsibility for the profitable management of a **234-bed acute care hospital** in suburban Boston. In this capacity, my responsibilities are vast, ranging from the **daily operations** of the hospital and all **patient care programs** to a host of **administrative, regulatory,** and **financial affairs**. In fact, I am currently working on a **Certificate of Need** application for $35 million to fund development of a new **rehabilitation facility** and several **community outreach** programs to enhance the public's use of our hospital for **preventative care and education.**"

What is the most valuable skill you bring to our company?

"The fact that I am both a **doctor** and an **administrator** is the greatest skill I bring to your facility. This allows me to manage from both a hands-on **health care delivery** perspective as well as that of a **manager**, concerned with **dollars, resources, person-**

nel, and **facilities**. The interrelationship of the two is what has been at the foundation of my entire career success."

What do you consider to be your most significant achievement or contribution?

"As a **physician**, I would have to say that my greatest achievement is the positive impact I've made in the lives of hundreds of patients, many of whom had resigned themselves to living with **chronic neurological conditions**. Through the tremendous advances in the field of **neurology** and the latest **treatment protocols**, I've been able to give them back **quality of life** and time. However, knowing that you're equally interested in my **health care administration** background, let me also note that I've been a pioneer in the **managed care** arena, working with **insurance companies, providers,** and **health care facilities** to create programs responsive to our community's needs."

CARL WATSON, M.D.
2649 North Wabash Avenue
Chicago, Illinois 60610

Home (312) 480-9809   Office (312) 916-4125

February 4, 2003

James L. Lewis
Lewis & Associates
100 West 49th Street, 15th Floor
New York, NY 10019

Dear Mr. Lewis:

Currently a Director of Memorial West Hospital / Medical School, I am exploring new management opportunities in the emerging health care, managed care, pharmaceutical and biotechnology industries. With more than 15 years of health care management experience, strong clinical qualifications and current attendance in Kellogg's MBA program (expected in 2002), I am seeking the opportunity to combine my skills for a top-level management position.

Beginning my career as a Medical Doctor and Radiologist, I quickly expanded the scope of my responsibility to include a diversity of business management functions – from strategic planning, staffing, and budgeting to pioneering programs in technology, quality, and performance improvement. In sum, I manage the "business" of medicine.

Notable achievements include recognition by JCAHO for my efforts in quality and regulatory affairs, development of innovative management and professional training programs, publication of research in more than 60 journal articles, and introduction of state-of-the-art information, radiologic, and medical systems. I have helped to build a department at Memorial that is not only recognized for its clinical expertise, but just as significantly for its management, financial, technological, and quality achievements.

With the addition of my MBA degree, I am now ready to transition my qualifications into the private sector where I can participate in the development, operations, and leadership of a successful organization. If you are working with a client company seeking a candidate with my qualifications, I would welcome a personal interview. Please note that I am interested in relocating to New York and that my compensation requirements are flexible. Thank you.

Sincerely,

Carl Watson

Carl Watson, M.D.

Enclosure

HOWARD M. JOHNSON, MPA

Hjohn@mcimailnet.net
9863 Constable Road
Wilmington, Delaware 19832
Residence: 302-786-5433   Fax: 302-786-6935

HEALTH CARE INDUSTRY EXECUTIVE
Managed Care / Hospitals & Clinics / Multi-Site Facilities

Cross-functional management expertise in the strategic planning, development, and operations of health care facilities and comprehensive delivery systems. Combines leadership success in:

- Integrated Health Care Delivery
- Staffing, Training & Development
- Budgeting & Cost Reduction
- Project & Time Management

- Government Relations & Liaison Affairs
- Contract Negotiations & Mediation
- Regulatory Reporting & Compliance
- Resource & Technology Acquisition

Excellent organizational, communication, and analytical skills. Delivered innovative, cost-sensitive and high-quality managed care programs to replace traditional health care services. Adjunct University Professor.

PROFESSIONAL EXPERIENCE:

INMATE HEALTH SERVICES, INC.   1993 to Present
(National Contract Health Care Services Delivery Organization)

Regional Vice President – Wilmington, DE (1993 to Present)

Senior Executive with full responsibility for the strategic planning, staffing, financial affairs, resources, day-to-day operations, and P&L performance of a comprehensive managed health care delivery system for the Wilmington Prison System. Operate six facilities delivering care to 5,600 inmates and providing 100,000 clinic visits each year. Control $17 million annual operating budget. Direct a staff of 175 FTEs, Director of Nursing, Director of Medical Records, Regional Medical Director, and administrative personnel. Provide oversight to a team of 20 physicians and 15 physician assistants.

- Delivered strong cost reductions in labor, material, equipment, and overhead. Transitioned from breakeven in 1995 to 16% operating margin in 1996 with 10%+ projected for 1997.

- Spearheaded development of innovative health care services and programs including:

  - **In-House Specialty Health Care Practices** (e.g., general surgery, optometry, ophthalmology), reducing cost of services by an average of 5-7% annually.
  - **Managed Care** with a focus on cost reduction and quality control/assurance.
  - **Chronic Care** to reduce costs while improving quality of monitoring/management care.
  - **Pharmacy Utilization** to improve service and drug availability.

- Proactively managed litigation, medical malpractice, and employee law. Worked closely with the City of Wilmington Law Department on consent decrees regarding medical care.

- Conceived/led in-house staff training and development programs on topics ranging from patient care standards to cost control, quality management, and government liaison affairs.

- Structured and negotiated favorable union contracts and wage agreements.

- Established cooperative partnerships with the City of Wilmington Public Health Department and area hospitals to expand medical resources and provide timely follow-up of public health issues and referrals. Personally managed sensitive governmental and political liaison affairs.

HOWARD M. JOHNSON, MPA
Page Two

INMATE HEALTH SERVICES, INC. *(Continued):*

Regional Manager – Atlanta, GA (1993)

Regional Health Care Administrator for the Sheriff's Department, three health care facilities, and 3,000 inmates. Directed a staff of five administrators/managers and 75 FTEs. Personally managed liaison affairs with local government agencies, attorneys, social service organizations, and others.

- Led the organization through an aggressive restructuring, transitioning from loss to 18% profit within nine months. Resolved immediate crisis and restored client credibility.

- Resolved critical non-compliance issues with client contract, improved utilization management, implemented quality assurance initiatives, and controlled overhead costs. Restaffed key management positions.

INSTITUTIONAL MEDICAL SERVICES, INC.   1990 to 1993
(National Contract Health Care Services Delivery Organization)

Health Service Administrator – Philadelphia, PA (1991 to 1993)

Orchestrated successful operating and financial turnaround of health care unit servicing the medical needs of 1,200 inmates. Regained accreditation from the American Correctional Association following redesign and quality improvement of all service delivery and preventative care programs. Directed a staff of 35+.

Hospital Administrator – Greenville, SC (1990 to 1991)

Senior Administrator of a 35-bed inpatient care hospital within the confines of the South Carolina State Penitentiary. Full responsibility for facilities management, purchasing, budgeting, regulatory reporting, staffing, and complete health care delivery system.

KAISER PERMANENTE HEALTH CARE PROGRAM, Rockville, MD
1979 to 1990

Medical Facility Administrator

Eleven-year management career with full P&L, operating, administrative, staffing and service delivery responsibility for a full-service outpatient health care facility, one of the earliest HMOs in the U.S. Serviced a population of more than 35,000 patients annually.

EDUCATION:

Executive Development Program, Stanford University, 1989

Master's of Public Administration, University of Virginia, 1979
Minor in Health Care Administration & Finance. Dean's List.

Bachelor of Business Administration, University of Virginia, 1976
Minor in Economics. Dean's List.

10

Hospitality

Sample Job Titles

Assistant Food and Beverage (F&B) Manager

Banquet Captain

Banquet Manager

Banquet Sales Manager

Cashier

Catering Manager

Certified Food and Beverage Executive (CFBE)

Certified Hotel Administrator (CHA)

Chef

Club Manager

Conference Center Manager

Director of Food and Beverage (F&B)

Executive Chef

Front Office Manager

General Manager

Guest Services Manager

Housekeeping Manager

Marketing Manager

Multi-Unit Operations Manager
Operations Manager
Regional Director
Resort Manager
Restaurant Manager
Rooms Division Manager
Sales Director
Sales Manager
Service Staff Manager
Sous Chef
Special Events Director
Unit Manager
Waiter/Waitress

KeyWords and KeyWord Phrases

Amenities: Created a world-class **amenities** program to attract VIPs, corporate executives, and other business travelers.

Back-of-the-House Operations: Redesigned **back-of-the-house operations**, implemented incentives to support customer service objectives, and delivered a 12% reduction in annual operating costs.

Banquet Operations: Expanded service programs to include full-scale **banquet operations**, catered food service, and other special events.

Budget Administration: Directed **budget administration**, forecasting, and allocation for over $34 million in annual guest service expenses.

Catering Operations: Expanded on-premise **catering operations** to include major off-premise events for the Baltimore Orioles, Baltimore Convention Center, and National Aquarium.

Club Management: Over 20 years experience in **club management** with exclusive private properties throughout Austria, Switzerland, and Germany.

Conference Management: Recruited to plan, design, construct, staff, and operate the first-ever **conference management** center in Nigeria ($8.8 million joint public-private venture).

Contract F&B Operations: Negotiated over $20 million in **contract F&B operations** for corporate centers in Atlanta, Charleston, and Tampa.

Corporate Dining Room: Profitably operated the 200-seat **corporate dining room** at Federal Express headquarters.

Customer Retention: Designed promotional and marketing communications to improve **customer retention** in the group and business travel markets.

Customer Service: Pioneered innovative **customer service** standards unique to the hospitality industry and successfully positioned Abrams Hotels as #1 in exclusive guest amenities.

Food & Beverage Operations (F&B): Senior Executive with full P&L responsibility for the entire **food & beverage operation** of Lyman Hotels worldwide (2,000 properties in 84 countries on 5 continents).

Food Cost Controls: Implemented stringent **food cost controls** and reduced annual expenditures by $2+ million.

Front-of-the-House Operations: Created unique customer incentives and standards that drove strong gains in customer service throughout all **front-of-the-house operations**.

Guest Retention: Created and launched the "Guest Value" program that increased **guest retention** by more than 30% over two years.

Guest Satisfaction: Demonstrated the worth of "Guest Value" (unique customer service and loyalty program) with an average 95% **guest satisfaction** rating.

Hospitality Management: Built and operated profitable **hospitality management** programs worldwide for Hyatt, Hilton, and several prestigious European properties.

Inventory Planning/Control: Forecasted annual product requirements and directed departmental **inventory planning and control** functions.

Labor Cost Controls: Restructured front- and back-of-the-house staffs, implemented stringent **labor cost controls**, and saved $4.5+ million annually.

Meeting Planning: Directed **meeting planning** for annual sales conventions for major corporate clients (e.g., IBM, Xerox, 3M, Andersen, Gould).

Member Development/Retention: Launched unique print and broadcast advertising programs, direct mail campaigns, and other communications to accelerate **member development** and improve **member retention**.

Menu Planning: Directed **menu planning** for more than 200 special event programs at Madison Square Garden (total cost of more than $75 million).

Menu Pricing: Restructured **menu pricing** and improved profit on average ticket by 5%.

Multi-Unit Operations: Held full responsibility for **multi-unit operations** through Wisconsin, Iowa, and Minnesota (total of 250 employees and over $45 million in annual sales).

Occupancy: Improved **occupancy** ratings by 27% within the highly competitive corporate travel market in Chicago.

Portion Control: Standardized **portion control** procedures to reduce escalating costs.

Property Development: Management team representative for **property development** and construction programs of hotels, restaurants, and conference centers throughout emerging Latin American markets.

Purchasing: Managed over $300 million in annual food and beverage **purchasing**.

Resort Management: Senior Operating Executive with full P&L responsibility for **resort management** and operations at six properties in the Western Caribbean.

Service Management: Spearheaded customer-driven **service manage-ment** and improvement programs to sustain competitive market lead.

Signature Property: Built and operated the 345-room Belvedere Property in Munich, Germany, creating what is now recognized as the Lederre Hotel Group's **signature property**.

Vendor Sourcing: Expanded **vendor sourcing**, identified low-cost suppliers, and reduced overall purchasing costs by 8%-10% annually.

VIP Relations: Introduced top-flight **VIP relations** and amenities services catering to high net worth individuals and corporate executives on long-term travel assignments.

KeyWord Answers to Interview Questions

Tell me about yourself.

"When I arrived on-site at the Meridien Hotel, there was an empty building. It was lovely, brand new, and on beautiful grounds. But there was nothing inside – no **employees**, no **guests**, no **F&B**, no **front desk**, no **housekeeping** ... nothing. Then the owner said, "Here's your hotel and three administrative people to help you. Can you have the hotel up and running within two months?" Well, long story short, we did it. Two months to the day after I arrived, we held our **grand opening** to a huge audience and **100% capacity** the first night! So, if you ask me about myself, it's that I'm the "hotel start-up guy," able to quickly, cost-effectively, and efficiently launch **new properties** to rave reviews, strong **financial perfor-mance**, and a keen commitment to the finest in **guest services**."

What is the most valuable skill you bring to our company?

"Undeniably, my best skills are my abilities to **organize** and **prioritize**. Whether I'm opening a new hotel, introducing a new **PC-based reservations management system**, or designing **guest amenities**, I have consistently delivered projects **on time** and **within budget** because of my ability to **plan**, **organize**, **prioritize**, and **execute**. This is the value and strength I bring to all of my operations and my special projects, and is what I will deliver to you and your stockholders."

What do you consider to be your most significant achievement or contribution?

"Without a doubt, my greatest achievement is the opening of the Meridien Hotel in just two months. This was a **249-room resort property** with complete **spa facilities,** three **F&B outlets,** and **18 acres of grounds and landscaping.** Starting with nothing, I opened a hotel 60 days later with a staff of 72. We were truly amazed. During that time, I did everything ... **budgeting, hiring, training, management development, menu planning and pricing, purchasing, security,** and, most significantly, **marketing.** In fact, by opening day we had more than $500,000 in **business meeting commitments** for the first 30 days."

FRANK NELSON, JR.
425 Armadillo Avenue
Rosemont, Texas 77877
299-432-3927

February 14, 2003

Paul Kirwin
President - Country Inns & Suites
Country Hospitality Worldwide
P.O. Box 59159
Minneapolis, MN 55459-8203

Dear Mr. Kirwin:

Congratulations! I've been watching the development of your new property in Rosemont, Texas and can tell you that the entire community is looking forward to the grand opening. We've needed a property of this type in Rosemont for several years (as I'm sure your demographics indicated), and I know that the project will be extremely profitable if well led.

I'm a local resident of Rosemont with a wealth of business experience worldwide. Having recently relocated permanently to the area, I would welcome the opportunity to interview with you or a member of your staff for the position of General Manager with the local property. Let me tell you why I am the "perfect" candidate (albeit atypical):

- 15+ years of general management experience in facilities development and management, including planning, budgeting, logistics, purchasing, equipment, materials, and technology.

- Outstanding communication and people-to-people interaction skills. I am well known throughout the local market, have extensive contacts throughout both the professional and civic communities, and recently completed a yearlong leadership training course with the City.

- Ability to "get the job done" no matter the circumstance. This was critical throughout my career, often working in environments with stringent deadlines and financial expectations.

- Strong qualifications in training, development, and leadership with direct responsibility for hundreds of employees, supervisors and managers, and multi-million dollar budgets.

- In-depth understanding of customer service, customer loyalty, and customer retention.

I am available at your convenience for a personal interview and guarantee that the strength of my leadership skills and operating performance will position Rosemont for strong and profitable growth.

Sincerely,

Frank Nelson

Frank Nelson, Jr.

Enclosure

JOHN P. LANDAU, CHA

3859 Wabash Avenue, #12B
Chicago, Illinois 60616
(847) 437-8621
jpland@planet.com

HOSPITALITY INDUSTRY EXECUTIVE
Private Clubs, Hotels and F&B Operations

- Member Development & Retention
- Sales/Marketing Management
- Quality Customer Service
- Human Resource Affairs

- Finance/Budget Administration
- Project Management
- Marketing Pricing/Analysis
- New Product/Service Development

Consistently successful in increasing revenues, member service/satisfaction, and profitability.

DISTINGUISHING CREDENTIALS:

- Certified Hotel Administrator, 1990
- Fluent English, French (mother tongue) and Spanish. Conversational German.
- Proficient in the use of PC-based lodging, reservation, F&B, and financial management systems.

PROFESSIONAL EXPERIENCE:

CHICAGO ATHLETIC CLUB, Chicago, Illinois   1991 to Present

Manager

Senior Operations Executive with full management responsibility for the Club's member-only, 3-star hotel (218 rooms and suites). Direct all related staffing, guest service, pricing, financial analysis/reporting, quality, and property management operations. Consult with Board and F&B management personnel to coordinate integrated operations, service, and marketing programs.

- Initiated a series of operational improvements which increased revenue from $2.9 million in 1991 to $4.8 million (66% gain) in 1996. Improved bottom-line profitability by $1.9 million (135%).

- Designed and led several high-caliber service and management training programs.

- Launched the introduction of new quality and performance standards, in conjunction with supporting program of employee incentives and recognition.

Concurrently, serve as Manager of the Travelers Island Facility for the past two years. Hold full operating and P&L responsibility for the facility (18 tennis courts, pro shop, dining room, terrace, snack and cocktail lounge, bath house, and 120-berth marina), guest/member relations, and service quality. Drive forward efforts to enhance member service and retention.

- Authored new policies and procedures manual, realigned staffing patterns, implemented a series of cost reduction initiatives, and closed 1996 with expenses less than 1993.

- Created a service, quality, and procedures training program for newly hired personnel.

JOHN P. LANDAU, CHA - *Page Two*
jpland@planet.com

HOTEL LESTER, Chicago, Illinois   1990 to 1991
(Hotel Member of Relais & Chateaux)

Resident Manager

Full P&L responsibility for one of the most exclusive properties in Chicago (68 full-service suites). Directed the entire operation, all financial affairs, all facilities management programs, and the complete F&B operation (including main dining room, room service, and banquet facilities). Achieved a significant increase in banquet sales through personal negotiation and management of key customer relationships. Operated within the highest standards for quality and service.

SUNRISE HOTELS INTERNATIONAL   1985 to 1989

Hotel Manager / Project Manager, Chicago, Illinois (1988 to 1989)

Special Projects Director managing a diversity of corporate assignments involving new property development, property acquisition/feasibility analysis, and property turnaround/ reorganization. Supervised financial analysis, prepared cash flow projections and debt service pro formas, and provided financial support for potential acquisitions in Florida, New York, and South Carolina.

- Directed a complete renovation and re-opening of the Sunrise Hotel in Boca Raton.

- Wrote corporate operations manual for affiliated hotels and restaurants.

Resident Manager, Sunrise Hotel, Chicago, Illinois (1985 to 1988)

Directed operations of this 3-star, 368-room, 220-employee hotel and of a large F&B operation (two restaurants, one bar and seven banquet rooms). Led a 5-person senior management team. Directed human resources, labor relations, training, purchasing, budgeting, guest relations, security, facilities, and daily business operations. Managed strategic planning and execution of sales, marketing, and business development campaigns.

- Contributed to dramatic growth and expansion with revenue increasing 135% to over $9.5 million and gross operating profit increasing 700% to $3.5 million.

- Directed $4.5 million renovation of the TowerSuite (12 units) and four banquet rooms.

HYATT INTERNATIONAL   1970 to 1985

Area Operations Analyst, Caribbean-Central America (1979 to 1985)

Unique management assignment conducting ongoing operational, profit, quality, and performance reviews of the seven Hyatt properties in the Caribbean-Central American Region. Worked cooperatively with on-site management teams to facilitate operational improvements.

- Initiated changes in work procedures, departmental responsibilities, and administrative systems that saved thousands of manhours per year and reduced net operating costs by $500,000+.

- Launched the introduction of several well-targeted quality and service enhancements.

Hotel Operations Analyst, Caracas Hyatt, Caracas, Venezuela (1975 to 1978)
Purchasing Director / F&B Controller, Bogota Hyatt, Bogota, Colombia (1970 to 1975)

EDUCATION: Diploma - Ecole Hoteliere S.S.H., Lausanne, Switzerland
Diploma - Business Management, Lausanne, Switzerland
Certified Hotel Administrator, American Hotel & Motel Association

11

Human Resources

Sample Job Titles

Benefits and Compensation Administrator
Certified Professional in Human Resources (PHR)
Certified Senior Professional in Human Resources (SPHR)
Certified Trainer
Chief Human Resources Officer
Corporate Recruiter
Corporate Trainer
Country Human Resources Manager
Director of Human Resources
Director of Organizational Development
EEO Specialist
Employee Assistant Program (EAP) Manager
Employee Relations Administrator
Employee Relations Manager
Employment Manager
Employment Specialist
Human Resources Assistant
Human Resources Generalist

Human Resources Manager
International Employment Manager
International Human Resources Director
Labor Relations Specialist
Management Development Specialist
Management Recruiter
Manpower Planning Manager
Organizational Development Director
Pension Plan Administrator
Personnel Administrator
Personnel Division Director
Personnel Manager
Professional Recruiter
Recruiter
Staffing Manager
Technical Employment Manager
Trainer
Training and Development Manager
Training Specialist
Vice President of Human Resources
Wage and Salary Analyst

KeyWords and KeyWord Phrases

Americans With Disabilities Act (ADA): Expanded regulatory compliance programs to incorporate new federal **ADA** regulations and initiated $12 million capital investment program to upgrade facilities to meet access requirements.

Benefits Administration: Expanded in-house **benefits administration** function to include pension plans, 401(k) plans, tuition reimbursement programs, LOA programs, and joint spouse maternity leave programs.

Career Pathing: Introduced the concepts of **career pathing**, leadership development, and succession planning into Federal Express in an effort to increase executive staff recruitment and retention.

Change Management: Pioneered innovative **change management** programs focused on core productivity, efficiency, and safety improvement programs.

Claims Administration: Directed a 12-person **claims administration** function responsible for all health insurance, disability, and workers' compensation claims.

College Recruitment: Managed a nationwide **college recruitment** program to attract talented young engineers and technical designers.

Compensation: Benchmarked best practices worldwide to create Knudsen's domestic and international **compensation** programs.

Competency-Based Performance: Created a **competency-based performance** analysis and appraisal system to identify top performers and facilitate progressive career movement.

Corporate Culture Change: Pioneered **corporate culture change** initiatives impacting more than 10,000 employees at 54 manufacturing facilities and 122 sales offices throughout Europe, Asia, and Latin America.

Cross-Cultural Communications: Introduced in-house language training programs to strengthen staff competencies in **cross-cultural communications**.

Diversity Management: Forged the introduction of **diversity management** programs and initiatives to expand hiring, training, and promotion of minority candidates.

Electronic Applicant Screening: Spearheaded project to implement the first **electronic applicant screening** process in the industry, complete with resume scanning and keyword scanning technology.

Employee Communications: Designed and produced multimedia **employee communications** for new hire orientation, training, and leadership development.

Employee Empowerment: Championed implementation of **employee empowerment** and participative management programs to increase management/staff relations and cooperation.

Employee Involvement Teams: Formed six **employee involvement teams** to support HR's efforts in employee downsizing, reorganization, and consolidation.

Employee Relations: Expanded **employee relations** initiatives to include in-house EAP and counseling programs.

Employee Retention: Designed performance-based incentives for a 200-person hourly workforce and increased **employee retention** by better than 26%.

Employee Surveys: Wrote, administered, and reported results of corporate-wide **employee surveys** investigating employee satisfaction and personal career objectives.

Equal Employment Opportunity (EEO): Achieved/surpassed all **EEO** and Affirmative Action regulations.

Expatriate Employment: Spearheaded a worldwide **expatriate employment** and human resources function incorporating recruitment, training and development, succession planning, and compensation.

Grievance Proceedings: Administered over 100 **grievance proceedings** as the direct intermediary between union and management officials.

Human Resources (HR): Senior Executive with full operating responsibility for design, development, and leadership of comprehensive **human resources** and organization development function.

Human Resources Generalist Affairs: Administered all **HR generalist affairs**, including recruitment, selection, training, manpower planning, benefits, claims administration, employee relations, and succession planning.

Human Resources Partnerships: Forged innovative **human resources partnerships** with key operating divisions worldwide to drive common vision and achieve financial objectives.

Incentive Planning: Spearheaded **incentive planning** functions for sales and support personnel through ITI's worldwide field organization.

International Employment: Created a comprehensive **international employment** organization responsible for all generalist HR functions and a complex expatriate compensation program.

Job Task Analysis: Conducted a sophisticated **job task analysis** study to delineate all core competencies, functions, and requirements of each of the company's 22 different job classifications.

Labor Arbitration: Negotiated favorable resolutions to several high-profile **labor arbitration** proceedings negatively impacting Bethlehem Steel's long-term market viability.

Labor Contract Negotiations: Directed 6-person cross-functional team responsible for **labor contract negotiations** with Teamsters officials.

Labor Relations: Created a proactive **labor relations** function that successfully thwarted several work stoppages and proposed walk-outs.

Leadership Assessment: Developed quantifiable tools for **leadership assessment** of top operating management.

Leadership Development: Pioneered innovative **leadership development** programs to accelerate career advancement of high-potential management candidates.

Management Training & Development: Identified organizational needs and created a 4-part **management training and development program**.

Manpower Planning: Created **manpower planning** methodologies to staff new production facilities in Iowa and Utah.

Merit Promotion: Designed a performance-driven **merit promotion** program to reward top producers.

Multimedia Training: Partnered with Technology Services Division to create **multimedia training** and leadership programs integrating voice, data, and other electronic systems.

Multinational Workforce: Managed a 42-person **multinational workforce** with personnel from Germany, Switzerland, Austria, Japan, Mexico, and the U.S.

Organization(al) Design: Defined new corporate vision and established new **organizational design** to streamline management tiers and advance staff to supervisory positions.

Organization(al) Development (OD): Spearheaded **OD** initiatives incorporating change management, employee empowerment, participative leadership, and process reengineering.

Organization(al) Needs Assessment: Conducted worldwide **organizational needs assessment** to define core drivers in fast-paced technology industries.

Participative Management: Energized staff and supervisors to successfully transition to **participative management** organizational structure.

Performance Appraisal: Created a comprehensive **performance appraisal** system based on pre-established performance criteria.

Performance Incentives: Designed a complete portfolio of **performance incentives** awarded for measurable gains in production yield, quality performance, and customer satisfaction.

Performance Reengineering: Led fast-paced **performance reengineering** initiatives to keep pace with rapid market expansion and customer growth.

Position Classification: Designed a corporate-wide **position classification** system with associated salary grades, levels, and incentive structures.

Professional Recruitment: Spearheaded an aggressive **professional recruitment** program to identify top industry performers in sales, marketing, and international business development.

Regulatory Affairs: Administered **regulatory affairs**, compliance, and reporting with state and federal agencies governing HR operations.

Retention: Designed staff incentives and increased employee **retention** by better than 45%.

Safety Training: Accelerated the corporation's commitment to safe work practices with the introduction of a plant-wide **safety training** program.

Self-Directed Work Teams: Created **self-directed work teams** responsible for full product line management, from initial R&D through manufacturing and customer delivery.

Staffing: Redefined **staffing** levels to assimilate new technologies and reduce annual payroll expenditures.

Succession Planning: Created **succession planning** models adopted by national association as best in practices model for the entire industry.

Train-the-Trainer: Developed curriculum and instructional materials for **train-the-trainer** programs in technology, telecommunications, and electronic commerce.

Training and Development: Planned and launched start-up of worldwide **training and development** division to support the company's expansion into emerging product technologies and markets.

Union Negotiations : Led sensitive **union negotiations** governing salary and benefit programs for all two million members of the United Autoworkers Union.

Union Relations: Forged positive **union relations** through cooperative design of safe work practices and full compensation for on-the-job injuries.

Wage and Salary Administration: Developed a corporate-wide **wage and salary administration** program to ensure equitable compensation across all geographies and job classifications.

Workforce Reengineering: Led a massive **workforce reengineering** initiative to reduce Terminal's worldwide staff by 30% by the end of 1999.

KeyWord Answers to Interview Questions

Tell me about yourself.

"I'm an **HR generalist** with nine years experience in all core HR functions ... **interviewing, hiring, job placement, employee relations, compensation, benefits, employee recognition**, and **training and development**. My greatest successes, however, have been in **workforce downsizing**, which, unfortunately, I know is one of your greatest needs. First with Motorola and then with Alcatel, I've orchestrated the **layoff** of more than 3,000 employees over the past five years. It certainly is not a very pleasant experience, but it's a reality of business today and a reality that I'm particularly adept at managing. I've accomplished this by creating in-house **outplacement** programs that provide employees with the tools and resources that they need to manage successful **job searches** and find new employment. By adding a real human touch, everyone has benefited."

What is the most valuable skill you bring to our company?

"My ability to **build rapport** is what I consider to be my most significant attribute. I have excellent **interpersonal relationship** and **communication** skills, and am comfortable in virtually every situation – from the board room to the manufacturing floor. What's more, I have a real appreciation for each and every employee, realizing that any business is only as strong as the commitment of its **workforce**. As an **HR professional**, it is my job to make those employees feel valued through their individual contributions."

What do you consider to be your most significant achievement or contribution?

"I've previously addressed my accomplishments in **workforce downsizing**, so let me focus here on my success in **training and development**. One of the greatest advantages to working with a company the size of Motorola is the **diversity of the workforce** and, in turn, the diversity of training I developed. One month I'd be working on designing a **training program** to introduce a new assembly process on the manufacturing floor; the next month I'd be creating a **leadership training program** for the **senior management team**. In total, I designed and delivered more than 30 different programs to more than 2,000 employees."

EUGENE S. THOMPSON, CCP

P.O. Box 156	Home (202) 624-1465
Washington, DC 21056	Office (202) 783-2210
Email: est@aol.com	Fax (202) 783-3322

August 18, 2003

Jeffry Lawrence, President
Inacomp Technology Manufacturing
122 Kroger Drive
Spokane, WA 99056

Dear Mr. Lawrence:

Strong human resources leadership can have a tremendous impact on corporate and organizational value. By building an effective HR infrastructure, providing strategic HR leadership, and controlling escalating compensation and benefit costs, you can immediately improve the financial performance, productivity, and viability of your organization. This is the value I deliver.

An accomplished HR executive with strong qualifications in all core generalist functions, I have been instrumental in strengthening performance through my efforts in:

- Union, Management, and Labor Relations
- Domestic and International Staffing
- Employee Training and Development
- Safety Management & Control
- Benefits and Compensation Design
- HRIS Technology
- Quality and Productivity
- Employee Relations
- Regulatory Compliance
- Employee Law and Litigation

I am a proactive business manager, credited with the development of innovative productivity, efficiency, quality and performance management programs with strong bottom-line results. Further, my ability to build cooperation – between union and non-union personnel – between employees and operating management teams – between field and headquarters organizations – has been critical to our overall performance.

Although secure in my current position, I am confidentially exploring new professional challenges and opportunities. Thus my interest in discussing your search for a Corporate Human Resources Director. I appreciate your consideration and look forward to speaking with you in the next few days.

Sincerely,

Eugene S. Thompson

Eugene S. Thompson, CCP

Enclosure

SAMUEL P. ROBINSON

3023 South Fifth Street
Washington, D.C. 22302

Home (202) 633-4015
Office (202) 252-2300

SENIOR HUMAN RESOURCES PROFESSIONAL
Expertise in Strategic HR Planning, Generalist HR Affairs, Organizational Development, & Change Management

Successful management career as a Senior HR Manager for four corporations and multiple operating units. Provide innovative, results-driven leadership to balance HR with operating and financial demands. Characterized as a mentor, teacher, leader, and executive advisor. Pioneered organizational effectiveness and change management.

PROFESSIONAL EXPERIENCE:

PINEVIEW LTD., Washington, D.C.   1993 to 2002

Vice President - Human Resources (1995 to 2002)

Senior HR Executive with full responsibility for the strategic planning, development and leadership of all HR, employee relations, labor relations, EH&S, and organization development initiatives for three operating companies in the food, specialty chemicals, and pharmaceutical businesses. Scope of responsibility impacted more than 550 employees in seven operating locations (R&D, manufacturing, sales, administration) in the U.S. and Finland. Appointed Corporate Officer in 1995.

CHALLENGE: Lead organization from a traditional labor relations function to an integrated, comprehensive human resources organization with focus on strategic and business unit planning, leadership development, and long-term growth/ expansion.

RESULTS
- Developed results-oriented operating management. Reengineered 10% of workforce, effectively utilizing higher-skilled personnel.

- Created Division Training Committee and introduced leadership, cultural awareness, and team-building concepts and programs.

- Championed a successful EH&S program design, implementation and employee communications/training initiative.

- Captured over $200,000 in benefit cost reductions, avoided an additional $1.2 million in SERP funding, and implemented employee recognition and awards programs.

- Realigned senior management compensation programs, created format for gainsharing, introduced mid-management incentives, tied variable compensation to business plans, and initiated modified Hay evaluation instrument for pharmaceutical business unit.

Vice President - Human Resources - Pineview Products Company (1993 to 1995)

CHALLENGE: Transition 335-employee, $125 million agricultural business into a specialty chemical manufacturer with strong organizational infrastructure, professional business practices, and talented operating, marketing, and financial leadership.

RESULTS
- Redefined organizational requirements and championed management transition to new, more profitable marketing strategy.

- Recruited new senior management team and conducted aggressive recruitment campaigns.

- Launched pilot reengineering project and delivered a $650,000 savings.

- Introduced industry standards for EH&S program management/ regulatory compliance.

- Revitalized safety training program; reduced lost-time accidents from 24 to 3.

SAMUEL P. ROBINSON - *Page Two*

AIR SYSTEMS, INC., Chester, Pennsylvania   1980 to 1993

Fast-track promotion through a series of increasingly responsible HR management positions with several of the corporation's largest operating divisions. Throughout entire career, directed complete generalist affairs including recruitment, staffing, training/development, compensation, benefits, employee relations, succession planning, and HR strategy. Highlights:

Manager - Human Resources - Field Operations (1990 to 1993)

CHALLENGE: Drive forward reengineering, job realignment, change management and organization development initiatives for multiple businesses with 7,000 employees in 120+ locations.

RESULTS
- Introduced concept to merge two of the largest operating businesses to create long-term productivity and performance improvements.

- Created communications strategies to strengthen self-directed work teams.

Manager - Human Resources - Polymers & Polyurethanes (1988 to 1990)

CHALLENGE: Provide strong and decisive HR leadership for a $625 million division with 1,200 employees at 11 operating locations (including 200+ professional R&D organization).

RESULTS
- Spearheaded division-wide HR planning, job realignment, employee involvement, team-building, and organization development projects.

- Directed major plant divestiture and re-employment of all 125 employees.

Manager - Human Resources - Chemicals Manufacturing (1985 to 1987)

CHALLENGE: Introduce improved HR strategies, services, and programs into the division's six largest operating units with 1,400 employees.

RESULTS
- Implemented large organization development, training, and leadership development programs.

- Realigned and strengthened compensation programs and salary administration.

- Taught Zenger Miller Frontline Leadership and Crosby Quality programs.

Plant Human Resources Manager (1983 to 1985) for the company's largest chemical manufacturing facility. Complete generalist and labor relations responsibilities.

Area Personnel Manager (1980 to 1983) directing HR policy, recruitment, wage and benefits, and labor negotiations for 500+ employees at five manufacturing sites.

MONTANA POWER AND LIGHT COMPANY, Helena, Montana   1975 to 1979

Labor Relations Administrator recruited to establish effective business relationships between the utility and its contractors. Orchestrated favorable labor concessions never before won in the nuclear industry. Established labor policies and programs impacting 1,500+ PP&L and contract personnel.

EDUCATION:

INDIANA UNIVERSITY	**BS Degree - Business Management** (1975)
HARVARD BUSINESS SCHOOL	**Strategic Human Resources Management**
UNIVERSITY OF MICHIGAN	**Labor Relations Management**

12

Human Services

Sample Job Titles

Administrator

Agency Director

Agency Manager

Associate Director

Behavioral Specialist

Case Worker

Client Advocate

Clinician

Counselor

Director of Human Services

Director of Social Services

Executive Director

Human Services Professional

Human Services Specialist

Psychiatrist

Psychologist

Rehabilitation Specialist

Service Delivery Manager

Social Services Administrator
Social Worker
Substance Abuse Counselor
Vocational Trainer

KeyWords and KeyWord Phrases

Adult Services: Expanded traditional programming to include a complete portfolio of **adult services** (e.g., in-home health care, sports, recreation, day care).

Advocacy: Spearheaded regional **advocacy** to increase awareness of the need for expanded human services, counseling, and substance abuse programs.

Behavior Management: Created an integrated **behavior management** model demonstrated to offset the impact of Tourette Syndrome on unintended vocalizations.

Behavior Modification: Innovated **behavior modification** programs successful in controlling the physical outbursts of dually diagnosed adolescent clients.

Casework: Directed all **casework** planning, staff assignment, and client review proceedings prior to court appearances.

Client Advocacy: Forged aggressive **client advocacy** programs to expand vocational training opportunities through state-funded agencies.

Client Placement: Administered **client placement** in mental health and rehabilitation facilities throughout the state of New Jersey.

Community-Based Intervention: Organized **community-based intervention** for repeat offenders indigenous to the local area.

Community Outreach: Spearheaded successful **community outreach** programs linking local residents with privately funded and publicly administered human service programs.

Counseling: Directed clinical intervention teams responsible for individual, group, and family **counseling** in state-wide residential facilities.

Crisis Intervention: Directed **crisis intervention** with potentially suicidal patients in a state-funded facility.

Diagnostic Evaluation: Managed interdisciplinary medical and nursing team responsible for comprehensive **diagnostic evaluation** of all incoming clients.

Discharge Planning: Coordinated cross-functional medical, nursing, rehabilitative, and counseling team managing **discharge planning** and follow-up care.

Dually Diagnosed: Conducted a longitudinal research study of **dually diagnosed** children through adolescence and adulthood to identify common characteristics and effective treatment protocols.

Group Counseling: Facilitated **group counseling** sessions with inmates from correctional institutions throughout the state system.

Human Services: Senior Executive with full responsibility for the strategic planning, staffing, budgeting, and administration of a large **human services** organization.

Independent Life Skills Training: Developed novel strategies to improve programs for **independent life skills training** and living.

Inpatient: Increased reimbursable income from **inpatient** population by 23% over two years.

Integrated Service Delivery: Assembled cross-functional clinical team to provide a centralized program for **integrated service delivery**.

Mainstreaming: Advocated and won legislative support for introduction of educational **mainstreaming** programs.

Outpatient: Controlled $250 million in private donations allocated for the delivery of comprehensive **outpatient services** to elderly residents of the inner city.

Program Development: Spearheaded strategic alliances with research centers and universities nationwide to facilitate **program development**, delivery, and success.

Protective Services: Issued judicial orders for **protective services** in alleged cases of child and sexual abuse.

Psychoanalysis: Completed 12 years of in-depth **psychoanalysis** with leading psychiatrists utilizing both traditional and non-traditional therapies.

Psychological Counseling: Managed health care team responsible for **psychological counseling**, crisis intervention, and long-term treatment planning.

Psychotropic Medication: Authorized to dispense **psychotropic medication** in emergency situations.

School Counseling: Founded and managed Wisconsin State's **School Counseling** and Health Services program.

Social Services: Directed a 200-employee **social services** organization with $100 million in annual funding from government, not-for-profit, and private organizations.

Social Welfare: Lobbied for the successful passage of favorable **social welfare** designed to obliterate the region's rapidly expanding inner city problems.

Substance Abuse: Designed proactive **substance abuse** and rehabilitation programs that were successful in reducing the negative behaviors associated with prolonged addiction.

Testing: Administered a comprehensive psychological, emotional, cognitive, and behavioral **testing** program.

Treatment Planning: Coordinated **treatment planning** and intervention for both inpatient and outpatient populations.

Vocational Placement: Coordinated **vocational placement** for all incoming program participants.

Vocational Rehabilitation: Designed the first-ever **vocational rehabilitation** programs in cooperation with Xerox, IBM, Westinghouse, AlliedSignal, and other major corporations.

<u>**Vocational Testing**</u>: Designed **<u>vocational testing</u>** tools to accurately identify each individual's technical, analytical, and mechanical competencies.

<u>**Youth Training Program**</u>: Forged strategic partnerships with area colleges and universities for an innovative **<u>youth training program</u>** designed to advance the educational standards and expectations of the local population.

KeyWord Answers to Interview Questions

Tell me about yourself.

"I've committed my professional life to helping those in need. Although I certainly don't mean for that to sound as sugary as it does, it really is at the foundation of my career. A graduate of Kent State, I experienced much of the emotional turmoil of the late 1960s and it set my future direction. You know the generation. So, with my goals firmly established, I began my career as a **Social Worker**, first with a **state government agency** and later with a **nonprofit organization**. Now, as **Executive Director** of CareFirst, a **residential facility** for **youth offenders**, I hold full management responsibility for a **142-bed secure facility** on a 25-acre farm. I continue to work as a **Case Manager** with oversight responsibility for **youth placement** within the facility, **psychiatric care**, **medical care**, **vocational training**, **family counseling**, and more. Additionally, I manage a $2.8 million annual **operating budget** and a **staff** of 189."

What is the most valuable skill you bring to our company?

"My **commitment** – to my clients, their families, and my staff – is my most valuable skill. It's why I work in the environments that I do which are often hostile and threatening. In the past, I've considered alternative careers, but realized that this is where I belong. I want to work with and support these young **offenders**, knowing if I can make a small difference in their lives, that it's been well worth it. Again, I'm sounding sugary and certainly don't mean to, but **commitment** really is the greatest value I bring to you, your residents, and your institution."

What do you consider to be your most significant achievement or contribution?

"The innovative **vocational training programs** that I've developed throughout my career are my proudest accomplishments. While working for the California State **Department of Youth Services**, I designed a program to train **youth-at-risk** in PC systems repair. Over a five-year period, more than 500 teens graduated from that program. More recently, I've created electronics training, automotive repair, and office skills training programs that have been delivered to more than 1,000 of our residents over the past six years."

LESLIE R. SILVERMAN
19 Leesville Pike
Altoona, PA 19890
441-388-8273
lessilver@mindspring.com

March 3, 2003

Don Atwood
Director
Hancock Center For Social Services
19 Elm Street
Elmwood, PA 19836

Dear Mr. Atwood:

Recruited to Clearwater Rehab Consultants in 1992, I was challenged to create, build, and manage a residential rehabilitation program for chronic youth offenders, most of whom were diagnosed with a combination of psychological, behavioral, and emotional problems. Since our beginning, my team and I have serviced over 2,000 youth offenders. Most remarkably, our recidivism rate is less than 10%, clearly demonstrating the effectiveness of both our residential and follow-up programs.

Previously, as an Adolescent Case Worker with the Pennsylvania Department of Social Services, I also worked with chronically delinquent youth. This required constant coordination with the legislative and judicial systems, with other social service agencies, and with a myriad of care-provider organizations. It was a great five years that provided the foundation for all that I have accomplished thus far.

A mutual colleague of ours, Eric Green of SPSA Systems, informed me that the Hancock Center is just getting ready to launch a similar residential care and treatment program, working with the specific types of populations I have serviced so effectively over the years. As such, please accept this letter and enclosed resume as application for the position of Director – Youth Residential Services.

I am available at your convenience for a personal interview and will phone your office next week to arrange a mutually agreeable time. Thank you in advance.

Sincerely,

Leslie R. Silverman

Leslie R. Silverman

Enclosure

BENJAMIN F. SMITH
bennie@jets.com
9348 Pioneer Square, #4
Seattle, Washington 98332
Home (206) 356-8732   Office (206) 983-3252

PROFESSIONAL QUALIFICATIONS:

PROJECT MANAGER / COUNSELOR / ADMINISTRATOR / HUMAN SERVICES PROFESSIONAL experienced in the design, planning, and delivery of programs for substance abusers, criminal offenders, economically disadvantaged, handicapped, and other special needs populations. Qualifications include:

- Strong skills in proposal writing, public speaking, and program management
- Well-developed counseling, communication, and crisis management skills.
- Over 10 years of general business and administrative management experience.
- Extensive qualifications in personnel training and supervision, budgeting, resource/funds allocation, and documentation/recordkeeping.

PROFESSIONAL EXPERIENCE:

Volunteer Additions Counselor   1993 to Present
THE HAVEN, Seattle, Washington

Provide individual counseling to substance abusers at this drug and alcohol outpatient facility. Work with clients referred by the courts, social workers, rehabilitation centers and other human service agencies/professionals. Design individualized treatment plans and objectives, maintain/update all client documentation, consult with Director regarding case management, coordinate crisis intervention services, and expedite external referrals for inpatient admissions.

- Assist Director with the preparation of fundraising solicitations to support program operations and service expansion.
- Designed and implemented effective counseling programs designed specifically to meet the needs of a diverse client population with various substance addictions.

Co-Owner & Field Service Manager   1986 to Present
HEATING SUPPLY, Seattle, Washington

Own and operate a heating contracting business that has become a leader in furnace retrofit and installation work in the Seattle metro area. Prepare work orders and estimates, schedule and supervise work crews, coordinate equipment and material acquisitions, and manage customer service/relations.

- Increased company sales 500% since 1987.
- Wrote proposals, capability statements, and operating plans to secure government contracts.

BENJAMIN F. SMITH - *Page Two*

Project Manager   1981 to 1986
INSTITUTE FOR HUMAN DEVELOPMENT, Seattle, Washington

Directed a large-scale furnace retrofit pilot project undertaken as part of the Institute's program to assist Seattle's economically disadvantaged citizens. Demonstrated average fuel savings of 21% on initial 200 installations and authored final report which was instrumental in changing federal legislation concerning the use of energy assistance funds.

- Prepared documentation, negotiated and secured funding from private foundations and local government to continue agency operations.
- Managed $2 million annual energy conservation project that completed 8000+ heating system retrofits in four years. Supervised a staff of 12 field and administrative personnel in addition to 30+ contractors.

Volunteer Proposal Writer   1983
LYNWOOD PRISON, Lynwood, Washington

Authored winning proposal to establish a skills training program (e.g., carpentry, plumbing, home repair, building maintenance) on-site at Lynwood Prison. Determined budget, staffing, material and other resource requirements to develop in-house training curriculum and fully equipped shop. Wrote training curriculum, program objectives, schedules, and skills performance criteria.

- Prepared proposal that was successfully funded by local government and operated by the prison for several years.

Senior Planner   1974 to 1980
OFFICE OF EMPLOYMENT & TRAINING, Seattle, Washington

Wrote annual plan to provide the unemployed and economically disadvantaged citizens of Seattle with skills and vocational and educational training opportunities. Surveyed local economic trends, industry trends, and labor shortages to determine appropriate training programs offered by public and private organizations throughout the region. Consulted with Director regarding funding approval and policy recommendations. Supervised research, strategic planning, and program development activities.

- Wrote several proposals that won in national competition and brought an additional $20 million in discretionary funding to the City. Proposals included special training programs for the handicapped, offenders, welfare recipients, and non-native English language speakers.
- Designed a public awareness program to educate the local business community and improve employment opportunities for ex-offenders. Hosted several high-profile business meetings and seminars, coordinated media coverage, and launched public education initiatives.

EDUCATION:

M.A., Economics, University of Washington, 1974
B.A., Economics, Seattle Pacific University, 1971
Postgraduate Courses, Psychology & Psychotherapy, University of Washington, 1992 and 1993

13

Information Systems and Telecommunications Technology

Sample Job Titles

Applications Development Analyst
Applications Development Manager
Certified Computer Professional (CCP)
Chief Information Officer (CIO)
Chief Knowledge Officer (CKO)
Chief Technology Officer (CTO)
Communications Technician
Computer Analyst
Computer Applications Engineer
Corporate Technology Officer
Data Administration Manager
Data Center Manager
Database Administrator
Database Manager
Director of Computer Operations

Director of End-User Computing

Director of Information Management

Director of Software Development

Director of Technical Support Operations

E-Business Manager

E-Commerce Manager

Enterprise Network Engineer

Executive Vice President (EVP) of Technology

Global Information Systems (IS) Manager

Global Information Technology (IT) Manager

Global Systems Director

Information Center Manager

Information Systems (IS) Administrator

Information Technology (IT) Director

Internet Administrator

LAN Administrator

Management Information Systems (MIS) Director

Network Administrator

Network Development Analyst

Programmer

Programmer/Analyst

Project Leader

Research and Development (R&D) Director

Senior Information Systems (IS) Officer

Senior Project Manager

Senior Systems Analyst

Systems Engineer

Systems Manager

Systems Requirements Manager

Telecommunications Analyst

Telecommunications Manager

Telecommunications Technology Director

Vice President of Management Information Systems (MIS)

Vice President of Information Technology (IT)
Vice President of Research and Technology
Vice President of Voice and Data Communications
WAN Administrator
Web Designer
Webmaster

KeyWords and KeyWord Phrases

Advanced Technology: Recruited to Tandem Computers to spearhead the design, development, and delivery of **advanced technology** solutions for major banks and financial institutions nationwide.

Applications Development: Led a 22-person **applications development** team designing new software programs to meet transactional requirements.

Architecture: Directed systems **architecture** design across multiple platforms to ensure optimum integration and information access.

Artificial Intelligence (AI): Forged TI's launch into the emerging **AI** industry.

Automated Voice Response (AVR): Introduced **AVR** technology to expedite customer support and field service operations.

Backbone: Designed Ethernet **backbone** to support both LAN and WAN transmissions.

Benchmarking: Guided systems **benchmarking** across multiple industries, technologies, and applications.

CASE Tools: Pioneered the introduction of **CASE tools** to further accelerate development of advanced systems technology.

Capacity Planning: Evaluated existing technologies and defined **capacity planning** requirements for the next five years.

CD-ROM Technology: Expanded Time-Life's product offerings to include **CD-ROM technology** for delivery of both print and video publications.

Cellular Communications: Built and managed a large-scale **cellular communications** sales and marketing division in partnership with AT&T.

Client/Server Architecture: Transitioned from mainframe to **client/ server architecture**, reducing systems costs by 15% and increasing systems accessibility by better than 25%.

Computer Science: Graduated top of the class from MIT with a joint **Computer Science** and Engineering degree.

Cross-Functional Technology Team: Led a 45-person **cross-functional technology team** challenged to build the company's first-ever telecommunications systems.

Data Center Operations: Supported **data center operations** worldwide with the introduction of emerging hardware, software, and networking technologies.

Data Communications: Managed a 24/7 **data communications** and data support center.

Data Dictionary: Designed a comprehensive **data dictionary** for use by all technical and non-technical staff in their joint systems development efforts.

Data Recovery: Introduced time-sensitive **data recovery** processes and virtually eliminated all data losses.

Database Administration: Created a formal **data administration** function to control all IT development projects and daily systems operations.

Database Design: Led 6-person IT team in **database design** and documentation projects.

Database Server: Replaced obsolete technology with leading edge **database server**, expedited data processing, and eliminated systems duplication.

Desktop Technology: Launched Xerox's entry into the rapidly expanding **desktop technology** market.

Disaster Recovery: Authored Seagram's in-house **disaster recovery** processes.

Document Imaging: Forged strategic alliance with emerging technology venture to provide Octel with the latest advances in **document imaging** technology.

E-Commerce: Built new **e-commerce division** to capitalize on emerging market opportunities and closed $250,000 in first-year sales.

E-Learning: Created the first-ever **e-learning** programs introduced by IBM as part of their corporate management training and development program.

Electronic Data Interchange (EDI): Spearheaded introduction of **EDI** technology with major retailers nationwide (e.g., Wal-Mart, Sears, Target, Sam's Club).

Electronic Mail (Email): Introduced **email** to improve headquarters communications with field sales teams worldwide.

Emerging Technologies: Senior Operating Executive challenged to revitalize operations and lead the corporation's launch into **emerging technologies** designed specifically for the health care and human services industries.

End User Support: Expanded help desk staff to strengthen **end user support** programs.

Enterprise Systems: Advised senior executives regarding the functionality and utility of **enterprise systems** technology.

Ethernet: Implemented **Ethernet** to expand global communications capabilities between headquarters, field offices and client locations worldwide.

Expert Systems: Led design and development of **expert systems** for sophisticated data collection, analysis, and reporting processes.

Fault Analysis: Created the industry's first **fault analysis** technology, now a $2 billion revenue center for Xytoc Computer Systems.

Fiber Optics: Managed in-house laboratory operations at Eastman Kodak to develop next-generation **fiber optics** technology and beat competition to the market.

Field Support: Restaffed and retrained **field support** team to improve quality of customer technology installations and technical training.

Firewall: Designed and installed multi-layer, technologically sophisticated **firewall** technology for secure government operations.

Fourth Generation Language: Developed **fourth generation language** used in advanced scientific applications.

Frame Relay: Transitioned to **frame relay** technology to accelerate MIS capabilities.

Geographic Information System (GIS): Pioneered the use of **GIS** technology in the UPS global organization.

Global Systems Support: Established new business unit to provide **global systems support** to AI users worldwide.

Graphical User Interface (GUI): Developed **GUI** application to merge common technologies across diverse platforms.

Hardware Configuration: Directed engineering team responsible for **hardware configuration** and field installation at customer sites.

Hardware Development/Engineering: Redesigned **hardware development and engineering** protocols in response to changing user requirements.

Help Desk: Staffed and operated a 24/7 **help desk** supporting both internal and external customers.

Host-Based System: Reengineered **host-based system** to accommodate new technology installations and upgrades.

Imaging Technology: Negotiated $12 million acquisition of advanced **imaging technology**.

Information Technology (IT): Senior **IT** Executive with full operating and systems planning responsibility for a newly formed technology consortium between Tandem and Carnegie Mellon.

Internet: Managed Ford's entire **Internet** presence, including 22 different websites, active server pages and browsers, firewalls, and a host of other leading-edge technologies.

Joint Application Development (JAD): Accelerated **JAD** projects with the introduction of an experienced front-line technology management team.

Local Area Network (LAN): Invested over $3 million to develop **LAN** technology to link all corporate sales offices and distribution centers.

Mainframe: Joined IBM in its earliest stages of designing the first **mainframe** computer technology to be launched into the commercial market.

Management Information Systems (MIS): Senior **MIS** Executive with full P&L responsibility for Allied's $400 million Technology Systems Division.

Multimedia Technology: Introduced **multimedia technology** (e.g., electronic commerce, videoconferencing, CD-ROM, Internet) to capitalize upon high-growth market opportunities.

Multiuser Interface: Designed **multiuser interface** to expand systems capabilities.

Multivendor Systems Integration: Orchestrated a complex **multivendor systems integration** project to deliver advanced navigational technologies to the U.S. Armed Forces.

Network Administration: Senior Manager responsible for **network administration**, technology acquisitions, budgeting, staffing, and performance improvement.

Object Oriented: Advanced **object oriented** systems technologies into non-traditional development projects.

Office Automation (OA): Forged strategic alliance with DRG Computers to deliver **OA** technology throughout the Department of Energy, Department of Commerce, and U.S. State Department.

Online: Accelerated development of **online** technology to keep pace with regional and national competition.

Operating System: Redefined **operating system** requirements to upgrade technology performance and strengthen data quality.

Parallel Systems Operations: Managed **parallel systems operations** during conversion from IBM to Digital equipment.

PC Technology: Replaced obsolete mainframes with advanced **PC technology**.

Pilot Implementation: Managed **pilot implementation** of new AI and robotics technologies.

Process Modeling: Orchestrated a large-scale **process modeling** project in preparation for new technology installation.

Project Lifecycle: Administered **project lifecycle** from initial systems planning and technology acquisition through installation, training, and operations.

Project Management Methodology: Defined **project management methodology** to optimize technology resources and applications.

Rapid Application Development (RAD): Facilitated introduction of **RAD** processes to expedite systems implementation.

Real Time Data: Created platform for **real time data** collection, analysis and worldwide dissemination.

Relational Database: Designed **relational database** technology as part of the corporation's transition to advanced systems operation.

Remote Systems Access: Developed technology to provide **remote systems access** for sites worldwide.

Research & Development (R&D): Planned, staffed, budgeted, and directed operations of a sophisticated technology **R&D** center.

Resource Management: Controlled **resource management** and allocation of $100 million in hardware, software, and network technologies.

Satellite Communications: Designed sophisticated **satellite communications** systems for a highly sensitive government control with high-speed voice and data transmission for worldwide deployment.

Software Configuration: Pioneered innovative **software configuration** models that led to a major evolution within the financial software industry.

Software Development/Engineering: Led 22-person cross-functional project team challenged to revitalize and expand **software development and engineering** capabilities.

Systems Acquisition: Negotiated over $50 million in **systems acquisitions** to fund expansion and diversification.

Systems Configuration: Managed **systems configuration** for all new technology acquisitions and internal development projects.

Systems Development Methodology: Reengineered **systems development methodology** to integrated CASE tools, AI, and fourth generation language.

Systems Documentation: Led team responsible for technical and non-technical **systems documentation**.

Systems Engineering: Directed a team of Ph.D. scientists in the development of **systems engineering** processes, protocols, and standards.

Systems Functionality: Tested operations to ensure optimum **systems functionality** and availability.

Systems Implementation: Guided **systems implementation** across multiple platforms at 34 locations.

Systems Integration: Elevated the stature of the **systems integration** team with the provision of service-driven, quality-driven customer performance standards.

Systems Security: Introduced leading-edge **systems security** and intellectual property protection technologies.

Technical Documentation: Revised all **technical documentation** governing client/server architectures and systems operations.

Technical Training: Wrote curriculum, trained instructors, and directed **technical training** programs for user groups nationwide.

Technology Commercialization: Transitioned EL Labs from an R&D facility into an advanced **technology commercialization** organization.

Technology Integration: Spearheaded **technology integration** of all new system acquisitions and in-house development projects.

Technology Licensing: Negotiated over $200 million in **technology licensing** and transfer agreements with business partners throughout Asia Pacific.

Technology Needs Assessment: Conducted organization-wide **technology needs assessment** for Andersen's Global Consulting Division.

Technology Rightsizing: Revitalized operations and led an aggressive **technology rightsizing** effort to divest non-essential assets.

Technology Solutions: Pioneered **technology solutions** to meet the needs of complex customer service, logistics, and distribution operations.

Technology Transfer: Established strategic alliances with major R&D facilities nationwide and coordinated **technology transfer** between researchers and commercial systems vendors.

Telecommunications Technology: Credited with the development, engineering, and market launch of advanced **telecommunications technology** integrating LAN, WAN, and satellite systems.

Teleconferencing Technology: Saved the corporation $4 million in travel expenses through implementation of in-house **teleconferencing technology**.

User Training & Support: Recognized for success in the delivery of **user training and support** programs that outpaced the competition and provided 24-hour support to customers nationwide.

Vendor Partnerships: Structured and negotiated **vendor partnerships** to facilitate joint systems development projects.

Voice Communications: Acquired AT&T's premier systems to enhance **voice communications** technologies.

Web Hosting: Evaluated 22 different **web hosting** services, selected most technologically advanced provider, and negotiated annual hosting, server, and maintenance support contract.

Webcasting: Expanded multimedia marketing and advertising campaigns to include weekly **webcasting** of both audio and video programming.

Webinar: Designed and taught the first **Webinar** training program in the U.S. Government (U.S. Dept. of Commerce, 250 attendees, 90-minute training session).

Wide Area Network (WAN): Invested over $2.8 million in **WAN** technology to link operating divisions worldwide.

KeyWord Answers to Interview Questions

Tell me about yourself.

"I am a **product designer and engineer**, successful in taking projects from **theoretical concept** through **technical design** and **prototype development** to final **market launch**. Beginning my career with HP in 1988, I was involved in the initial **technical, functional,** and **applications design** of HP's entire **platform of PC technology**. Recruited to IBM in 1994, I continued with the development of four new **PC platforms**, several **new applications,** and a sophisticated **client/server infrastructure** to support regional utility operations. In summary, I've participated in and/or led more than 20 **new product development programs** for products now generating combined **annual revenues** of $750 million for IBM."

What is the most valuable skill you bring to our company?

"My most valuable skill is my ability to **fast-track projects**. In fact, 16 of the 20 projects I've been involved in during my tenure with IBM have been delivered **ahead of schedule** and at a minimum of $50,000 **under budget**. Not only do I consider this to be my strongest skill, so does IBM! They've honored me with numerous **corporate awards** for my **technical, project management,** and **financial contributions** to the company."

What do you consider to be your most significant achievement or contribution?

"Without a doubt, my most notable accomplishment has been the **cost savings** I've produced for IBM. As I mentioned previously, I've delivered several projects well **under budget** for a total **cost savings** of more than $2.8 million over the past three years. When you consider the time, expense, personnel, and technical resources involved in **developing new technologies,** this has been a remarkable achievement in a time of over-inflated prices, challenging economic conditions, and intense competition. Obviously, I also consider the **technologies** I've developed and brought to market equally notable achievements."

DENNIS L. CARTERET
121 Grand Avenue ▪ Elmtree, MA 02765 ▪ (713) 982-3876 ▪ DennisL24@aol.com

May 24, 2003

Joseph Barnes
Managing Director
IT Investment Trust
29 Marshall Boulevard
Boston, MA 02930

Dear Mr. Barnes:

Building successful and profitable Internet and E-commerce ventures is my expertise. Highlights include:

▪ Currently launching the start-up of a B2B and B2C venture in partnership with AOL, Pillsbury.com, Mrs. Fields, and other major players. Structured and negotiated innovative funding and marketing alliances to advance a high-profile "go to market" campaign. *Projecting first year profitable revenues of $12 million.*

▪ Negotiated Board funding, wrote business plan, negotiated multi-million dollar advertising campaign, and orchestrated the operations start-up of a new .com venture (subsidiary of well-established manufacturer). *Delivered first year revenues of $2.5 million.*

I bring to your organization years of senior leadership experience with bottom-line P&L responsibility for virtually all core business functions – from strategic planning, investment funding, and new business development to operations, marketing, branding, logistics, finance, HR, and information technology. My management style is direct and decisive, yet I am flexible to responding to constantly changing organizational, competitive, market, staff, and technology demands.

Currently, I am exploring new executive opportunities with a high-tech organization poised for aggressive and significant growth. Aware of the quality of your organization and your commitment to market expansion, I would welcome a personal interview and can guarantee that the quality and depth of my experience will add measurable value to your organization.

Thank you.

Sincerely,

Dennis L. Carteret

Dennis L. Carteret

Enclosure

MARILYN P. CLAYTON
1520 Main Street
Colorado Springs, Colorado 82160
Phone: (303) 402-3322   www.technology.com/consult   Email: consult@aol.com

---

MULTIMEDIA TECHNOLOGIST & PROGRAM/PROJECT DIRECTOR
Delivering Advanced PC- & UNIX-Based Programs, Systems & Technologies

Combines cross-functional, cross-technology experience in the design, staffing, budgeting and delivery of advanced systems and applications. Successful in developing and integrating technologies to support broad-ranging operating, financial, and organizational needs. Core competencies include:

- Multimedia Content Design
- Computer-Based Training & Authoring
- Program Development & Management
- Product Development & Marketing

- Interactive Technology
- Technical & Non-Technical Training
- Cross-Functional Team Leadership
- Client Training & Management

TECHNOLOGY SKILLS & EXPERTISE:

Multimedia Authoring Tools
GAIN/Momentum (UNIX under Motif)
ICON Author (PC)
WISE (PC)
TICCIT (Digital)
TenCORE

Office Productivity Tools (PC/Mac)
Microsoft Office (Word, Excel, PowerPoint)
Framemaker
Lotus Notes
ACT!
Filemaker Pro

Web Site Development (Mac)
Netscape Navigator Gold
HTML

Graphics Development Tools (Mac)
Adobe Acrobat/Illustrator
DeBabilizer

PROFESSIONAL EXPERIENCE:

MULTIMEDIA TECHNOLOGY CONSULTANT   1996 to Present
Independent Consultant specializing in the design, development, and delivery of advanced PC- and UNIX-based technology programs. Project highlights include:

- **Swedish Mobile** – Supported implementation of computer-based, interactive, training systems for American Management Systems' ForCe 2000 telecommunications software.
- **Sprint** – Managed needs analysis, design, navigation design, interface design (using lobbying/building metaphor), Design Specification Document and prototype development for billing system training and technology support systems.

LRX INCORPORATED, Denver, Colorado   1992 to 1996

Product Director
Senior Director leading the development of an interactive, multimedia, computer-based training CD-ROM for a computer-aided design 3D modeling software program.

- Directed project from initial concept, feasibility, and market analysis through development, pricing, staffing, training, and software vendor partnership. Led cross-functional project team of designers, artists, programmers, editors, and support staff.
- Defined systems approach, interface design, content, and marketing strategies.
- Established 800 number technical support team, all marketing communications and promotions, user manuals, and ACT! customer tracking database to support product launch.

MARILYN P. CLAYTON (Page 2)

Senior Technology Designer
Subcontracted to Techniflight Corporation to develop a multimedia tutorial for Lear jet introductory flight training (using GAIN/Momentum UNIX-based authoring tool from Sybase). Subsequently contracted for full-time commitment to the FOCUS: Hope Project in Detroit, Michigan, an innovative, technologically sophisticated university curriculum for the Center for Advanced Technology.

- Facilitated development of state-of-the-art engineering systems/strategies for CAD/CAM, tool crib controls, and quality assurance applications.

RADIUM SYSTEMS, INC., Fairfax, Virginia   1985 to 1991

Group Manager & Senior Technology Designer
Joined Radium Systems as the first Instructional Designer in the corporation. Over the next six years, spearheaded the growth and expansion of the department to 21 professionals delivering UNIX-based, multimedia programs and technologies to government and commercial clients worldwide. Member of Corporate Strategic Planning Team.

- Introduced applied Instructional System Development (ISD) approach to design seven multimedia courses in advanced electronic systems deployment (total contract value exceeding $2.6 million). Computer-based training was integrated into an HP-based part task trainer.
- Performed human factors critical task analyses, wrote functional system requirements, and designed text and graphics.
- Led team in development/delivery of technology programs using PC-based WICAT authoring tool (WISE) to design integrated systems for the Republic of China Navy.
- Proposal Manager for 10+ competitive RFPs and Statement of Qualification documents.

Program Manager
Led development of three advanced technology programs valued from $500,000 to $7 million. Directed preparation of Statement of Work, managed customer negotiations, calculated labor and material costs, negotiated subcontractor and consulting agreements, and managed projects through to on-budget completion.

LOGISTIX, INC., Washington, D.C.   1983 to 1985

Staff Analyst
Developed technology training programs for workstations, word processing, spreadsheet, database, graphics, and integration packages. Explored expert systems technology for job aid applications.

NATIONAL INFORMATION SYSTEMS, Baltimore, Maryland   1979 to 1983

Marketing Support Trainer
Programming Team Leader

EDUCATION:

Graduate Studies in Multimedia Development & Human Computer Interface Design
UNIVERSITY OF COLORADO

Graduate Studies in Human Factors Engineering & Industrial Psychology
THE AMERICAN UNIVERSITY

BS - English & Instructional Technology
THE AMERICAN UNIVERSITY

14

International Business

Sample Job Titles

Area Sales Executive
Business Development Director
Business Development Executive
Business Development Manager
Country Sales and Marketing Manager
Director of International Business Development
General Manager
Global Accounts Manager
Global Business Manager
Global Marketing Director
Global Sales Director
Global Trade Manager
Import/Export Manager
International Business Advisor
International Business Consultant
International Marketing Executive
International Sales Executive

International Trade Representative
Managing Director
Regional Sales and Marketing Manager
Senior Vice President of Business Development
Senior Vice President of International Trade
Vice President of Global Sales and Marketing
Vice President of Import and Export Trade

KeyWords and KeyWord Phrases

Acquisition: Identified candidate, directed due diligence, structured transaction, and negotiated the largest **acquisition** ($26.4 million) in the history of the corporation.

Barter Transactions: Pioneered Xytac's first-ever **barter transaction** programs to expand international trade opportunities.

Channel Development: Guided marketing and distributor **channel development** throughout emerging Latin American markets.

Competitive Intelligence: Created statistical models and reports of **competitive intelligence** for products, technologies, services, and market reach.

Corporate Development: Championed **corporate development** initiatives including mergers, acquisitions, strategic alliances, joint ventures, and co-marketing partnerships.

Cross-Border Transactions: Negotiated complex **cross-border transactions** between Vietnamese suppliers and Taiwanese distributors.

Cross-Cultural Communications: Developed training seminars to enhance the **cross-cultural communications** competencies of Xerox's international sales, marketing, and service organizations.

Diplomatic Protocol: Demonstrated expertise in **diplomatic protocol** and relations with high-ranking officials from the PRC, Taiwan, and Singapore.

E-Commerce: Integrated an interactive, online, **e-commerce** and product ordering system to complement field sales, marketing, and business development efforts.

Emerging Markets: Planned and executed strategy to expand focus throughout **emerging markets** worldwide.

Expatriate: Designed compensation and benefit programs for **expatriate** and foreign national employees in South Africa.

Export: Redesigned and streamlined logistics, warehousing, and distribution operations to expand **export** programs throughout the European continent.

Feasibility Analysis: Conducted a complex, in-country **feasibility analysis** project to determine potential market and profitability for Latin American manufacturing.

Foreign Government Affairs: Built cooperative working relationships with officials to strengthen the organization's **foreign government affairs** practices and support cooperative initiatives.

Foreign Investment: Lobbied before state and federal legislatures to advance **foreign investment** opportunities in Central and South America.

Global Expansion: Challenged to plan and execute a large-scale **global expansion** and marketing initiative to transition Farm Bureau from a national to international organization.

Global Market Position: Evaluated competitive activity, competitive products, emerging technologies, and new markets to determine the corporation's **global market position**.

Global Marketing: Recruited to plan and orchestrate IBM's **global marketing** and business development initiatives across five continents.

Global Sales: Recruited in-country sales teams and built/led a **global sales** organization that consistently exceeded revenue, profit, and market share quotas.

Import: Redesigned internal documentation processes, expanded transportation programs, and increased **import** revenues by more than 37% within first year.

Intellectual Property: Designed contracts, agreements, and other legal documents to protect the corporation's **intellectual property** from unauthorized licensing and distribution.

International Business Development: Senior Marketing Executive with full strategic and tactical responsibility for leading the corporation's worldwide **international business development** programs.

International Business Protocol: Demonstrated proficiency in **international business protocol** across diverse cultures, economies, and markets.

International Financing: Structured a three-party **international financing** agreement between Aramco, Bechtel, and Caterpillar for $16 million development project in Saudi Arabia.

International Liaison: Trained new sales recruits in **international liaison**, marketing, and business development skills.

International Licensee: Structured and negotiated Apple Computer's first-ever **international licensee** agreement for product marketing in Eastern Europe.

International Marketing: Drove Martin Marietta's **international marketing** projects throughout Asia and Latin America.

International Sales: Created a worldwide **international sales** organization through direct, VAR, reseller, and mass merchant channels.

International Subsidiary: Established and managed **international subsidiary** to provide manufacturing, distribution, sales, and marketing leadership for the entire PacRim region.

International Trade: Captured **international trade** opportunities worldwide and increased technology sales by more than 225% over four years.

Joint Venture: Negotiated a complex **joint venture** agreement for the development of a $8.2 million cement manufacturing plant in Thailand.

Licensing Agreements: Worked with corporate counsel to structure **licensing agreements** with distributors worldwide.

Local National: Designed recruitment, training, benefit, and compensation systems for **local nationals**.

Market Entry: Spearheaded **market entry** into Brazil, negotiated $8.9 million in first year sales, and outpaced the competition.

Marketing: Directed classical **marketing**, market research, and strategic planning functions at corporate headquarters for six independent operating companies.

Merger: Facilitated **merger** and integration of all information technology, order processing, billing, and product delivery programs for Time Warner's first international acquisition.

Multi-Channel Distribution Network: Designed organizational infrastructure and created a **multi-channel distribution network** to expand product reach throughout the reseller and retail markets.

Offshore Operations: Championed development of **offshore operations** to reduce labor and overhead costs associated with food products manufacturing.

Public/Private Partnership: Negotiated **public/private partnership** agreements between U.S. manufacturers and Australian government officials to introduce advanced telecommunications technologies.

Technology Licensing: Structured and executed complex **technology licensing** agreements between manufacturers and distributors throughout France, Germany, and the U.K.

Start-Up Venture: Led **start-up venture** through planning, staffing, and budgeting to full-scale operation within first 120 days.

Strategic Alliance: Negotiated **strategic alliance** with Motorola to develop joint technology and avionics programs.

Strategic Planning: Directed long-term **strategic planning** projects for 16 corporations working cooperatively to transition from domestic to global marketing/business development.

Technology Transfer: Identified opportunity to expand market penetration and led a series of sophisticated **technology transfer** programs throughout Europe, Asia, and Africa.

KeyWord Answers to Interview Questions

Tell me about yourself.

"Born and raised in Brazil, I emigrated to the United States when I was 18 to attend the University of Michigan where I earned my degree in **International Business Management**. Following graduation, I was hired by Pepsico and successfully completed their two-year **sales management** training program. During this time, I began to work in **international marketing** and **business development** with the Latin American Division. Over the next six years, I earned several promotions to my current position as **International Sales Manager** for Brazil, Argentina, and Chile. In this capacity, I manage a complex, **multinational sales region**, **cross-border transactions**, **import/export operations**, and the **hiring**, **training**, and **supervision** of a 22-person **foreign national workforce**. In addition, I spearhead a **management task force** responsible for **emerging markets development**, **joint ventures, strategic alliances**, and **product licensing.**"

What is the most valuable skill you bring to our company?

"Obviously, my ability to immerse myself within the Latin American **culture** is one of my most significant skills. It's always easier for a "local" to do business with a "local," which is why Pepsico promoted me into my current position. The market was not producing, sales were down, customers were unhappy, and the company needed an immediate **solution**. That solution was me. By putting a native Latin American into the position, I was able to **restore credibility** with our customers and turn the market around in less than six months. As we all know, **sales** is all about **relationship management.**"

What do you consider to be your most significant achievement or contribution?

"Without a doubt, the most significant achievement of my career has been my **revenue performance**. Over the past five years, my teams and I have generated over $28.5 million in **sales** within the **intensely competitive** Latin American market. This is a result of our ability to **build customer relationships, launch** innovative **promotional and marketing campaigns,** and **strengthen customer loyalty**. What's more, Pepsi is now **ranked #1** in all three Latin American markets."

IGOR SCHWARTZ
390 Springflower Circle
Alpharetta, Georgia 39089
Phone: (770) 492-0387   igrschw@mindspring.com   Fax: (770) 492-0898

March 14, 2003

Vladmir Scholwenski
Global Enterprises, Inc.
22 Valencia Avenue
Long Beach, CA 98029

Dear Mr. Scholwenski:

For more than 10 years, I have watched as the former Soviet Union and the entire Eastern European region struggle to transition to a free market economy, principally in Russia and Ukraine. Unfortunately, what I've witnessed is:

- Eastern European political bureaucracies and business environments that have been ineffective in responding to these extraordinary changes.
- Russian and Ukrainian businesses that are burdened with tax regulations, permit regulations, and other government-imposed obstacles to their performance and productivity.
- The entire world's inability to productively and profitably enter these markets, principally due to their lack of understanding of the intricacies of doing business within these difficult markets.

Through my efforts, I've acquired substantial expertise working with countries in the midst of transitioning to free markets, and understand the unique challenges they are facing. Further, being of Russian heritage, I can appreciate the tremendous obstacles facing this nation and others, merging my background with my 20+ years of life in the US in a free democracy.

Please also note that I have an extensive network of contacts with honest, credible, and progressive leaders in the academic, scientific, educational, military, government, political, business, cultural, and civic communities, particularly in Russia and Ukraine. These individuals have been instrumental in supporting my commercial business efforts throughout the region.

To have the opportunity to participate in establishing policies and programs involving the restructuring of the Eastern European markets would be the most rewarding path for my own professional career. As such, I would welcome a chance to speak with you about opportunities where I could provide cultural, economic, and business value.

Sincerely,

Igor Schwartz

Igor Schwartz

Enclosure

PAUL MANDAU
49 Dawson Avenue
Albany, New York 10303-3556
Phone / Fax (914) 921-3245
mandau.paul@mandau.com

SENIOR GENERAL MANAGEMENT / BUSINESS DEVELOPMENT
MARKETING & SALES MANAGEMENT
U.S., Europe, Latin America, Middle East, Far East, & Africa

Strong executive career leading successful start-up, turnaround, and fast-track growth marketing corporations worldwide. Combines expertise in business development, product positioning, and market expansion with strong operating, financial, HR and manufacturing management record. Fluent in French and Spanish. Conversational in Portuguese, Arabic, Greek and Slovak. MBA Degree.

Contributed to significant revenue/profit growth through decisive and proactive management. Specialist in start-ups, turnarounds, and strategic alliances in emerging markets.

PROFESSIONAL EXPERIENCE:

PRINCETON COSMETICS, White Plains, New York   1995 to 2001

Director - International Business Development

Recruited to plan and orchestrate aggressive market development and business development initiatives throughout emerging markets worldwide for this $75 million corporation. Challenged to build new market presence while reengineering and expanding existing international sales and distribution operations. Authored strategic marketing plans, tactical sales, and channel development initiatives. Led a team of sales/marketing managers.

- Built international sales revenues from $4 million to $7 million (75%). Projections indicate 115% growth over next 12 months.

- Identified and captured opportunities for explosive growth throughout the Pacific Rim. Negotiated strategic alliances with major distributors throughout Japan, China, Korea, and the Philippines. Evaluated feasibility of recommended joint venture in China.

- Structured and negotiated strategic alliance with South and West African business partners to expand presence within high-growth emerging markets.

- Revitalized sales, marketing, and distribution operations throughout Mexico after four years of stagnant sales. Projections indicate 400% growth over next 12 months.

BRAND ONE, INC., White Plains, New York   1991 to 1994

General Manager - Latin America

Reversed six-year negative P&L performance of 16 distributor markets throughout Latin America. Designed and led sales, product, and management training programs for 660 distributor sales, administrative, and support personnel. Personally developed and managed relationships with major accounts throughout the region.

- Generated net sales increase of $1.2 million (295%), operating profit growth of $600,000 (36%), and market share improvement to 89%.

- Increased volume 253% through increased distribution and design/implementation of innovative category and market support programs.

PAUL MANDAU - *Page Two*

SMITH & LEILSON DRUG, INC., New York, New York   1987 to 1990

Managing Director - Chile (1989 to 1990)

Full P&L, operating, and business development responsibility for an independent subsidiary with 139 employees. Scope of responsibility included the entire manufacturing operation (staffing, budgeting, capital expenditures, production planning/scheduling, quality, safety), all financial and administrative functions, and a high-profile sales and marketing organization.

- Reversed four-year sales, operating profit, and market share reduction. Grew sales to $12 million (175%), operating profit to $2.7 million (285%), and volume by 31%. Reduced cost of goods 19% and number of SKUs from 184 to 109.

- Recaptured market leadership in core OTC categories: analgesics (20%), antacids (23%), muscle relaxants (58%), and deodorants (21%).

Director - Latin American Business Development (1987 to 1988)

Revitalized Mexican and Brazilian sales/marketing organizations, initiated several successful new product introductions, and designed a series of existing product revitalizations on regional basis.

- Built sales to $213 million (18% increase) and operating profits to $15 million (105% increase) in a 27-subsidiary division.

PFIZER, INC., New York, New York   1975 to 1986

Rapid promotion through increasingly responsible offshore sales, marketing, and new business development management positions. Career highlights included:

Associate Director - International Business Development (1985 to 1986)

Headquarters assignment with newly formed senior management group established to develop and implement international business expansion opportunities. Directed start-up of Turkish joint venture ($40 million in first year sales), expanded licensing agreements in Pakistan and Bangladesh, and converted West African importing operations to manufacturing subsidiaries.

Managing Director - Egypt (1981 to 1984)

Directed start-up of the first U.S. company to open direct operations in Egypt. Held full P&L responsibility for 24 manufacturing and administrative personnel, and a countrywide sales distribution network. Built revenues to $2 million despite government-subsidized competition.

Business Development Director - Argentina (1980)

Closed non-performing joint venture in Chile and transitioned into a profitable trading company. Renegotiated licensing agreement in Haiti, and led negotiations for Argentine acquisition.

Marketing & Sales Director / New Products Director / Product Manager (1975 to 1979)

- Increased revenues in metropolitan France and French West Africa from under $60 million in 1969 to $200 million in 1974 through new product launches.

- Increased Colombian sales from $60 million in 1977 to $100+ million in 1979.

- Built revenues in Greece from $6 million to $25 million within two years.

EDUCATION: CALIFORNIA STATE UNIVERSITY
MBA, International Business, 1976
BS, Business Management, 1975

15

Law and Corporate Legal Affairs

Sample Job Titles

Arbitrator
Assistant District Attorney
Associate
Associate Attorney
Associate Counselor
Attorney
Contracts Attorney
Corporate Counsel
Corporate Secretary
Counsel
District Attorney
General Counsel
General Managing Partner
Judicial Law Clerk
Law Clerk
Lawyer
Legal Assistant

Legal Counsel

Litigator

Managing Partner

Mediator

Paralegal

Partner

Personal Injury Attorney

Real Estate Attorney

Senior Attorney

Senior Counsel

Senior Partner

Trial Attorney

Vice President of Corporate Law and Administration

KeyWords and KeyWord Phrases

Acquisition: Directed legal and contract negotiations for over $200 million in corporate, product, and technology **acquisitions** during Tandem's rapid growth and global expansion.

Adjudicate: **Adjudicated** employee claims alleging harassment, unfair promotion, and discriminatory hiring practices.

Administrative Law: Served as Westmoreland County's only **administrative law** judge for 10 consecutive years.

Antitrust: Successfully defended **antitrust** lawsuit brought by Apple alleging use of their proprietary technologies in Xerox's latest generation of laser printers.

Briefs: Wrote **briefs**, memoranda, petitions, correspondence, motions, and other legal documentation for the firm's real estate practice.

Case Law: Researched **case law** in preparation of Iowa's first industrial espionage criminal case.

Client Management: In addition to all trial responsibilities, accountable for client development and **client management** with major corporations.

Contracts Law: Specialized in **contracts law** with particular emphasis on international trade, technology licensing, and multinational joint ventures.

Copyright Law: Administered Random House's **copyright law**, infringement, and litigation affairs.

Corporate Bylaws: Wrote **corporate bylaws** following the spin-off of Larabie's banking division to create a new corporation with new board of directors and new management team.

Corporate Law: Held full responsibility for the strategic planning and leadership of the entire **Corporate Law** Department, encompassing both domestic and international legal affairs.

Corporate Recordkeeping: Appointed Board Secretary responsible for **corporate recordkeeping**, shareholder communications, and year-end reporting.

Criminal Law: Built and managed a successful **criminal law** practice specializing in the prosecution of repeat offenders.

Cross-Border Transactions: Negotiated **cross-border transactions** for the sale of IBM technology into emerging Mexican markets.

Depositions: Administered **depositions** for all legal proceedings conducted under the jurisdiction of the Montgomery County Circuit Court.

Discovery: Directed **discovery** in representation of alleged malpractice incident.

Due Diligence: Managed **due diligence** for all corporate mergers, acquisitions, joint ventures, and strategic alliances worldwide.

Employment Law: Restructured **employment law** division to meet regulatory requirements and corporate policy for retention and promotion.

Environmental Law: Resolved complex **environmental law** issues arising from improper handling of hazardous waste and disposal.

Ethics: Created vision and established corporate **ethics** committee to advance community-based fundraising, support, and services.

Family Law: Practiced **family law** with an emphasis on the placement and custody of minors.

Fraud: Investigated alleged incidents of **fraud** perpetrated by previous CFO during his 10-year tenure with the corporation.

General Partnership: Structured and transacted all legal contracts for the formation of a real estate **general partnership**.

Intellectual Property: Wrote corporate legal requirements, standards, and use provisions for the transfer of **intellectual property** rights.

Interrogatory: Prepared formal written responses to over 400 **interrogatory** questions during initial discovery procedures.

Joint Venture: Formed **joint venture** between ABC and PBS for the funding, production, and distribution of environmental programming.

Judicial Affairs: Mediated resolution in **judicial affairs** proceedings between two conflicting municipalities.

Juris Doctor (JD): Awarded **Juris Doctor** degree in 1989 as #1 in 420-person graduating class.

Labor Law: Earned a nationwide reputation for expertise in **law labor**, labor negotiations, and mediation.

Landmark Decision: Led legal team in **landmark decision** on corporate taxation passed down by the U.S. Supreme Court.

Legal Advocacy: Provided aggressive **legal advocacy** and representation to human services agencies throughout Minnesota.

Legal Research: Conducted extensive **legal research** and analysis to uncover relevant case law from the early 1930s.

Legislative Review/Analysis: Managed **legislative review/analysis** of changing regulations, identified impact on business operations, and communicated reporting requirements to division vice presidents.

Licensing: Negotiated over $400 million in **licensing** and technology transfer agreements.

Limited Liability Corporation (LLC): Established Bahamian-based **LLC** to protect real estate investment assets and sale proceeds.

Limited Partnership: Formed a **limited partnership** for the development of a 122-room resort in Grand Cayman.

Litigation: Personally managed all complex **litigation** arising from contractual disputes and non-performance.

Mediation: Directed successful **mediation** with union officials and averted potential work stoppage.

Memoranda: Wrote legal **memoranda** for submission to U.S. Claims Court disputing alleged non-compliance.

Mergers: Structured, negotiated, and transacted six **mergers** in 1995 with total investment value of $44 million.

Motions: Drafted **motions** requesting several continuances in response to witness-scheduling obligations.

Negotiations: Managed sensitive **negotiations** between plaintiffs and defendants to resolve issues prior to trial.

Patent Law: Specialized in **patent law** of industrial products, technologies, and components.

Personal Injury: Refocused legal practice from family law to **personal injury** in response to changing client requirements for legal advice and representation.

Probate Law: Managed **probate law** of wills and estates with combined assets of more than $500 million.

Real Estate Law: Recruited to establish DYD's first-ever, in-house **Real Estate Law** Department to manage expanding real estate investment projects and control over $1 billion in assets.

Risk Management: Expanded corporate **risk management** program to include administration of all pension and 401(k) plans.

SEC Affairs: Administered this Wall Street investment firm's **SEC affairs**, reporting, and compliance program.

Settlement Negotiations: Transacted disposition of $1 million in assets through **settlement negotiations** between family members and corporation.

Shareholder Relations: Designed and produced a portfolio of corporate communications to strengthen **shareholder relations** and restore credibility.

Signatory Authority: Held **signatory authority** for all corporate financial and legal documents.

Strategic Alliance: Pioneered the corporation's first-ever **strategic alliance** with an emerging telecommunications service provider.

Tax Law: Directed local, state, federal, and international **tax law** for IBM.

Technology Transfer: Negotiated over $340 million in **technology transfer** agreements with business partners in Mexico, Colombia, and Brazil.

Trade Secrets: Devised strategy to protect the corporation's **trade secrets** following notification of an alleged industrial espionage ring.

Trademark: Revitalized the corporation's commitment to security and authored new **trademark** protection policy.

Transactions Law: Fast-track promotion throughout corporate legal career with an emphasis in domestic and international **transactions law**, contracts, and intellectual property.

Trial Law: Maintained a 90%+ winning rate in all **trial law** proceedings.

Unfair Competition: Investigated and mediated alleged incidents of **unfair competition** in the aerospace and semiconductor industries.

Workers' Compensation Litigation: Successfully resolved 12 pending **workers' compensation litigation** cases to the satisfaction of both management and union officials.

KeyWord Answers to Interview Questions

Tell me about yourself.

I am a **Corporate Attorney** with a wealth of experience in **corporate law** and **litigation, intellectual property, technology licensing, copyright law, contract law**, and **international trade**. Following graduation from Temple University School of Law, I began my legal career as an **Associate** with Marsh, McClennan and Associates. Within two years, I was recruited to McAlister, Banner and Smith, where I started to specialize in the technology industry and related **corporate legal affairs**. During my tenure with McAlister, I negotiated some of the first-ever **technology transfer agreements** on behalf of AT&T. My relationship with AT&T was so strong that they actively recruited me for over a year until I accepted my current position as **Corporate Counsel** for the $2.8 billion technology division. In this capacity, I orchestrate all **corporate legal affairs** for operations in 62 countries worldwide with a total workforce of more than 50,000.

What is the most valuable skill you bring to our company?

My **negotiating skills** are, by far, my strongest skill. Couple that with my ability to quickly **build rapport** with other **attorneys, bankers, financiers, venture capitalists, corporate executives**, and **regulators**, and you have uncovered what is at the basis for my entire career. Despite often conflicting agendas, tight financial constraints, and critical concerns about protecting **proprietary** information and technology, I have been able to negotiate **large-dollar contracts** to the benefit of all involved parties. In fact, based on my expertise, I have often been personally selected by AT&T's **Board of Directors** to handle the company's most complex and most sensitive **negotiations**.

What do you consider to be your most significant achievement or contribution?

During AT&T's 1998 expansion into India, I personally **negotiated contracts** with both **government officials** and the **management team** at the helm of India's entire telecommunications infrastructure. This was an unbelievably challenging **negotiation** involving more than 55 people, eight companies and 16 government agencies.

AT&T received all regulatory approvals within a record-breaking 120 days, I negotiated several **joint ventures**, and AT&T is now the **market leader**.

JENNIFER YEARWOOD, ESQ.

8751 Ravine Road ■ Fayetteville, North Carolina 27066
(919) 637-0815 ■ Yearwood@attorney.net

March 11, 2003

George Lutz, President
Prudential Healthcare
1908 Woodland Avenue
Salem, MA 04453

Dear Mr. Lutz:

As Corporate Counsel / General Counsel for several start-up and high-growth corporations, I have provided critical legal, technical, financial, "deal making," and operating expertise. Currently, as Counsel for an emerging HMO in North Carolina, my challenges have included:

- Development of improved contract strategies and negotiating positions.
- Management of complex due diligence reviews for proposed joint ventures and mergers.
- Implementation of PC technology to automate legal affairs and documentation.
- Review/analysis of complex legislative initiatives impacting the HMO's operations.

Prior to joining the HMO, I progressed rapidly through my earlier corporate counsel positions, working in cooperation with senior operating management of several prestigious corporations. Achievements were notable and included:

- Delivering a 40% reduction in overhead costs through internal reengineering and process improvement.
- Directing legal formation and operations start-up of new technology venture.
- Revitalizing one organization's marketing programs and negotiated/closed $50+ million in leasing transactions.
- Spearheading start-up of new corporation and negotiated $20+ million in equity sales.

My role as Corporate Counsel has transcended all core business functions within each organization. In addition to managing planning, corporate development, transactions, and litigation, I have functioned as a participating partner in the operations, marketing, and financial success of each organization.

My goal is an in-house Corporate Counsel position with an emerging health care provider organization in need of strong, decisive, and proactive leadership. As such, my interest is in meeting with you to explore such opportunities with Prudential Healthcare. I appreciate your consideration and look forward to speaking with you. Thank you.

Sincerely,

Jennifer Yearwood

Jennifer Yearwood, Esq.

Enclosure

WARREN T. COLLINS
39349 South Bay Street ▪ San Francisco, California 96375
Home (415) 493-7459 ▪ Office (415) 246-5894 ▪ Email: WTC225@mcimail.com

CORPORATE GENERAL COUNSEL
Technology Licensing / Mergers & Acquisitions / Joint Ventures / Patents & Trademarks
Litigation & Claims Defense / Corporate Finance / Human Resource Affairs / Contracts

PROFESSIONAL EXPERIENCE:

PFIZER, INC., Redwood Valley, California   1989 to Present
(Fortune 500 specialty pharmaceutical, medical device, surgical equipment, and optical products manufacturer with over 20 major operating subsidiaries worldwide and 1996 revenues of $1.5 billion)

Associate General Counsel & Assistant Secretary (1989 to Present)
Regional General Counsel - Japan (1991 to Present)
Recruited back to previous employer as Senior Counsel responsible for worldwide intellectual property (IP) affairs and licensing, with an IP portfolio of 7,500+ trademarks and 1,500 patents. Direct a staff of 11, including five attorneys and three paralegals. Manage $5 million operating budget.

- Deputy to General Counsel for administration of Corporate Legal Department of 25, including 11 attorneys and six paralegals.

- Structure and negotiate licensing contracts with global pharmaceutical companies, biotechnology companies, and universities for product acquisitions. Negotiate co-promotion, distribution, and supply agreements worldwide.

- Direct all patent and trademark origination, enforcement, and defense actions worldwide. Travel throughout Europe, Japan, Australia, and North America.

- Provide legal consultation for merger, acquisition, and joint venture transactions. Select And direct outside counsel worldwide.

Concurrent appointment as **Corporate Counsel** for Allergan's operations in Japan and as a **Board Member** for two Japanese subsidiaries. Directed all general legal affairs through a multinational legal team (e.g., IP, contracts, leases, joint ventures, employment agreements, claims, and litigation).

NOTE: *Accelerated number of patent awards through improved legal process. Ranked by IPO as one of the top 200 organizations worldwide in number of U.S. patents granted in 1996.*

LEGAL & BUSINESS CONSULTANT, Golden City, California   1984 to 1989

Independent Consultant to CEOs, COOs, Presidents, and Boards of Directors of emerging technology, pharmaceutical and consumer products industries. Provided expertise in patent law, portfolio valuation, technology valuation, regulatory affairs, and new venture start-up.

- Retained for one-year interim assignment as **General Counsel** for Biomedics (biotech R&D venture) to guide the development of in-house legal and patent departments.

- Developed consulting relationship with the California Cancer Research Foundation regarding intellectual property, portfolio evaluation, patents, and related legal actions/claims.

- Developed and obtained first FDA approval (ANDA) of a generic product for a widely used branded surgical scrub for start-up company. Took venture through development and approval, thereafter negotiating successful sale.

WARREN T. COLLINS - *Page Two*

MERIWETHER RESEARCH & DEVELOPMENT COMPANY, San Jose, California
1981 to 1984

Executive Vice President, General Counsel, CFO & Secretary
Joined Meriwether Research to direct this drug development company's IPO following its spin-off from Allergan Pharmaceuticals. Raised $25 million and placed stock on NASDAQ (managed by Merrill Lynch). Achieved market capitalization of $250 million.

Held full accountability for all IP, general and corporate legal, financial, accounting, and human resource affairs for the corporation. Managed a large out-licensing effort for drug development candidates and adjuncts, corporate financial and strategic planning, budgeting, contracts, joint venture and long-range corporate development functions. Directed a staff of 15.

- Patented and licensed CLEOCIN-T, FDA-approved prescription antibiotic for acne. Product delivered $50+ million in annual revenues to licensee (Upjohn).

- Raised an additional $5 million in revenues through negotiation of strategic R&D partnerships with major multinational and regional pharmaceutical companies in Japan and Europe.

PFIZER , INC., Irvine, California   1973 to 1981

General Counsel - Allergan International Division (1977 to 1981)
Assistant General Counsel & Assistant Secretary (1975 to 1981)
Senior Legal Counsel directing Allergan's IP, corporate development, contracts, and in-licensing and out-licensing programs worldwide. Spearheaded the start-up of new company subsidiaries, manufacturing operations, and joint ventures in the U.K., France, Italy, Japan, and Ireland.

Vice President & General Counsel - Nelson Research (1973 to 1975)
Directed corporate development, merger, acquisition, licensing, contracts, and drug development programs worldwide. Guided top scientists in early-stage development of computer-assisted drug design technologies. Directed the award of over 50 patents with numerous foreign corresponding patents and licenses.

EDUCATION:

JD (Honors), George Washington University National Law Center
MBA, Pepperdine University School of Business and Management
BS (Chemistry), University of California at Berkeley

PROFESSIONAL ACTIVITIES:

Bar Admissions	State Bar of California, U.S. Patent and Trademark Office Bar, U.S. Supreme Court
Associations	American Intellectual Property Law Assn., Licensing Executives Society, American Corporate Patent Counsel, Editorial Board (Managing Intellectual Property)
Publications	Editorial Board Member & Contributing Writer to "Managing Intellectual Property," European-based monthly legal publication: – *"Patent Practitioners - Don't Let GATT Get You,"* March 1995 (republished by IP section of California State Bar) – *"Intellectual Property and Pharmaceuticals,"* Patent Yearbook, 1995
Presentations	Presentations sponsored by the Practicing Law Institute (PLI) in San Francisco, 1993, published by PLI in its "Global Intellectual Property Series": – *"Patent Litigation in Civil Law Countries"*; *"Contact Lens Care Litigation"*

16

Manufacturing and Operations Management

Sample Job Titles

Assembly Technician
Assistant Manufacturing Manager
Assistant Operations Manager
Assistant Plant Manager
Assistant Production Manager
Director of Manufacturing
Director of Operations
Distribution Manager
Engineering Manager
Facilities Manager
General Manager
Group Manager
Inventory Control Analyst
Inventory Control Manager
Logistics Manager
Manufacturing Associate
Manufacturing Engineer

Manufacturing Manager

Manufacturing Operations Manager

Materials Manager

Operations Manager

Operations Superintendent

Pilot Plant Manager

Plant Manager

Plant Superintendent

Process Manager

Product Line Manager

Production Control Manager

Production Manager

Production Supervisor

Production Worker

Project Manager

Quality Assurance Analyst

Quality Manager

Shift Supervisor

Superintendent

Union Representative

Vice President of Distribution

Vice President of Logistics

Vice President of Manufacturing

Vice President of Operations

Vice President of Production

KeyWords and KeyWord Phrases

Asset Management: Directed **asset management** functions for 20 manufacturing facilities, two distribution centers, and 68 sales offices nationwide, with total asset value exceeding $2.1 billion.

Automated Manufacturing: Transitioned Playtex from a labor-intensive production operation into a state-of-the-art **automated manufacturing** facility.

Capacity Planning: Facilitated **capacity planning** to consolidate Canadian, Mexican, and U.S. operations into one centralized production operation.

Capital Budget: Controlled a $280 million **capital budget** allocated for technology acquisition.

Capital Project: Brought Johnson's most significant **capital project** in the past 10 years from concept through planning, staffing, and budgeting to full-scale operations and on-time completion.

Cell Manufacturing: Transitioned from traditional line production to **cell manufacturing**, delivering a 22% improvement in product quality and 35% gain in daily production yields.

Computer Integrated Manufacturing (CIM): Spearheaded implementation of **CIM**, CAD, JIT, and SPC systems/technologies to accelerate production output and strengthen quality performance.

Concurrent Engineering: Introduced **concurrent engineering** processes that significantly enhanced transition from R&D to prototype manufacture to full-scale production.

Continuous Improvement: Implemented **continuous improvement** processes and achieved a 24% gain in product quality ratings.

Cost Avoidance: Created environment that rewarded individual employees for contributions to long-term **cost avoidance** and profit growth.

Cost Reductions: Captured over $2 million in material **cost reductions** through expanded vendor sourcing.

Cross-Functional Teams: Championed development of **cross-functional teams** to address critical productivity, efficiency, and quality issues negatively impacting production yields and customer satisfaction.

Cycle Time Reduction: Created formal production schedules, retrained supervisory staff, and impacted a measurable program of **cycle time reduction**.

Distribution Management: Architected the corporation's first nationwide **distribution management** and warehouse control program.

Efficiency Improvement: Guided **efficiency improvement** initiatives throughout all core production planning, production scheduling, and manufacturing operations.

Environmental Health and Safety (EHS): Forged strategic partnership with Human Resources to create a performance-driven **EHS** program for all 10 IBM manufacturing facilities in the Northeast.

Equipment Management: Designed **equipment management** protocols to divest obsolete technology and redeploy advanced equipment resources to high-growth product lines.

Ergonomically Efficient: Redesigned manufacturing plant and created **ergonomically efficient** workstations, reducing extended employee absences and saving over $250,000 in annual workers' compensation costs.

Facilities Consolidation: Advised Manufacturing Manager in design and implementation of a nationwide **facilities consolidation** program.

Inventory Control: Implemented **inventory control** models and processes which reduced on-hand inventory assets by more than $3 million.

Inventory Planning: Launched a large-scale **inventory planning** function in cooperation with Emerson, 3M, and AlliedSignal to control Joyner's annual inventory expenses.

Just-In-Time (JIT): Modified Raytheon's **JIT** processes for implementation throughout all Motorola divisions, affiliates, and subsidiaries.

Labor Efficiency: Improved **labor efficiency** ratings by 12% through in-house training and staff development efforts.

Labor Relations: Managed sensitive **labor relations** initiatives during six-month union contract negotiations.

Logistics Management: Created an integrated **logistics management** program assimilating all purchasing, inventory, distribution, and warehousing functions.

Manufacturing Engineering: Recruited to build and direct the corporation's <u>**Manufacturing Engineering**</u> Division in an aggressive effort to upgrade production facilities, processes, and technologies.

<u>**Manufacturing Integration**</u>: Coordinated <u>**manufacturing integration**</u> of five acquisitions into core production operations.

<u>**Manufacturing Technology**</u>: Acquired over $5 million in <u>**manufacturing technology**</u> and robotics to fully automate the entire production operation.

<u>**Master Schedule**</u>: Designed <u>**master schedule**</u> for annual and five-year manufacturing plans.

<u>**Materials Planning**</u>: Revised <u>**materials planning**</u> programs to incorporate six new product lines into all production and distribution sites nationwide.

<u>**Materials Replenishment System (MRP)**</u>: Introduced <u>**MRP**</u> II system to support start-up of ISO 9000 certification process.

<u>**Multi-Site Operations**</u>: Challenged to revitalize <u>**multi-site operations**</u>, reduce labor and material costs, upgrade quality performance, and strengthen customer loyalty.

<u>**Occupational Health & Safety (OH&S)**</u>: Designed Layton's first <u>**OH&S**</u> program, achieving compliance with both state and federal regulations governing hazardous materials handling and transportation.

<u>**On-Time Delivery**</u>: Improved <u>**on-time delivery**</u> from 56% to 98% within first year.

<u>**Operating Budget**</u>: Challenged to reduce $8.7 million annual <u>**operating budget**</u> through facilities, staff, and technology consolidation.

<u>**Operations Management**</u>: Senior <u>**Operations Management**</u> Executive with full P&L responsibility for six manufacturing plants and a staff of more than 2,000.

<u>**Operations Reengineering**</u>: Orchestrated an aggressive <u>**operations reengineering**</u> initiative and delivered a 22% improvement in production output, 10% reduction in material costs, and 34% improvement in key account retention.

Operations Start-Up: Recruited by CEO to plan and orchestrate **operations start-up** of clean room manufacturing facility.

Optimization: Worked to identify and implement methods to enhance **optimization** of production yields and finished product.

Order Fulfillment: Managed a 52-person **order fulfillment** operation supplying major customers in North America, Latin America, Europe, and Asia.

Order Processing: Reengineered and upgraded **order processing** systems, achieving 99% same-day delivery.

Outsourcing: Pioneered Lytec's first-ever assembly **outsourcing** operation and captured 12% reduction in labor costs over first six months.

Participative Management: Forged implementation of **participative management** strategies in cooperation with management teams, union officials, and hourly union personnel.

Performance Improvement: Guided a series of **performance improvement** programs that transitioned LTR from #4 to #1 in the industry.

Physical Inventory: Eliminated the need for annual **physical inventory** inspections through introduction of JIT systems/processes.

Pilot Manufacturing: Introduced new electronic technology into **pilot manufacturing** plant prior to full-scale production.

Plant Operations: Challenged to revitalize **plant operations**, eliminate redundancy, automate repetitive functions, and improve bottom-line profitability.

Process Automation: Led an aggressive **process automation** program that computerized 115 manual processes and virtually eliminated all documentation requirements.

Process Redesign/Reengineering: Spearheaded an aggressive **process redesign/reengineering** program that increased manufacturing yields by 22%, reduced staffing requirements by 35%, and contributed to a 44% improvement in YTD profits.

Procurement: Revitalized **procurement** operations, introduced international sourcing to supplement domestic vendor programs, and controlled $245 million in annual purchasing contracts.

Product Development & Engineering: Assembled cross-functional project team challenged to re-invent Myer-Rand's complete **product development and engineering** organization.

Product Rationalization: Initiated a large-scale **product rationalization** process to identify top performers and eliminate non-producers.

Production Forecasting: Designed a PC-based model to accelerate **production forecasting** and planning processes.

Production Lead Time: Slashed **production lead times** by more than 60% following implementation of computerized planning and scheduling technologies.

Production Management: Recruited to revitalize **production management** competencies in a downtrending market and industry.

Production Plans/Schedules: Established bi-annual **production plans and schedules** in cooperation with plant managers and production supervisors nationwide.

Production Output: Recruited the industry's most notable troubleshooter, provided technical and labor resources, and supported his efforts in enhancing **production output**, product quality, and cost savings.

Productivity Improvement: Credited with a 34% gain in **productivity improvement** and product reliability.

Profit & Loss (P&L) Management: Senior Manufacturing Executive with full **P&L management** responsibility for the strategic planning, staffing, assets, and field operations of Raydoc's entire manufacturing organization.

Project Budget: Allocated $2 million **project budget** to renovate warehousing and distribution facilities throughout Ohio.

Purchasing Management: Redesigned **purchasing management** and contracting processes for a net $2 million annual cost savings.

Quality Assurance/Quality Control: Devised and implemented an integrated **quality assurance/quality control** process that improved finished product quality ratings by more than 30%.

Quality Circles: Led six **quality circles** challenged to eliminate obstacles to quality control and improve overall performance of operations, products, and components.

Regulatory Compliance: Achieved/surpassed all **regulatory compliance** standards as per OSHA, FDA, DOT, and other state and federal agencies.

Safety Management: Architected the corporation's first-ever **safety management** program and delivered a 24% reduction in lost time accidents over first two years.

Safety Training: Developed curriculum, trained instructors, and supervised a plant-wide **safety training** program.

Shipping & Receiving Operation: Restructured business processes to create a performance-driven, customer-driven **shipping and receiving operation**.

Spares & Repairs Management: Established in-house **spares and repairs management** function to reduce reliance on, and costs associated with, third-party vendors.

Statistical Process Control (SPC): Implemented **SPC** into all core design, engineering, and manufacturing operations.

Technology Integration: Spearheaded $2.8 million **technology integration** project into Gryner's German and French manufacturing operations.

Time and Motion Studies: Conducted a series of **time and motion studies** that identified and virtually eliminated all production inefficiencies.

Total Quality Management (TQM): Credited with the design and implementation of a fully integrated **TQM** program that positioned TerraLand as #1 in timbering operations.

Traffic Management: Created a global **traffic management** function to coordinate product distribution throughout Europe, Asia, and emerging African nations.

Turnaround Management: Challenged to plan and orchestrate an aggressive **turnaround management** initiative to transition Xylog from loss to sustained profitability despite intense market competition.

Union Negotiations: Participated in strategy planning and consensus building for favorable **union negotiations**.

Value-Added Processes: Implemented **value-added processes** to support Frester's global acquisition and operations integration programs.

Vendor Management: Structured a sophisticated **vendor management** program with measurable quality, productivity, and efficiency objectives.

Warehousing Operations: Redesigned **warehousing operations**, reduced staffing requirements 12%, and improved net profitability 28%.

Work in Progress (WIP): Reduced **WIP** by 30% through introduction of cellular manufacturing and robotics technology.

Workflow Optimization: Engineered **workflow optimization** processes for a 34% improvement in daily production output.

Workforce Management: Credited with the creative design and integration of innovative **workforce management**, motivation, and incentive programs.

World Class Manufacturing (WCM): Transitioned HGM Computers from a small technology venture into a **world class manufacturing** operation recognized as one of Fortune's 100 fastest growing enterprises.

Yield Improvement: Introduced improved production processes and delivered 22% gain in **yield improvement**.

KeyWord Answers to Interview Questions

Tell me about yourself.

"Building top-performing **manufacturing operations** is my expertise. When I was challenged to orchestrate a **Greenfield produc-**

tion plant, I was able to staff the facility, install the equipment, **design manufacturing flow**, and get the first product out the door within three months. When I was asked to manage a complex **turnaround**, I introduced leading-edge **manufacturing processes** including **work cells, continuous flow**, and **cycle-time reduc-tions**. Currently as **Plant Manager** of a **high-growth manufac-turer**, I am spearheading the introduction of **advanced robotics**, **ISO 14000**, a sophisticated **master scheduling** program, and a number of other high-profile initiatives. In summary, I am the executive who gets things done, **increases revenues, improves profits**, and drives **long-term growth**."

What is the most valuable skill you bring to our company?

"The greatest value I bring to your organization is the diversity of my experience ... from **start-ups** to **turnarounds** to **high-growth production plants**. Each of these types of organizations has its own unique challenges and opportunities. It has been my responsi-bility to identify the challenges, implement effective **solutions**, and capitalize upon opportunities that allowed us to grow, improve our **bottom-line profit performance**, and dominate the markets in which we have operated."

What do you consider to be your most significant achieve-ment or contribution?

"When I arrived at McCampbell's Plastics Production, the company was in crisis. Costs were out of control, technologies weren't working, the management team had resigned itself to mediocrity, and customers were running out the door. At that point, I recruited **new management talent**, brought in experts to resolve the tech-nological issues, and launched a massive **public relations** effort to recapture our lost **market share**. Within one year, I was able to **halt losses, increase revenues 42%, cut costs 25%**, and regain better than 90% of our original **customer base**."

KEVIN LAIRD, JR.
28 Granite Street
Littleton, CO 32033
(303) 654-4533

February 21, 2003

Louis Wesley, President
Langley Production Machinery
1213 Long Meadows
Middleburg, OH 43565

Dear Mr. Wesley:

As General Manager / Vice President of Manufacturing / Operations Manager, I have consistently delivered results:

- 30% revenue growth, $1+ million cost reduction, and ISO 9002 certification for Goulder Systems.

- Successful turnaround of Tyler Cable with 90% increase in operating profits and $3 million cost reduction.

- Accelerated product development program that generated $5+ million in revenues for Alloy.

- $2+ million operating cost reduction for Bletcher's Powermatic Division.

Throughout my career, I have held full P&L responsibility for Production, R&D, Engineering, Quality, Warehousing, Distribution, Accounting, Human Resources, and MIS/Manufacturing Automation. In addition, I have directed staffs of 200+, reengineered workforces to cut costs while optimizing productivity, and provided strong management leadership in start-up, turnaround, and high-growth organizations.

My greatest strengths lie in my ability to evaluate existing operations and implement the processes, technologies, and systems to improve performance, meet customer objectives, and increase bottom-line profitability. Now I am looking for a new opportunity where I can continue to provide strong and decisive leadership.

I would welcome a personal interview to explore management opportunities with Langley Production Machinery and thank you in advance for your consideration.

Sincerely,

Kevin Laird

Kevin Laird, Jr.

Enclosure

LEWIS L. LAYNE
P.O. Box 3359
Marion, Illinois 60345-3359
(847) 278-8712

SENIOR MANAGEMENT EXECUTIVE
Global Manufacturing / Multi-Site Plant Operations / Industrial Engineering

Talented Management Executive with 20 years of experience building and leading manufacturing operations throughout the U.S. and abroad. Recognized as a subject matter expert on facilitating process change and implementation through training, direction, and motivation of operating staff and management teams.

- Strategic Business Planning & Reengineering
- Cost Containment and Profit Growth
- Management of Technology
- Quality & Performance Improvement
- Inventory and Supply Chain Management
- Production Processes and Controls

PROFESSIONAL EXPERIENCE:

LAYNE & ASSOCIATES, Marion, Illinois – 1994 to Present

Managing Partner

Founded an exclusive consulting practice working with leading firms to provide expertise in manufacturing operations, supply chain management, and management of technology. Lead cross-functional project teams in the analysis, redesign, and implementation of operating enhancements to create world class manufacturing organizations. Key projects and highlights include:

- *Petrochemical Operation, Bombay, India.* Led the assessment of the reliability performance of a world-scale petrochemicals operation. Focused efforts on performance improvement processes and the maintenance, storeroom, and purchasing functions. Proposed reorganization and establishment of controls to improve reliability. **RESULTS**: Identified $25 million profit improvement and increased plant throughput by 12%.

- *Diesel Engine Manufacturer, Cape Town, South Africa.* Contracted for a 7-month on-site assignment to improve production planning and inventory control functions for the leading diesel engine manufacturer in Africa. **RESULTS**: Implemented a plan-do-review process with team centers and key performance indicators. Increased customer service levels from 70% to 95% and reduced inventories from 77 to 45 days on-hand.

- *Kellogg Graduate School / Northwestern University, Chicago, Illinois.* While completing Masters program, participated in management of technology research project sponsored by General Motors, Kodak, and Rockwell International. **RESULTS**: Developed process-based model for management of technology. Conducted high-level evaluations of existing management of technology processes and identified potential best practices for use throughout industry.

ALEXANDER & ALEXANDER – 1988 to 1994

Management Consultant

Recruited to join this global consulting group based on expertise in the design and delivery of value-added process improvements for major Fortune 500 and international corporations. Managed the complete project cycle including client assessment, engagement planning, proposal development, and project delivery. Key clients included Johnson & Johnson, Mobil Oil, Dole Foods, Ford, Kraft/General Foods, Procter & Gamble, and Merck Pharmaceuticals.

LEWIS L. LAYNE - Page Two

- Identified potential $55 million cost savings for General Motors through manufacturing benchmarking throughout the Saginaw Steering Systems Division.
- Spearheaded the design/implementation of a comprehensive maintenance planning and scheduling process for Dole Foods. Reduced manpower by 40% within seven months.
- Assessed and redesigned work processes throughout Novacor's maintenance planning and scheduling department. Reduced work backlogs by 80%.
- Facilitated the consolidation of Golden Cat's multi-site operations from four distinct facilities into three as part of a corporate-wide capacity and consolidation analysis.

REESE LABORATORIES – 1977 to 1988

Progressed through several increasingly responsible engineering and plant management assignments with this $12 billion multinational health care products supplier. Promoted based upon consistent success in operations management, cost control, and business process reengineering.

Plant Engineering Section Head - Corporate Headquarters (1983 to 1988)

Operations Supervisor for biohazardous, pharmaceutical, and clean room environmental systems of a 2.5 million sq.ft. complex of 40 buildings. Led team of 14 engineers and technical support personnel responsible for environmental systems maintenance and operation. Challenged to establish group and develop procedures for new and existing facilities to meet environmental standards.

- Managed the installation of state-of-the-art automated facilities management system. Facilitated the start-up of one million sq.ft. of new operations.
- Reduced operating costs by $300,000 through efficient operation of environmental systems.

International Manufacturing Engineer (1979 to 1983)

Promoted to the $4 billion International Manufacturing Division. Implemented a cost reduction program for 35 manufacturing plants including program design, measurement, reporting of results, and training. Led the assessment of 10 manufacturing facilities worldwide. Reduced operating expenses by $2 million annually. Received Presidential Award for outstanding performance.

Engineering Management Trainee (1977 to 1979)

Selected from a competitive group of candidates for a two-year management training program while completing master's degree. Completed four assignments within the Corporate Engineering Division including the utilities, projects, design, and maintenance departments.

EDUCATION & CERTIFICATIONS:

M.S., Industrial Engineering, THE UNIVERSITY OF CHICAGO, 1997
Major: Operations Research; Minor: Management of Technology
M.B.A., NORTHWESTERN UNIVERSITY, 1987
Major: Finance; Minor: Marketing
M.S., Mechanical Engineering, NORTHWESTERN UNIVERSITY, 1980
B.S., Mechanical Engineering, THE UNIVERSITY OF CHICAGO, 1976

Certified in Production & Inventory Management, APICS
Certified Management Consultant, IMC
Registered Professional Engineer, Illinois

17

Public Relations and Corporate Communications

Sample Job Titles

Advertising Director

Advertising Manager

Communications Analyst

Communications Director

Community Relations Manager

Conference Manager

Corporate Communications Specialist

Creative Director

Director of Corporate Communications

Editor

Events Manager

Graphic Artist

Graphic Designer

Journalist

Legislative Affairs Director

Lobbyist

Marketing Associate

Marketing Manager
Media Relations Director
Meetings Manager
Photographer
Political Affairs Director
Promotions Manager
Press Manager
Public Affairs Director
Public Affairs Officer
Public Relations Director
Special Events Manager
Trade Show Manager
Vice President of Advertising
Vice President of Corporate Communications
Vice President of Creative Services
Vice President of Public Relations
Writer

KeyWords and KeyWord Phrases

Advertising Communications: Designed, wrote and produced a complete portfolio of print and multimedia **advertising communications** for key corporate clients (e.g., Exxon, Johnson & Johnson, Sears, Neiman-Marcus, Lazarus).

Agency Relations: Directed **agency relations** with major advertising, marketing, direct mail, and print production companies.

Brand Management: Full P&L responsibility for **brand management** of Baxter's #1 global product line ($340 million Xytol brand).

Brand Strategy: Refocused **brand strategy** to meet changing consumer demographics and buying preferences.

Broadcast Media: Established proactive working relations with major **broadcast media** to favorably manage press communications during major corporate downsizing.

Campaign Management: Brand Manager with full responsibility for **campaign management** and execution of nationwide market launch of Tide Extra, now a $400 million product line ranked #2 in market share.

Community Affairs: Partnered with community leaders in support of high-profile **community affairs**, revitalization, and funding activities.

Community Outreach: Expanded regional health care advertising programs to include direct **community outreach** and community teaching programs.

Competitive Market Lead: Revitalized Palmolive Liquid Soap product line and captured a strong and sustainable **competitive market lead**.

Conference Planning: Guided **conference planning** and special event programs with full responsibility for logistics, menus, guest speakers, agendas, facilities, and on-site security.

Cooperative Advertising: Negotiated **cooperative advertising** partnerships with major retailers and captured a 15% reduction in annual print and broadcast costs.

Corporate Communications: Spearheaded the design, development, and production of a series of high-profile **corporate communications** to create the company's first fully integrated corporate identity.

Corporate Identity: Designed logos, letterheads, home pages, videos, and customer communications with a consistent and recognizable **corporate identity**.

Corporate Sponsorship: Identified market opportunity and negotiated a $2 million **corporate sponsorship** with Atlanta Allied Resources to fund Bill Tuttle's NASCAR racing team.

Corporate Vision: Defined new **corporate vision** and authored business plan incorporating critical organizational development, process reengineering, and change management programs.

Creative Services: Selected suppliers and negotiated third-party **creative services** contracts for graphics design, copyrighting, photographic, and print production services.

Crisis Communications: Managed sensitive **crisis communications** with major media worldwide.

Customer Communications: Won a 1992 industry award for "creative excellence" in design of outbound **customer communications** campaign.

Direct Mail Campaign: Wrote copy and coordinated production/mailing of 20,000-piece **direct mail campaign** to existing customer base that delivered $750,000 in repeat sales.

Electronic Advertising: Pioneered Mattel's launch into emerging **electronic advertising** and communications technologies.

Electronic Media: Integrated **electronic media** with traditional print promotions to expand corporate advertising and communications campaigns throughout emerging markets.

Employee Communications: Created a proactive **employee communications** campaign to link management expectations with employee incentives and performance goals.

Event Management: Directed site selection, budgeting, entertainment, and on-site **event management** functions for over 200 meetings, conferences, training symposia, and social programs annually.

Fundraising: Achieved/surpassed all **fundraising** objectives and delivered $2 million in donations to the American Red Cross.

Government Relations: Directed **government relations** program critical to the success and continued funding of advanced telecommunications R&D projects.

Grassroots Campaign: Won support of local advocacy group and spearheaded **grassroots campaign** successful in defeating proposed legislation.

Investor Communications: Created a high-impact, high-profile **investor communications** program that restored Apple's credibility throughout the Wall Street community.

Issues Management: Counseled President and CEO on critical **issues management** and response to media inquiries.

Legislative Affairs: Orchestrated **legislative affairs** programs in cooperation with local, state, and federal legislators to support the passage of the 1990 Free Commerce Act.

Logistics: Led 16-person special events team responsible for all **logistics**, including travel, lodging, local transportation, meals, and conference agenda.

Management Communications: Designed monthly **management communications** program to update all supervisory and management personnel on changing regulatory requirements and documentation procedures.

Market Research: Conducted nationwide competitive **market research** to drive strategy for next generation products.

Marketing Communications: Designed and produced all corporate **marketing communications**, advertisements, promotions, incentives, POS displays, and home pages.

Media Buys: Directed **media buys** for over $2 billion in annual television advertising.

Media Placement: Negotiated front page **media placement** with *Forbes*, *Fortune*, and *Time*.

Media Relations: Maintained positive **media relations** despite widespread coverage of environmental pollutants and leakage incidents.

Media Scheduling: Coordinated **media scheduling** in cooperation with new product roll-out team to accelerate new launch and distribution.

Meeting Planning: Directed **meeting planning** for training and leadership development programs for the Center for Creative Leadership.

Merchandising: Designed award-winning consumer products **merchandising** programs that contributed substantially to Macy's 20% sales gain in 1996.

Multimedia Advertising: Produced **multimedia advertising** and customer communications programs to more competitively position Lerner against emerging suppliers.

Political Action Committee (PAC): Led GE's political action committee over a 10-year period, significantly improving the corporation's ability to influence favorable legislation.

Premiums: Designed **premiums** as a direct competitive incentive against mature product brands.

Press Releases: Wrote corporate **press releases** for distribution to all major print and broadcast media throughout North America, Latin America, and Europe.

Print Media: Launched a new **print media** campaign that provided Sears with competitive market and price distinction.

Promotions: Developed POS **promotions** that increased Coke's sales in all regional Wal-Mart locations by an average of 12% over six months.

Public Affairs: Challenged to restore regulatory confidence with a pro-active **public affairs** and communications program.

Public Relations: Dominated the market with successful **public relations** initiatives targeted to major manufacturers, distributors, vendors, resellers, and mass merchants.

Public Speaking: Managed **public speaking** engagements before investors, bankers, shareholders, and directors to support further investment in emerging health care products.

Publications: Directed in-house writing team that delivered 35 technical, marketing, and employee **publications** in 1996.

Publicity: Won major media **publicity** with the donation of $2 million to the National Gallery of Art.

Sales Incentives: Created performance-driven **sales incentives** to drive field teams to a better than 35% increase over last year's sales numbers.

Shareholder Communications: Revitalized **shareholder communications** program and restored credibility despite poor market and revenue performance.

Special Events: Planned, staffed, budgeted, advertised, and managed **special events** nationwide to raise money for local AIDS charities and health care research programs.

Strategic Communications Plan: Authored the corporation's first-ever **strategic communications plan**, defined corporate vision, and charted course of action over next five years.

Strategic Planning: Member of six-person senior executive team responsible for annual **strategic planning**, business development, and market expansion.

Strategic Positioning: Elevated Midol's ranking in the HBA products industry through **strategic positioning** and product redefinition.

Tactical Campaign: Guided field sales, marketing, and support teams in the implementation of **tactical campaigns** designed to accelerate profitable revenue growth.

Trade Shows: Represented emerging technology ventures at Comdex and other industry **trade shows** nationwide.

VIP Relations: Launched a high-profile and successful **VIP relations** program to strengthen partnerships with major corporate, industrial, government, and not-for-profit clients.

KeyWord Answers to Interview Questions

Tell me about yourself.

"For the past 12 years, I've been responsible for the **strategic design** and **tactical execution** of a full range of **public relations programs** – programs targeted to our **corporate and institutional clients**, programs targeted to the **general public** for our retail division, and programs targeted to increase **media awareness and coverage**. My expertise lies in my ability to coordinate project teams encompassing **creative and graphic design**, **strategy**, and **field implementation**. As a result of my efforts and those of other PR professionals within the organization, we have increased our **market awareness**, strengthened **customer loyalty**, expanded the reach of our **corporate identity campaigns**, and launched into **e-commerce** for our most recent PR efforts. Equally notable has been my performance in **issues management,** often dealing with complex, time-sensitive issues involving **product reliability and performance.**"

What is the most valuable skill you bring to our company?

"Undeniably, my greatest strength is my ability to assemble and **lead project teams** through all facets of **campaign design and execution.** Whether working with a small group of three to four individuals or a multi-divisional team of 20+, I have consistently provided the **leadership** necessary to achieve **project milestones.** I manage by **consensus,** rewarding each individual team member for their contributions to the overall project. Just as important, however, let me also mention that I have outstanding **oral and written communication skills,** a must for every **PR professional.**"

What do you consider to be your most significant achievement or contribution?

"I am most proud of my work on the ThinkPad **launch campaign.** Working with a team of 12 other **PR and corporate communication experts,** we designed a **multimedia campaign,** integrating **print, television, radio,** and the **Internet** to facilitate a **global market launch.** As a result of our efforts, in tandem with those of the **field sales organization,** we far exceeded our initial **revenue goals,** bringing in over $12 million in ThinkPad sales within the first 60 days."

THOMAS HUANG
11 Delaware Avenue ▪ Toledo, OH 49382 ▪ Phone: 444.323.9283
thuang234@missionimpossible.com

March 14, 2003

Larry Nelson
Martinson Manufacturing, Inc.
909 Toledo Avenue
Toledo, OH 49322

Dear Mr. Nelson:

Twenty years ago, technology innovations virtually sold themselves. With a bit of advertising here and there, a company was set to launch a new product. Today, however, things have changed dramatically, and marketing has become one of the most vital components to any technology venture. With both global competition and new product roll-outs at an all-time high, it is no longer enough to just develop a product. What is required is an astute marketer with technological expertise. And that is precisely who I am.

Working with some of the world's leading technology companies (e.g., Schlumberger, Emerson, AMERCOM), I have led innovative R&D programs with responsibility for marketing, commercialization, joint ventures, partnerships, and licensing. Most significant have been my financial results:

- For Emerson, I drove the development of eight new products generating total revenues in excess of $20 million annually.
- For ATMAN, a German-based company, I increased European market sales from $2 million to $10 million.
- For AMERCOM, I developed and commercialized 20 new products and achieved a 70% win rate on competitive contracts.
- For Schlumberger, I reengineered existing product technology and saved over $1.5 million in company operating costs.

These achievements are indicative of the quality and caliber of my entire professional career – identify market opportunities, drive technology development, and create profitable sales and marketing programs. It goes without mentioning that the strength of my hands-on technology skills has been vital to my success in business development and revenue generation.

Since leaving Emerson last year, I have continued to focus my efforts on technology development and global marketing, and would be pleased to share specific engagements with you during an interview. Currently, I am exploring new career opportunities in technology marketing and would be delighted to meet with you.

Sincerely,

Thomas Huang

Thomas Huang

Enclosure

REBECCA L. CORCORAN

PR4You@winning.com
210 East Chestnut Hill
Philadelphia, PA 19831
Home (215) 862-9724
Office (215) 831-8030

MARKETING / MEDIA & PUBLIC RELATIONS / SPECIAL EVENTS / SPORTING EVENTS
Creating High-Impact Images, Concepts, Services, Programs, & Opportunities to Build Revenues, Corporate Sponsorships, and Fundraising Contributions

Dynamic management career leading the conceptualization, creative design, planning, staffing, budgeting, and promotion of successful marketing and special events programs worldwide. Expert in identifying market demand and building sustainable market presence. Skilled strategic planner, business manager, and sales/marketing director. Strong organizational, communication, public speaking, and negotiations qualifications. Conversational French.

PROFESSIONAL EXPERIENCE:

Senior Associate   1991 to Present
THE POLETTI GROUP, Philadelphia, PA

Invited to join an elite real estate sales organization specializing in the marketing and sale of high-end residential properties throughout metropolitan New York.

- Achieved Million Dollar Roundtable each year. Promoted to Senior Associate after first year.
- Closed over $5 million in transactions within first five months of 1995. Ranked as one of the top sales producers in the organization.

Concurrent with The Poletti Group, chaired/co-chaired a series of high-profile fundraising and special events programs nationwide:

- Co-chaired the 1997 **Hot Springs Hospital Charity Luncheon**, one of the largest and most widely covered events in the region. Increased fundraising by 25%. Selected to co-chair the 1998 event.
- Chaired the 1996 campaign for **Science Service**, a widely publicized event launched to increase awareness of the innovative science scholarship and academic opportunities for young teenage candidates sponsored by the organization. Created a series of dynamic marketing and public relations materials to increase market visibility. Worked collaboratively with Honorary Chairperson Joan Rivers.
- Co-chaired the **Annual Red Cross Ball** (1990 to 1995), a prominent social event with celebrity sponsors including Deirdre Hall, Marla Maples, and Marylou Whitney. Increased attendance from 250 in 1990 to 800+ in 1995 with Fortune 500 corporate sponsors.

Special Events Director   1990 to 1991
LONDON DOWNS POLO & COUNTRY CLUB, London Downs, NY

High-profile management position directing integrated marketing, special events, media, and promotions programs for the Club, the Polo Museum, and internationally sponsored sporting events. Concurrent responsibility for spearheading national and international real estate sales and marketing programs for Equestrian Estates (high-end residential sub-community). Ranked as the #1 revenue producer.

- Appointed to the International Advisory Board for the Polo Museum. Personally launched a series of highly successful fundraising and corporate sponsorship campaigns.
- Organized and executed an 800-person grand opening celebration with national and international media coverage.

Vice President of Marketing & Development   1988 to 1989
SILVER SERVICES, INC., Memphis, TN

Recruited to provide the direction, energy, strategy, and expertise to launch an integrated sales, marketing, and business development campaign for this retirement community corporation seeking to expand nationally. Authored first strategic marketing plan, directed $500,000 marketing and property development budget, and created a distinctive lifestyle community.

- Drove revenue growth by 20% within one year.

Regional Director of Marketing & Sales   1985 to 1988
NATIONAL RETIREMENT FOUNDATION, Memphis, TN

Fast-track promotion from Marketing Director to Marketing Director/Executive Director of a 175-unit, 20-acre upscale retirement community. Directed a staff of 54 and a $2.3 million annual operating budget. Created and successfully marketed a unique lifestyle and community culture that competitively positioned the property within the market and served as the corporate model for new project development. Promoted to Regional Director of Marketing & Sales (first in the history of the corporation) and given full responsibility for strategic planning, design, and management of all new business development, advertising, public relations, special events, and revenue generating programs for 12-14 projects nationwide.

- Led team that closed over $15.9 million in sales revenues in 1988.
- Maintained a high-profile position within the corporation. Led presentations to corporate investors, spoke at industry conferences and symposia, and directly managed press relations.

Co-Owner / General Manager   1974 to 1985
GRAY TRAVEL AGENCY, Memphis, TN

Co-founded a specialty travel and tour company with market focus on major specialty and sporting events worldwide (e.g., Melbourne Cup, the Olympics, World Championships). Designed unique tour packages for corporate clients, groups, and associations. Personally managed daily agency operations, staffing, sales/marketing, customer service, and contract negotiations. Built business to $2 million in annual sales.

PROFESSIONAL ACTIVITIES & AFFILIATIONS:

- **Independent Consultant** retained by Gross & Co. (1994 to Present), a newly formed investment banking firm in Atlanta, Georgia, to provide expertise in **investor solicitation and negotiations** for a new $42 million fund (limited partnership with six high-profile board members including Norman Schwartzkopf). Traveled with partners to Europe to meet with potential investors in April 1995. Currently creating a portfolio of marketing and business development materials.

- **Special Events & Tour Consultant** with Elite Travel Services in Palm Beach, Florida (1994 to Present). Currently developing and marketing several unique travel packages to upscale resorts, sporting events, and fundraising events worldwide (e.g., Princess Grace Foundation in Monte Carlo July 4th).

- **Founding Board Member of Equestrian Events, Inc.,** a nonprofit organization formed by the Governor of Tennessee in cooperation with the Tennessee Horse Park. Launched high-profile special events, fundraising programs, and corporate sponsorships for the prestigious events. Served as President for two terms, Vice President for two terms, and Secretary for two terms. Built fundraising budget from $1,500 to $450,000 over eight years.

EDUCATION:

BA Degree, Speech & Hearing Pathology / Graduate Studies, University of Kentucky

18

Purchasing and Logistics

Sample Job Titles

Buyer
Certified Purchasing Manager (CPM)
Contracts Administrator
Contracts Manager
Corporate Purchasing Director
Director of Acquisitions
Director of Purchasing
Field Purchasing Manager
Logistics Manager
Materials Analyst
Materials Manager
Purchasing Agent
Purchasing Director
Purchasing Manager
Resource Manager
Senior Buyer
Senior Product Analyst
Subcontracts Administrator

Supplier Manager
Supply Chain Manager
Vendor Relations Manager
Vice President of Materials and Resources
Vice President of Purchasing

KeyWords and KeyWord Phrases

Acquisition Management: Staffed and directed an **acquisition management** function responsible for over $2 billion in annual expenditures.

Barter Trade: Pioneered the development of an international **barter trade** program with Asian and European business partners to reduce domestic tax liabilities.

Bid Review: Managed a complex RFP and **bid review** process for the award of a $100 million health care research grant.

Buy vs. Lease Analysis: Developed PC-based models to enhance **buy vs. lease analysis** competencies.

Capital Equipment Acquisition: Directed over $50 million in **capital equipment acquisitions** during first year of $2 billion economic development program.

Commodities Purchasing: Managed a 12-person **commodities purchasing** business group responsible for electronics components acquisition in Japan, Korea, and the Philippines.

Competitive Bidding: Administered the entire **competitive bidding** and contract award process for the $2 billion renovation of the New York Harbor Tunnel.

Contract Administration: Directed **contract administration**, negotiation, and rebid functions for over $200 million in annual subcontracts.

Contract Change Order: Issued **contract change orders** to reflect design and engineering modifications.

Contract Negotiations: Led cross-functional teams responsible for all corporate **contract negotiations** for real estate acquisition and site development.

Contract Terms and Conditions : Standardized routine **contract terms and conditions** for all consumer lending relationships.

Cradle-to-Grave Procurement: Managed worldwide **cradle-to-grave procurement** contracts for the U.S. Army Materiel Command.

Distribution Management: Created a multi-channel **distribution management** program in cooperation with VARs, resellers, systems integrators, and major consulting firms.

Economic Ordering Quantity Methodology: Introduced **economic ordering quantity methodology**, EVA principles, and other sophisticated financial tools for purchasing, warehousing, inventory, and distribution.

Fixed Price Contracts: Administered **fixed price contracts** with the U.S. Army, U.S. Navy, IBM, Xerox, and Raytheon totaling over $40 million annually for the delivery of advanced navigational devices.

Indefinite Price/Indefinite Quantity: Managed **indefinite price/indefinite quantity** contracts for technology, communications, electronics, and underwater surveillance systems.

International Sourcing: Introduced **international sourcing** and partnered with Asian manufacturers to market the first-ever RBR devices in the U.S.

International Trade: Expanded **international trade** into emerging African markets to capitalize upon acquisition and divestiture opportunities in various mineral commodities.

Inventory Planning/Control: Re-invented Fram's **inventory planning and control** function, introduced JIT principles, streamlined documentation requirements, and cut inventory costs by 20% annually.

Just-in-Time (JIT) Purchasing: Successfully implemented **JIT purchasing** into 200 IBM manufacturing sites worldwide, resulting in a better than 5% reduction in annual purchasing and inventory holding costs.

Logistics Management: Created a fully integrated **logistics management** function consolidating purchasing, inventory, warehousing and distribution.

Materials Management: Established a formal **materials management** function to gain control of parts, inventory, spares, and WIP throughout 100,000 sq. ft. manufacturing plant.

Materials Replenishment Ordering (MRO) Purchasing: Introduced a series of productivity improvement programs including **MRO purchasing**, quality councils, and an aggressive cost reduction initiative.

Multi-Site Operations: Planned, staffed, budgeted, and directed all purchasing and contract functions for **multi-site operations** throughout Pennsylvania, Maryland, and New Jersey.

Negotiation: Demonstrated powerful **negotiation** skills in challenging situations.

Offshore Purchasing: Reduced annual costs by $22 million through introduction of **offshore purchasing** and vendor partnerships.

Outsourced: Pioneered Kelly's successful transition from in-house to **outsourced** telecommunications and telemarketing services.

Price Negotiations: Managed sensitive **price negotiations** during $2 billion acquisition of American Savings Bank by Maryland National Bank.

Procurement: Appointed Project Officer responsible for worldwide **procurement** of military armament and explosives.

Proposal Review: Led team responsible for **proposal review**, cost analysis, and evaluation for acquisition of $275 million avionics system.

Purchasing: Recruited to this emerging Internet venture to guide the development of a corporate **purchasing**, materials management, warehousing, and data delivery function.

Regulatory Compliance: Directed **regulatory compliance** functions encompassing FAR, DFAR, and state regulatory requirements.

Request for Proposal (RFP): Issued 200+ **RFPs** in support of Syntex's $300 million nuclear plant expansion and retrofit.

Request for Quotation (RFQ): Reviewed all **RFQ** submissions for $20 million health care services contract.

Sourcing: Expanded materials **sourcing** programs to include minority vendors in certified business districts.

Specifications Compliance: Reviewed contractor progress reports to ensure **specifications compliance** and accurate documentation.

Subcontractor Negotiations: Authorized general contractor to manage and administer all **subcontractor negotiations**.

Supplier Management: Created an integrated **supplier management** model based on partnership strategies and common visions.

Supplier Quality: Introduced a comprehensive **supplier quality** review and assessment process to strengthen quality of final consumer products.

Vendor Partnerships: Spearheaded profitable **vendor partnerships** to exploit common customer relationships and facilitate market expansion.

Vendor Quality Certification: Established a multi-year **vendor quality certification** program that contributed to a 22% increase in customer satisfaction/retention.

Warehousing: Managed a 22-site **warehousing** and product distribution organization to record performance, efficiency, and profit levels.

KeyWord Answers to Interview Questions

Tell me about yourself.

"I am a well-qualified **Purchasing Manager** with 15 years' experience in the automotive industry with Ford and Chevrolet. During my tenure with these companies, my scope of responsibility has increased dramatically. Initially only responsible for **purchasing** electronic and mechanical components, I soon became responsible for **vendor sourcing** in both **domestic and international markets**. Following that assignment, I was then trained in and assumed responsibility for all **vendor contract terms and conditions**. Now, as one of only six **purchasing managers** in a $500 million production facility, I manage the entire **supply chain** including **inventory planning and control, vendor quality assurance, contracts, purchasing**, and the **flow of materials** throughout the complex. In fact, last year I purchased over $68 million in **raw materials, technologies**, and **components**."

What is the most valuable skill you bring to our company?

"My **negotiating skills** are by far my strongest attribute. I NEVER accept the first price I'm given, knowing that if I can **strategically negotiate**, I will always be able to **reduce material costs**. Hand-in-hand with negotiating is one's ability to **communicate**, and I do that exceptionally well. My ability to **build rapport** and develop **cooperative working relationships** has been at the foundation of my success in **negotiating** and in fostering the long-term, profitable management of our **purchasing** and **supply chain management operations**."

What do you consider to be your most significant achievement or contribution?

"Without a doubt, my most significant contributions to both Ford and Chevrolet have been my successes in **cost reduction**. Most notably, Ford was paying over $2.5 million annually for a small electronic component. By **sourcing** another **vendor** and **negotiating a multi-year contract**, I was able to reduce that cost by 25% each year. With Chevrolet, I've delivered over $12 million in **annual cost savings** on several core components and am projecting an additional $5 million savings on all **technology expenditures** over the next two years."

PAUL A. SHELBY
141 Roundabout Drive
Morrison Township, Arkansas 83415
Home (554) 566-1285
Office (554) 358-5870

September 4, 2003

Charles Abbington
Vice President of Operations
Becthold Corporation
294 Washington Avenue
Dallas, TX 87451

Dear Mr. Abbington:

With 12 years' experience in purchasing management and material/supply sourcing, I bring to your organization strong qualifications and a record of consistent achievement in:

- Negotiating multi-million dollar, multi-year purchasing contracts – long term, fixed price, and minority supplier.
- Identifying quality suppliers and establishing favorable pricing, terms, and conditions.
- Transferring supply contracts from foreign to domestic sources to meet stringent quality and performance requirements.
- Directing sophisticated manufacturing engineering and tooling programs.

Most notably, I have captured millions of dollars in cost savings, including:

- $20 million purchasing cost reduction for Venture Systems.
- $5.5 million purchasing cost reduction for Chrysler Corporation.

I am most proud of my tenure with Venture Systems. Recruited in 1991, I built the organization's purchasing function from concept into a 10-person worldwide business unit responsible for over $550 million in annual procurement acquisitions. Our financial and operational successes were notable and included the introduction of innovative business strategies, procurement policies, and strategic vendor alliances.

Currently, I am exploring new professional opportunities and would welcome a personal interview as Vice President of Purchasing. Thank you.

Sincerely,

Paul A. Shelby

Paul A. Shelby

Enclosure

WENDELL T. HOLMES
3984 SW Shore Drive
Tampa, Florida 33598
(897) 314-5431

CAREER SUMMARY:

Over 15 years experience managing high-volume **PURCHASING / MATERIALS MANAGEMENT / INVENTORY CONTROL** operations. Qualifications include:

- Purchasing Department Management
- Staffing/Training/Supervision
- Quality/Productivity Improvement
- Inventory Planning/Forecasting

- Vendor Sourcing/Selection
- Contract Negotiations/Administration
- Competitive Bidding/Award
- Cost Reduction/Avoidance

Certified Purchasing Manager (CPM) Candidate.

PROFESSIONAL EXPERIENCE:

PREMIERE MANUFACTURING, INC., Tampa, Florida   1994 to Present

Senior Purchasing Agent

Recruited by previous employer (automotive components manufacturer) for a senior-level position at the corporation's world headquarters. Scope of responsibilities includes global vendor sourcing, vendor contract negotiations, materials planning, and inventory analysis. Focus efforts on reducing net purchasing costs and lowering inventory volumes while maintaining adequate stock on hand to meet daily production flow.

GTE TELEPHONE COMPANY, Orion, Ohio   1990 to 1994

Purchasing Manager - Florida

Senior Purchasing Manager with full responsibility for planning, staffing, budgeting, and directing the entire purchasing organization for the company's operations throughout the state of Florida. Supervised a staff of eight direct reports and 27 indirect personnel. Total annual purchasing exceeded $100 million.

- Managed operations during a period of significant growth (e.g., purchase orders increased from 12,000 to 40,000 annually, line items increased from 4,000 to 110,000).

- Realigned workforce of the Purchasing Department, reduced non-management staffing from 35 to 22 personnel, and saved the corporation $400,000 in annual payroll expenses.

- Established and staffed materials forecasting department to more effectively manage materials planning functions for company operations throughout the Southeast.

- Led design and implementation of a paperless purchasing and invoicing system that significantly upgraded the productivity, efficiency, and quality of the entire materials management organization.

- Saved $75,000 in annual office supply and material costs through aggressive vendor negotiations.

- Managed telephone refurbishing and scrap disposal contract projected to save $1 million annually.

- Negotiated development and subsequent administration of a cooperative educational program with Tampa Technical Institute for start-up of a CPM Certification Program for GTE personnel.

WENDELL T. HOLMES - Page Two

PREMIERE MANUFACTURING, INC., Lexington, Virginia   1987 to 1990

    Purchasing Agent

Scheduled and purchased all materials for press switch, solenoid, mini-pressure transducers, and molding department (e.g., stampings, metals, copper, brass, stainless steel, screw machine components, molded parts, tooling). Responsible for vendor research, sourcing, bidding, and documentation. Coordinated JIT purchasing averaging $1.7 million annually.

- Reduced R&D purchasing costs by $200,000 for one specific project (20% under projected costs).

- Saved $150,000 in costs on plastic components through negotiation of bulk purchasing agreements.

- Lowered product inventories by more than 25% annually ($250,000 estimated savings).

MELLON SYSTEMS, INC., Melbourne, Florida   1986 to 1987

    Senior Buyer

Fast-paced purchasing, vendor sourcing, and materials management position buying a diversity of commodities (e.g., primary electro/electromechanical products and metal fabricated materials, cabinetry, plant equipment, maintenance/repair supplies). Purchased for both the manufacturing and land/building divisions of the company. Held concurrent responsibility for research, selection, and contracting with technical service consultants.

STEWART OFFICE SUPPLY, Ft. Myers, Florida   1985 to 1986

    Sales Representative

Sold/marketed office equipment, furniture, and supplies to commercial, industrial, and institutional accounts throughout the region. Met with prospective clients to evaluate product requirements, led presentations, negotiated pricing, and closed final sales. Consistently met monthly quotas for sales revenues and new account development.

GTE TELEPHONE, Orion, Ohio   1973 to 1985

    Purchasing Supervisor

Fast-track promotion through a series of increasingly responsible purchasing and warehouse management positions. Final assignment as Purchasing Supervisor included direct responsibility for training/supervising a staff of six in Materials Repair/Return.

EDUCATION:

TAMPA TECHNICAL INSTITUTE
30 credit hours toward CPM Certification

NATIONAL MANAGEMENT ASSOCIATION
Management Training & Supervisory Development Courses

GTE, INC.
Management, Supervisory, Communications & Performance Development Courses

19

Real Estate, Construction, and Property Management

Sample Job Titles

Acquisitions Director
Asset Disposition Officer
Asset Manager
Broker of Record
Certified Property Manager (CPM)
Chief Executive Officer (CEO)
Chief Operating Officer (COO)
Director of Operations
Director of Property Management
Facilities Manager
General Contractor
Land Developer
Land Manager
Leasing Agent
Leasing Manager
Managing General Partner
Managing Partner

Portfolio Administrator

Portfolio Manager

President

Project Manager

Project Superintendent

Property Manager

Real Estate Agent

Real Estate Developer

Real Estate Director

Real Estate Sales and Marketing Manager

Real Property Administrator (RPA)

Registered Property Manager (RPM)

Sales Associate

Vice President of Acquisition

Vice President of Development

Vice President of Real Estate

KeyWords and KeyWord Phrases

Acquisition: Negotiated the **acquisition** of $200 million in investment property as part of Austin's downtown revitalization and economic development project.

Americans With Disabilities Act (ADA): Rewrote procedures for Building & Construction Division to incorporate recent **ADA** regulations for accessibility.

Asset Management: Responsible for **asset management** and disposition of over $2 billion in both commercial and multi-unit residential property.

Asset Valuation: Directed **asset valuation** of all proposed acquisitions, reviewed tenant leases, and made final purchase recommendations.

Asset Workout/Recovery: Led **asset workout** teams in recovering over $200 million in distressed real estate assets.

Building Code Compliance: Directed on-site inspection of all completed new construction projects to ensure **building code compliance**.

Building Trades: Supervised over 200 subcontractors representing all **building trades** during the construction of the $200 million Ivory Towers Project.

Capital Improvement: Planned, designed, budgeted, and directed $189 million in facilities renovation and **capital improvement** projects.

Claims Administration: Simplified a complex **claims administration** and reporting process, streamlined documentation requirements, and expedited funds disbursement.

Commercial Development: Managed over $500 million in **commercial development** projects including Class A office buildings, retail centers, and retirement communities.

Community Development: Appointed to gubernatorial committee responsible for guiding policy governing **community development** and revitalization.

Competitive Bidding: Coordinated **competitive bidding** for all subcontracted electrical, HVAC, and site work for the $20 million Haynes Industrial Project.

Construction Management: Directed **construction management** affairs for the renovation of the Inner Harbor Tunnel, a 5-year, $2.8 billion project.

Construction Trades: Supervised all **construction trades** and field crews of up to 400 at six major job sites throughout Dallas.

Contract Administration: Managed **contract administration** function for DOE-funded R&D facilities.

Contract Award: Reviewed competitive bids and managed **contract award** to best-price, best-quality supplier.

Critical Path Method (CPM) Scheduling: Introduced **CPM scheduling** and reduced manhours by 15%.

Design & Engineering: Led **design and engineering** teams responsible for proposal development and final contract delivery.

Divestiture: Directed **divestiture** of $50 million in non-performing real estate assets.

Engineering Change Orders (ECOs): Transmitted **ECOs** to all project personnel and coordinated follow-up with all trades.

Environmental Compliance: Reviewed all project plans and specifications to ensure stringent **environmental compliance** with corporate policy and federal regulations.

Estimating: Managed **estimating** and produced specifications for over $1 billion in annual real estate development and renovation projects.

Facilities Management: Senior Director responsible for **facilities management**, new construction, and renovation of over $200 million in corporate real estate assets.

Fair Market Value Pricing: Established **fair market value pricing** for all asset sales and liquidations.

Field Construction Management: Full supervisory responsibility for **field construction management**, crewing and schedule control on fast-track restaurant projects.

Grounds Maintenance: Directed 200-person staff and controlled $55 million annual operating budget for the Smithsonian's **ground maintenance** operations.

Historic Property Renovation: Founded real estate investment firm specializing in **historic property renovation** and resale to public agencies and municipalities.

Industrial Development: Partnered with business leaders to fund **industrial development** projects in major metropolitan areas throughout the Southwestern U.S.

Infrastructure Development: Managed $10 million investment in **infrastructure development**, including all site work, paving, and common areas.

Leasing Management: Designed and directed **leasing management** programs for large office complexes in Midtown Manhattan.

Master Community Association: Appointed as the Corporate Representative to the **Master Community Association**, working cooperatively with residents to develop bylaws, policies, and operating procedures.

Master Scheduling: Implemented a **master scheduling** program which measurably expedited schedule completion and compliance.

Mixed Use Property: Funded development of over $25 million in **mixed use property** as part of Baltimore's Inner Harbor revitalization.

Occupancy: Designed tenant incentive programs to optimize **occupancy** and retention.

Planned Use Development (PUD): Member of Jim Rouse's senior management team leading the development of one of the first **PUD** projects in the U.S. (Columbia, Maryland)

Portfolio: Challenged to strengthen the financial and competitive value of property **portfolio**, increase ROI, and improve investor credibility.

Preventive Maintenance: Designed a scheduled **preventive maintenance** program, virtually eliminating all major building and systems problems (calculated at a better than $250,000 annual cost savings).

Project Concept: Drove **project concept** for the first-ever downtown entertainment center in Morristown integrating creative arts, theatrical production, and recreational programming.

Project Development: Guided **project development** as the direct liaison between developer, investors, bankers, and community leaders.

Project Management: Senior Executive with full responsibility for all bidding, proposals, contract awards, and **project management** for Mattel's new facility construction projects.

Project Scheduling: Streamlined and expedited **project scheduling**, reporting, and documentation requirements.

Property Management: Directed leasing, tenant relations, and **property management** for a 202-tenant apartment complex with full amenities and service programs.

Property Valuation: Guided **property valuation** for all proposed land and commercial property acquisitions.

Real Estate Appraisal: Managed **real estate appraisal** for leased and sold properties.

Real Estate Brokerage: Launched new venture and built one of the most successful and most profitable **real estate brokerages** in Miami, Florida.

Real Estate Development: Formed limited partnerships to fund over $500 million in health care **real estate development** projects in revitalized inner cities.

Real Estate Investment Trust (REIT): Managed a $2.6 billion **REIT** for the Triple XXX Investment Group, improving investment returns by an average of 10%-12% annually.

Real Estate Law: Combined general management and **real estate law** expertise to return Andersen Properties to profitability.

Real Estate Partnership: Structured and negotiated **real estate partnership** with 3M to build R&D and manufacturing facilities throughout the Far East.

Regulatory Compliance: Achieved/surpassed all **regulatory compliance** objectives for 10 consecutive years.

Renovation: Directed 60-person crew on $500,000 million **renovation** and expansion of corporate training center.

Return on Assets (ROA): Improved **ROA** by 16% on all divested properties through more aggressive negotiations.

Return on Equity (ROE): Acquired, renovated, and divested six commercial properties for a 26% **ROE**.

Return on Investment (ROI): Negotiated acquisition of six industrial plants in Southwestern Mississippi, partnered with local manufacturers, and delivered a 49% **ROI** to principals.

Site Development: Managed preliminary $2 million **site development** project for a proposed 500-home residential subdivision.

Site Remediation: Directed **site remediation** projects to eliminate hazardous conditions and pollutants.

Specifications: Authored project **specifications** for the $2.8 million renovation of the Walker-Schmidt Fidelity Building in downtown Minneapolis.

Syndications: Structured, negotiated, and formed several real estate **syndications** in cooperation with private investor groups nationwide.

Tenant Relations: Significantly improved **tenant relations** through introduction of monthly tenant newsletter and monthly tenant meetings.

Tenant Retention: Renovated facility and improved **tenant retention** by 20% over previous year.

Turnkey Construction: Managed over $300 million in **turnkey construction** projects for client companies nationwide.

KeyWord Answers to Interview Questions

Tell me about yourself.

"As a **Project Manager** with Kidder Peabody, I hold full **profit and loss responsibility** for the **construction of mixed-use retail and commercial facilities** throughout the state of Virginia. Over the past five years, I've managed more than 25 **projects** with **budgets** ranging from $250,000 to more than $5 million and **worksite crews** of up to 200 each day. Twenty-four of those projects were delivered **on-time** and **within-budget**; the remaining project was halted due to **environmental remediation** issues that arose during final inspection. I have an expert knowledge of **building codes and regulations**, all **building trades**, **competitive bidding**, **contract administration**, and **owner/investor relations**. Most important, I'm an intensely hard worker."

What is the most valuable skill you bring to our company?

"The reason that I've been able to deliver all of my projects **on-time** and **within-budget** is because of my strong **planning** and **organizational skills**. When I've got 200 people on a **project**, a hundred phone calls a day, and more than a thousand other things to juggle, it is critical that I be able to quickly and accurately **prioritize** what needs to be done, when, and by whom. This is, by far, the most valuable skill I bring to you and to your **projects**."

What do you consider to be your most significant achievement or contribution?

"In 1999, I was asked to take over a **project** that had some serious challenges. Costs were way over **budget**, **project scheduling** was a disaster, **contracts** were never signed, and the **real estate developers** were ready to pull out. That's what I encountered my first day on the job. The next day I assembled everyone, from the **design architects** to the road paving crews, and outlined an entirely new **construction plan**. Six months later the **project** was delivered and the facility opened **on time**. In fact, because of my efforts and those of my crew, my company received a sizable **construction bonus**."

DANIEL R. POWELL
700 Lincoln Place
Baltimore, Maryland 21212
410.444.8736   d.powell@voyager.net

October 12, 2003

John Warner, President
Fidelity Capital Ventures
1000 Michigan Avenue
Washington, D.C. 22002

Dear Mr. Warner:

If you are active in real estate development, community development, and/or large-scale, mixed-used construction projects, you will be interested in my qualifications.

- 20+ years' experience in real estate development and management in the U.S. and international markets.

- Complete development and management responsibility for over $500 million in projects over the past 10 years.

- Leadership of more than $450 million in project funding and public/private partnership financing programs.

Most significant, however, is my ability to drive projects through complex community, political, and governmental channels. By providing a strong community vision and decisive action plan, I have won the support of community, political, business, and financial leaders – support critical to project funding, development, and profitable sale/leasing.

Please note that my expertise includes single and multifamily residential, commercial retail, commercial office, light industrial, health care facilities, technology centers, large-scale recreational facilities, and more.

I would welcome the chance to explore potential opportunities with your investment firm and/or any of your principal holdings, and appreciate your time in reviewing my qualifications. Thank you.

Sincerely,

Daniel R. Powell

Daniel R. Powell

Enclosure

LOUISE A. ROBINSON, RPA
LAR@inforworld.com

92 Adelaide Street
Belleville, Missouri 60133

Phone (601) 538-3229
Fax   (601) 538-3532

REAL ESTATE INDUSTRY PROFESSIONAL
Property Management / Marketing / Tenant Relations

Twenty years experience in commercial and residential real estate. Consistently successful in increasing revenues, occupancy, and income through expertise in building tenant relations and responding to tenant needs. Extensive qualifications in property/site renovation and construction, multi-year competitive leasing, multi-site property management, and cost control/reduction. Outstanding communication and interpersonal skills.

A consistently top-producer with outstanding revenue and profit results within intensely competitive markets.

PROFESSIONAL EXPERIENCE:

Property Manager   1992 to Present
A-ONE PROPERTIES, INC., Clifton, Missouri

> **Portfolio:**   *163,000 square feet of prime office space in a three-building complex on nine acres with large parking lots and extensive landscaping. Asset value of $13.5 million.*

Recruited as the Property Manager with full P&L responsibility for the entire portfolio. Scope of responsibility includes construction, renovation, tenant relations/retention, collections, outsourcing, contract negotiations, purchasing, monthly financial reporting, and general office/administrative affairs.

- Increased occupancy from 29% to 73% in less than three years through personal efforts in property improvement and extensive networking leasing efforts with realtors and brokers.

- Led the strategic planning and preparation of fiscal and calendar budgets. Maintained financial control of forecasted budget. Brought 1996 under budget.

- Managed, in conjunction with project manager, $1.5 million renovation of all common areas. Delivered project on time and within budget.

- Negotiated outsourcing contracts for facilities maintenance/repair, janitorial services, and property security. Consistently reduced expenses while increasing quality of service and tenant satisfaction.

Vice President / Property Manager   1991 to 1992
THE REAL PROPERTY CORPORATION, Lewis, Missouri

> **Portfolio:**   *230,000 square feet comprised of three office buildings and 11 luxury garden apartment complexes. Asset value of $36 million.*

Led the successful turnaround of the portfolio to meet investor and owner financial objectives. Held full responsibility for marketing, construction and renovation, tenant relations, cash flow management, financial reporting, and general administrative affairs. Spearheaded a high-profile marketing and public relations initiative to upgrade tenant quality. Directed a staff of 30.

- Worked with architects and contractors in the space planning and tenant fit-up of all leased space.

- Managed a large-scale renovation to upgrade the facilities, properties, and common areas of the portfolio as part of the initiative to increase tenant retention and improve market competitiveness.

LOUISE A. ROBINSON, RPA – *Page Two*

PROFESSIONAL EXPERIENCE (*Continued*):

- Negotiated/directed all maintenance and improvement work including electrical systems, HVAC, elevators, and grounds. Designed a preventive maintenance program to reduce expenditures.

Chief Operating Officer   1990 to 1991
GRIFFITH MANAGEMENT CORPORATION, Wayne, Missouri

> ***Portfolio:***   *Mid-sized commercial office building. Asset value of $4.5 million.*

Recruited for one-year special project to direct a complete facilities renovation to transition property into the 1990s. Directed a number of site improvement projects, expanded and upgraded existing spaces, and designed tenant/owner communication programs.

- Worked with leading brokers to increase occupancy by 30%-35% through extension of existing tenant leases and negotiation of new, long-term tenant leases. Increased property value by 28% in one year.

Association Manager   1988 to 1990
HILLS VILLAGE ASSOCIATION, Bedminster, Missouri

> ***Portfolio:***   *153-acre, 1,492-unit association with 4,000+ residents.*

Challenged to manage a master community association for one of the largest planned urban developments (PUD) in the U.S. Established policies and procedures, developed organizational infrastructure, and created cooperative working relationships between home owners, builders, and investors.

President / Broker / Managing Partner / Property Manager   1979 to 1988
THE ROBINSON MANAGEMENT GROUP, INC., Montclair, Missouri

As President of The Robinson Group, represented sellers, buyers, and investors in commercial real estate sales transactions totaling several million dollars. As President of Bamberger Management Company, held full P&L responsibility for the management of 2,500 residential and commercial units at 12 properties throughout the region.

EDUCATION & PROFESSIONAL CERTIFICATIONS:

Certified Property Manager (CPM) Candidate, Institute of Real Estate Management, Current

Real Property Administrator (RPA), Building Owners and Managers Association, 1993

Registered Property Manager (RPM), International Real Estate Institute, 1993

New Jersey Licensed Real Estate Broker, since 1975

PROFESSIONAL AFFILIATIONS:

National Association of Corporate Real Estate Executives (NACORE)

Building Owners and Managers Association International (BOMA)

Institute of Real Estate Management (IREM)

Industrial and Commercial Real Estate Women (ICREW)

International Real Estate Institute (IREI)

20

Retail

Sample Job Titles

Assistant Store Manager

Associate Store Manager

Buyer

Department Manager

Director of Retail Operations

Director of Retail Sales

District Manager

District Vice President

General Manager

Hardgoods Manager

Loss and Prevention Specialist

Manager-in-Training

Merchandise Manager

Personnel Scheduling Coordinator

Regional Manager

Retail Sales Associate

Retail Sales Manager

Senior Buyer

Senior Merchandiser

Senior Sales Associate

Softgoods Manager

Store Manager

Store Operations Manager

Vice President of Retail Operations

Vice President of Retail Sales

KeyWords and KeyWord Phrases

Buyer Awareness: Conceived and directed production of new creative campaign to increase **buyer awareness** and solidify market positioning.

Credit Operations: Restructured **credit operations**, implemented more stringent credit authorization procedures, and reduced bad debt by 12% in FY96.

Customer Loyalty: Created Neiman's first-ever **customer loyalty** programs, positioning the organization as a pioneer in innovative customer service and delivery.

Customer Service: Revitalized the organization's commitment to **customer service**, introduced a series of customer premiums and incentive programs, and dominated retail market.

Distribution Management: Structured a multi-site **distribution management** and inventory control program to reduce product losses, cut staffing costs, and decrease transportation time.

District Sales: Recruited to turnaround **district sales** operations encompassing 54 retail stores, 500+ employees, and over $260 million in annual sales.

Hardgoods: Directed a $500 million retail **hardgoods** sales operation that achieved/surpassed annual revenue and profit goals by an average of 12%-15%.

In-Store Promotions: Led creative team responsible for design, production, and placement of **in-store promotions**, POS displays, and credit card incentive campaigns.

Inventory Control: Restructured documentation and reporting requirements for all incoming merchandise to improve **inventory control** and management competencies.

Inventory Shrinkage: Implemented internal control procedures and reduced **inventory shrinkage** by more than 8% annually (despite consistent and significant employee turnover).

Loss Prevention: Designed **loss prevention programs** that reduced customer theft by more than 20% and employee theft by 10%.

Mass Merchants: Negotiated $200 million in exclusive product sales with **mass merchants** nationwide (e.g., Wal-Mart, Rose's, Hill's).

Merchandising: Revitalized Macy's **merchandising** operations, recruited five experienced retail merchandisers, and contributed to a solid 10% increase in 1996 sales revenues.

Multi-Site Operations: Senior Business Executive responsible for **multi-site operations** throughout the Midwestern U.S., including 200 company stores, 150 franchise stores, and more than 3,000 employees.

POS Promotions: Designed award-winning POS **promotions** honored for excellence in "creative concept" and "tactical execution" at the industry's 1996 annual conference.

Preferred Customer Management: Created a **preferred customer management** program in cooperation with Sales, Merchandising, and Purchasing that drove sales growth within niche markets by more than 35%.

Pricing: Restructured product **pricing** and improved bottom-line profits throughout all departments by a minimum of 5%.

Product Management: Segmented product lines and introduced a new **product management** function focused on customer demand and product movement.

Retail Sales: Senior Operating Executive with full responsibility for the strategic planning, staffing, budgeting, MIS, warehousing, distribution, facilities, sales, and service operations of a $2.8 billion specialty **retail sales** chain.

Security Operations: Revitalized in-store **security operations**, retrained staff, and reduced in-store theft by 24%.

Softgoods: Recruited to rebuild Maxwell's **softgoods** operations to compete with leading specialty retailers and accelerate market gains.

Specialty Retailer: Raised $25 million in private financing to fund the acquisition and expansion of a four-store **specialty retailer** poised for strong market growth.

Stock Management: Introduced stringent **stock management** and documentation procedures to better control over $400 million in incoming merchandise annually.

Warehousing Operations: Restructured **warehousing operations** from company-owned to commercially leased facilities and reduced annual product storage costs by more than 18%.

KeyWord Answers to Interview Questions

Tell me about yourself.

"At age 18, my very first job was as a **Sales Associate** with The Gap. Six months later, I was promoted to **Assistant Store Manager**; six months later to **Store Manager**, the youngest ever in the history of the company. Well, I was hooked. I continued at The Gap part-time while attending the University of Michigan, where I earned my **Bachelor's Degree in Retail Management**. Following graduation, I was recruited to Saks Fifth Avenue where I've now worked for five years and am currently the **Merchandising Director** for the Saks Fifth Avenue store in New York City. I love my job and my career, but I'm ready for more responsibility with a smaller, growth-driven **retailer**."

What is the most valuable skill you bring to our company?

"My love of the industry is perhaps my greatest skill, along with my knowledge of virtually all **retail operations** ... **sales, buying, merchandising, customer service, promotions, special events, facilities management, security, inventory control, shrinkage, buyer awareness**, and much more. My experience with both The Gap and Saks has given me an exceptionally strong knowledge of diverse **retail operations**. Let me also mention that I also have very strong skills in **employee training, development,** and **leadership**."

What do you consider to be your most significant achievement or contribution?

"Personally speaking, my most significant achievement has been the rapid advancement of my career. Professionally speaking, in my current position with Saks, I've **reduced annual shrinkage** by more than 12%, a huge decrease over previous years. While working with The Gap, I was able to **increase annual sales** by an average of 15%-18% annually for four consecutive years."

LEONARD ERICSSON
12 Standish Drive
Poughkeepsie, Pennsylvania 19837
(924) 944-3928

May 12, 2003

Susan Gordon-Howell
Executive Vice President
Saks Fifth Avenue
2 Fifth Avenue
New York, NY 10090

Dear Ms. Gordon-Howell:

Throughout the past 12 years, I have built and profitably managed high-volume, multi-site sales and retail operations. My strength lies in my ability to merge all the finite elements of retailing – most critically, sales – with marketing, advertising, merchandising, inventory, personnel, customer service, finance, facilities, and the supporting business infrastructures. What makes my qualifications so unique is the fact that I have worked in a number of different retail situations – new ventures, acquisitions, turnarounds, and growth operations.

During my tenure with National Stores and two of its principal operating companies, I have repeatedly demonstrated my success by providing strong financial results. In one situation, sales grew to over $40 million; in another, revenues increased at a rate of better than 35% annually. This has been achieved largely as a result of my efforts in providing a strong strategic vision and a business structure to support success.

Currently secure in my position, I am confidentially exploring new management opportunities where I can continue to combine my strengths in sales leadership, retail operations, team building and market growth. I am accustomed to working within highly competitive markets and understand that store image and branding are vital to sustained growth. Further, I am both personally and professionally committed to quality performance and customer satisfaction.

Aware that you are currently seeking a Senior Operations Director to join your management team, I would welcome the opportunity to interview for the position. I guarantee that the depth and quality of my experience will be of measurable value to your operations. Thank you. I appreciate your confidentiality.

Sincerely,

Leonard Ericsson

Leonard Ericsson

Enclosure

CHARLES P. WILSON
1428 Ocean View Drive
New Orleans, Louisiana 33626

Phone: (514) 675-8723   CharlesLA@louisiana.rr.com

MANAGEMENT PROFILE
Multi-Site Retail & Service Operations / Franchise & Company-Owned Operations

Dynamic management career with start-up, turnaround, and high-growth organizations. Cross-functional expertise in business planning, marketing, operations management, human resources, and finance. Delivered strong revenue and profit results within highly competitive markets. PC proficient.

Characterized as a strong and decisive business leader. Excellent problem solving, communication, interpersonal relations, and "call to action" skills.

PROFESSIONAL EXPERIENCE:

KWIK LUBE INTERNATIONAL, INC.   1993 to Present

Regional Manager / District Manager

Returned to Kwik Lube after nine years of general management and P&L management positions with two large Louisiana-based franchisees. Hold direct P&L responsibility for up to 37 sales/service centers throughout Louisiana. Led a team of four District Managers.

Scope of responsibility includes marketing and new business development, management training and development, sales/service training, budgeting, accounting, auditing, and financial reporting. Challenged to introduce improved business and operating processes to drive revenue growth, reduce operating costs, and improve net profitability of multi-site operations.

- Delivered strong and sustainable financial results:
  - Met/exceeded all profit budgets each consecutive year.
  - Delivered 2.3% sales increase and 12.6% profit improvement in $14 million organization.
  - Delivered 4.2% sales increase and 13.3% profit improvement in $7 million organization.
- Ranked as the #1 region in the U.S. for customer satisfaction ratings.
- Currently spearheading start-up of new strategic partnership with Sears (nationwide program). Leading the development of three pilot operations in Louisiana to evaluate operational feasibility of new partnership. Delivered $500,000 in first year sales revenues.

SMITH PETROLEUM COMPANY (Kwik Lube Franchise)   1988 to 1993

General Manager

Promoted from District Manager to General Manager with full P&L responsibility for the management of 11 operating locations throughout the South Coast of Louisiana. Led a team of two District Managers directing daily sales and service operations. Focused efforts on building revenues and profitability. Redesigned and strengthened advertising/marketing programs, streamlined administrative processes, improved budget and financial controls, and upgraded recruitment and training programs. Launched reorganization and operations redesign initiative.

CHARLES P. WILSON - *Page Two*

SMITH PETROLEUM COMPANY *(Continued)*

- Built annual sales revenues from $3 million to $4.2 million, transitioned the operation from loss to breakeven and took negative cash flow to positive within one year.
- Facilitated implementation of POS technology with PC network to enhance internal sales controls and reporting capabilities.
- Designed incentive program and reduced operating costs by $500,000.
- Hired local advertising agency and directed multimedia print, broadcast, and direct mail campaigns.
- Led new store openings, divestitures, and aggressive turnaround initiatives.

GULF AUTOMOTIVE SERVICES (Kwik Lube Franchise)   1984 to 1987

Director of Operations

Recruited by owner to lead the franchisee through a period of rapid growth and expansion. Challenged to build organizational infrastructure, strengthen operations, recruit/train personnel, and spearhead aggressive marketing/business development initiatives. Held full P&L responsibility. Led a team of two District Managers.

- Led the organization through a period of accelerated growth and expansion, from 6 to 12 locations and from 36 to 100+ employees. Built annual sales from $1.5 million to $3.5 million.
- Facilitated profitable integration of three Pennzoil operations into existing franchise.

NOTE: In July 1987, Kwik Lube bought back the franchise. Remained as Director of Operations through March 1988, when acquired by Smith Petroleum Company.

KWIK LUBE INTERNATIONAL, INC.   1981 to 1984

Operations Consultant/Training Director (1983 to 1984)
Operations Assistant (1982 to 1983)
Unit Manager (1982)
Manager Trainee (1981 to 1982)

Fast-track promotion through early professional career. Highlights included:

- Consulted with franchise owners in the Baltimore, Philadelphia, and South New Jersey markets to provide expertise in operations, auditing, compliance, and new store openings.
- Led basic and advanced operations training courses for store managers and franchise owners to enhance their competencies in operations, product knowledge, inventory control, scheduling, expense control, and staffing/manpower planning.
- Managed new unit from pre-opening, staffing, initial marketing/business development, start-up, and grand opening through transition to independent franchisee.

EDUCATION: **BS Degree**, Bridgewater College, Bridgewater, Virginia, 1981
               The Dale Carnegie Course, 1984
               The Centers for Values Research Training, 1985

21

Sales and Marketing

Although the two functions of sales and marketing are uniquely distinct, Sales and Marketing are integrated here into one section due to the often significant overlap in position titles, functions, responsibilities, and achievements.

Sample Job Titles

Account Executive

Account Manager

Account Representative

Brand Manager

Business Development Representative

Chief Marketing Officer

Customer Representative

Customer Sales Associate

Director of Business Development

Director of Marketing

Director of Marketing Communications

Director of Marketing Support

Director of Sales

Director of Sales and Marketing

Director of Sales Support

District Manager

Division Sales Manager
E-Commerce Manager
Global Marketing Associate
Global Sales Representative
International Sales Manager
Key Account Executive
Key Account Manager
Major Accounts Manager
Major Accounts Representative
Manufacturer's Representative
Market Research Analyst
Marketing Associate
Marketing Director
Marketing Manager
Marketing Representative
National Account Executive
National Account Manager
National Sales Manager
Product Line Manager
Product Manager
Regional Sales Manager
Sales Associate
Sales Director
Sales Manager
Sales Representative
Sales Trainer
Sales Training Manager
Senior Account Executive
Senior Sales Associate
Senior Vice President
Technical Marketing Associate
Technical Sales Representative
Territory Sales Manager

Territory Sales Representative
Vice President of Business Development
Vice President of Sales and Marketing

KeyWords and KeyWord Phrases

Account Development: Spearheaded **account development** programs throughout emerging markets worldwide.

Account Management: Profitably directed **account management** programs for key customers nationwide including Pepsi, Rolex, and Time Warner.

Account Retention: Created innovative **account retention** programs to protect key customers against competition.

Brand Management: Instituted a formal **brand management** process to accelerate revenue growth within the company's core product line.

Business Development: Launched new **business development** initiatives throughout emerging Latin American markets.

Campaign Management: Directed copywriting, graphics, and multimedia production personnel to create an integrated **campaign management** strategy.

Competitive Analysis: Managed 6-person cross-functional marketing team responsible for **competitive analysis** and trend modeling within the mature hardlines market.

Competitive Contract Award: Favorably positioned negotiations to win **competitive contract award** against three major automotive manufacturers.

Competitive Market Intelligence: Compiled historical data, forecasts, and projections for a comprehensive **competitive market intelligence** study.

Competitive Product Positioning: Realigned sales and distribution channels to enhance **competitive product positioning** and accelerate revenue performance.

Consultative Sales: Deployed IBM's first-ever **consultative sales** and account management programs focusing on customer needs assessment, technology delivery, and long-term customer training/support.

Customer Loyalty: Initiated pioneering programs in **customer loyalty** to halt competition.

Customer Needs Assessment: Led organization-wide analyses to develop a comprehensive **customer needs assessment** and retention program.

Customer Retention: Improved **customer retention** ratings by 26% through the introduction of sales incentives, premiums, and targeted promotions.

Customer Satisfaction: Increased **customer satisfaction** ratings with the implementation of account management and retention strategies.

Customer Service: Managed a fully integrated **customer service** function comprised of personnel from Sales, Marketing, Order Fulfillment, Distribution, and Customer Training/Support.

Direct Mail Marketing: Orchestrated copywriting, design, and print production of a 20,000-piece **direct mail marketing campaign** to support new product launch.

Direct Response Marketing: Deployed multimedia advertising and promotions to create a high-impact **direct response campaign** with better than 72% customer response.

Direct Sales: Managed a 65-person **direct sales** organization throughout North America.

Distributor Management: Recruited, trained, and directed worldwide **distributor management** programs to augment direct sales team.

E-Business: Pioneered Lionel's entry into **e-business**, e-commerce, and e-trade, and delivered first year sales of more than $2.5 million.

Emerging Markets: Researched global sales trends and identified the top-performing **emerging markets** worldwide as the first step in new product placement and positioning.

Field Sales Management: Promoted to **field sales management** position responsible for 22 direct sales associates and a 65-person North American distribution network.

Fulfillment: Reengineered core business processes to enhance the order **fulfillment** and distribution process.

Global Markets: Introduced new product technology to launch Zenith into key **global markets**.

Global Sales: Built and managed American Airlines's most profitable **global sales** organization.

Headquarters Account Management: Assigned full P&L responsibility for **headquarters account management** of the Marriott business relationship.

High-Impact Presentations: Created multimedia, **high-impact presentations** to win a $5 million, 5-year customer contract.

Incentive Planning: Devised unique **incentive planning** program that drove individual sales performance by better than 10% in 1996.

Indirect Sales: Created **indirect sales** channels throughout the Mid-Atlantic, integrating the talents and resources of VARs, resellers, and other third-party distributors.

International Sales: Exploded **international sales** revenues with launch throughout Eastern Europe.

International Trade: Led AMAX's **international trade**, barter, and import/export programs.

Key Account Management: Innovated a unique **key account management** program targeted to the company's 10 largest multinational clients within North America.

Line Extension: Facilitated core product **line extension** in response to changing consumer market demands.

Margin Improvement: Streamlined field sales programs and consolidated functions, resulting in a 16% **margin improvement** on all major product lines.

Market Launch: Directed **market launch** of six new products in 1996, delivering total revenues of more than $2.8 million (125% of quota).

Market Positioning: Evaluated competitive activity and defined new corporate strategy for **market positioning** and revenue growth.

Market Research: Formalized Hill Brothers' **market research** function with the introduction of real-time data access to competitive trends, products, technologies, and markets.

Market Share Ratings: Created a unique customer premium program and improved **market share ratings** by 16% in FY96.

Market Surveys: Developed a portfolio of **market surveys**, customer questionnaires, and consumer buying observational tools to define long-term product positioning.

Marketing Strategy: Conceived the **marketing strategy** that drove Procter & Gamble to its most profitable year within the consumer goods and HBA industries.

Mass Merchants: Challenged to identify and capitalize upon sales opportunities within emerging **mass merchants** market.

Multi-Channel Distribution: Expanded sales penetration through development of **multi-channel distribution** programs in Latin America, South Africa, and the Pacific Rim.

Multi-Channel Sales: Led a **multi-channel sales** organization integrating direct, distributor, and VAR sales teams.

Multimedia Advertising: Launched Discovery's **multimedia advertising** program (e.g., print, broadcast, cable, Internet) in cooperation with one of New York's most prestigious advertising agencies.

Multimedia Marketing Communications: Integrated print, broadcast, cable, and Internet technologies to create high-impact, high-yield, **multimedia marketing communications** targeted to customers nationwide.

National Account Management: Integrated the resources, products, and technologies of all of Microsoft's customer sales divisions to create a fully integrated **national account management** organization.

Negotiations: Led high-powered **negotiations** for the successful award of a $6.2 million federal contract.

New Market Development: Hand-selected by CEO to spearhead Marriott's **new market development** program as the first step in a 10-year global expansion plan.

New Product Introduction: Led the development and market launch of all new **product introduction** programs for Mazda, exceeding revenue goals by 22% and strengthening the company's long-term market position.

Product Development: Spearheaded new **product development** programs, from concept through design, prototyping, and testing, to final market launch.

Product Launch: Led six new **product launch** campaigns within the emerging Eastern European markets, with one product generating $2.6 million in first year revenues (167% of quota).

Product Lifecycle Management: Directed "cradle-to-grave" **product lifecycle management** programs in cooperation with Engineering, Marketing, Sales, and Distribution.

Product Line Rationalization: Revitalized Sperry's **product line rationalization** program, divested two non-performing lines, and redeployed assets to focus on long-term growth markets.

Product Positioning: Evaluated competitive market trends and implemented **product positioning** strategies to ensure long-term and sustainable growth.

Profit & Loss (P&L) Management: Held full **P&L management** responsibility for the company's core product line and all line extensions.

Profit Growth: Reengineered field sales and distribution organizations despite corporate downsizing and delivered a 16% gain in **profit growth** (versus 5% industry-wide loss).

Promotions: Conceived, developed, and launched multimedia **promotions** that dominated the regional market.

Public Relations: Created Martin Marietta's corporate **public relations** function and produced an average of 10 press releases per month for the *Wall Street Journal* and *New York Times*.

Public Speaking: Traveled worldwide to lead **public speaking** engagements on behalf of the corporation during its transition from private to public ownership.

Revenue Growth: Exploded market penetration and drove a 46% gain in **revenue growth** within first six months.

Revenue Stream: Created new **revenue stream** with the introduction of products throughout the Far Eastern market.

Sales Closing: Dominated sales negotiations and favorably positioned **sales closing** against competition.

Sales Cycle Management: Spearheaded the entire **sales cycle management** process, from initial client consultation and needs assessment through product demonstration, price and service negotiations, and final sales closings.

Sales Forecasting: Introduced real-time data exchange between global sales offices to expedite annual **sales forecasting** functions.

Sales Presentations: Devised winning **sales presentations** utilizing multimedia demonstration techniques to consistently outperform competition.

Sales Training: Created a 6-month intensive **sales training** program in basic selling skills, competitive negotiations, and customer development/ retention.

Solutions Selling: Delivered **solutions selling** strategies to enhance revenue performance of field sales organization.

Strategic Market Planning: Facilitated annual **strategic market planning** sessions in cooperation with top-level executives, sales and marketing managers, product line managers, manufacturing director, and other key management staff.

Tactical Market Plans: Translated marketing strategy into **tactical market plans** to accelerate growth throughout North America.

Team Building/Leadership: Spearheaded first-ever **team building/ leadership** programs as the platform for merging the competencies of several distinct product lines and business units.

Trend Analysis: Devised innovative research and statistical methods to strengthen **trend analysis**, market analysis, and competitive analysis competencies.

KeyWord Answers to Interview Questions

Tell me about yourself.

"Building top-performing **sales regions** and **customer markets** is my expertise. Whether **launching a new product, developing a new market niche, penetrating a new territory**, or **revitalizing dormant sales**, I have consistently met or **exceeded all revenue goals**. With Turner Broadcasting, I **increased sales** in the Phoenix market by 22% the first year. With Metromedia Broadcasting, I **increased sales** in the Philadelphia market by 25% the first year, 28% the second year, and 45% the third year. Now, as **Commercial Account Sales Manager** with Paramount Distribution, I am targeting an 18% increase in my first year, after there's been no market increase for the past three years. So, as you can see, I'm a **producer** who loves to **sell, negotiate**, and **close**."

What is the most valuable skill you bring to our company?

"**Closing the sale** is my #1 skill. I can overcome virtually any **customer objection** and demonstrate the true value of what I'm selling. I am particularly effective when selling head-to-head against our **competition**, working just that bit harder to be sure that we get the sale. It is my **persistence, thoroughness**, and **customer relationship** style that has driven such significant **sales growth** in each and every one of my **markets**."

What do you consider to be your most significant achievement or contribution?

"The **revenue increases** I delivered while working for Metromedia Broadcasting are some of my most notable achievements. As you may recall in our earlier discussion about the company, I **increased sales** by 25% in year one, 28% in year two, and 45% in year three.

I was able to **revitalize the market, restore customer credibility, capture new accounts,** and firmly establish our **brand.** Then, using a **consultative sales process** to understand my **clients' needs, I positioned** Metromedia as the **market expert** within our industry."

NICHOLAS HENDERSON

2343 Jefferson Boulevard   Home (703) 642-4140
Arlington, Virginia 23068   Office (703) 859-6991

___

April 4, 2003

Vice President of Human Resources
XYAN, Inc.
1012 West Ninth Avenue, Suite 100
King of Prussia, PA 19406

Dear Sir/Madam:

As National Market Manager with AT&T, I bring to your organization 11 years of progressively responsible experience in the strategic planning, design, and leadership of winning sales, marketing, and business development programs. My notable achievements include:

- Design of two service-driven product extensions, including development of all marketing communications and full-scale market launch. **RESULT: $2 million in revenues within first year.**

- Creative concept and deployment of a series of promotional and marketing campaigns for the national introduction of a completely new product line. **RESULT: $3.5 million in monthly revenues within first year.**

- Realignment of pricing and market positioning strategies for AT&T's national account portfolio. **RESULT: Consistent wins over competition AND a measurable improvement in net profitability of each sales transaction.**

Complementing my ability to produce sales dollars are equally strong qualifications in training and leading professional sales teams, providing strategic market vision with appropriate tactical action plans, and responding to the constantly changing demands of the market. I lead by example and provide strong decision making, problem solving, and project management skills.

If decisive and action-driven leadership skills are your goals, we should meet. At that time, I would be pleased to provide specific information regarding my salary history and current salary requirements. Be advised that I am currently employed and respect your confidentiality in my search.

Sincerely,

Nicholas Henderson

Nicholas Henderson

Enclosure

MARGARET E. APPLEGATE

mea@aim.net
3984 Soldier Trail
Bellevue, Washington 98332
Phone (206) 488-8724   Fax (206) 488-7762

SENIOR SALES & MARKETING EXECUTIVE
Domestic & International Business Development

*Strategic Marketing Planning / Competitive Market Positioning / Multi-Channel Distribution
Sales Training & Team Leadership / New Product Launch / New Market Development*

Dynamic sales and marketing management career delivering state-of-the-art technology world-wide. Achieved strong and sustainable revenue, market and profit contributions through expertise in business development, organizational development and performance management. Keen presentation, negotiation, communication, and cross-cultural skills. Fluent in French (speaking, reading, writing). Understanding of Spanish and Italian. Member of American Management Association, International Trade Association, and Women in Technology.

PROFESSIONAL EXPERIENCE

Vice President - Americas Operations
International Software, Inc., Seattle, Washington (1995 to Present)

Recruited to $750 million NYSE company (one of the world's largest software providers with customer base including the top Fortune 500 corporations). Challenged to plan and orchestrate an aggressive turnaround and rejuvenation of the Americas sales organization.

Scope of responsibility includes all sales, marketing, business development, channel development, and customer management/retention operations throughout South America, Central America, Mexico, and the Caribbean. Lead a team of 12 regional managers, product specialists, and administrative personnel. Manage a 30-person direct sales force in Brazil.

- Transitioned Americas organization from 44% of plan in 1995 to 112% of plan in 1996 ($7 million to $14+ million).

- Expanded distributor base by more than 50% to increase market penetration and facilitate market launch of new product technologies and services.

- Provided strong organizational leadership and active participation in key account sales and business development. Resulted in a significant gain in employee morale, productivity, and sales production.

- Concurrent P&L responsibility for independent Brazilian-based sales and marketing company. Delivered 45% growth within less than one year through development of multinational customer base. Currently facilitating market introduction of EDI sales group with first year revenue projections at $1+ million.

Managing Partner
TechCom, Inc., Washington, D.C. (1994 to 1995)

Founded international software distribution company focusing on distributed and systems software productivity tools (emphasis on DB2, Oracle, and Sybase operating systems). Created marketing strategies, communications, promotional materials, reseller channels, and in-house sales programs. Developed partnering program for export/import of software services.

MARGARET E. APPLEGATE - *Page Two*

Director & General Manager - International Sales Operations
Global Systems Corporation, Washington, D.C. (1986 to 1994)

Fast-track promotion through four increasingly responsible international management assignments to final position as Senior Executive directing worldwide software sales and marketing operations for direct and reseller channels. Managed UK-based European operation and a team of sales, marketing, and technical support managers.

- Increased Global's international sales operation from a $3 million, six-country region to a $30 million, 50-country worldwide sales organization representing 53% of corporate revenue.

- Established international reseller network to market distributed computing solutions for UNIX platforms, including IBM AIX, HP-UX, Sun OS, and Sun Solaris.

- Expanded and restructured sales networks in Western Europe, Eastern Europe, South America, and the Pac Rim through development of distributor channels for Global's Performance Series for MVS and VSE.

- Renegotiated software agreement with European distributors, saving $5 million in contract dissolution compensation. Successfully renegotiated distribution agreements during product divestiture, resulting in a $9 million savings to Global.

- Reviewed and approved multinational software sales contracts with Fortune 100 companies.

- Honored for outstanding sales results and over-quota production for eight consecutive years.

Manager of Field Marketing - North American Sales Operations
Data Management, Inc., Alexandria, Virginia / Seattle, Washington (1979 to 1986)
(Acquired by International Software)

Marketing Executive with full responsibility for the design, development, and implementation of marketing programs for 15 U.S. offices and Canada on behalf of one of the world's largest independent software vendors. Liaison between North American Operations and International Division.

- Created innovative incentive programs and facilitated training programs for field sales and marketing teams. Coordinated week-long, annual worldwide sales and technical conference.

- Designed marketing collateral and promotional materials for use by North American sales offices.

- Expanded North American sales/marketing presence through participation in industry trade shows, conventions, and exhibits targeted to both commercial and federal sectors.

- Initiated nationwide seminar program to promote DMI's software products. Designed seminar materials, directed presentation programs, and spearheaded implementation of computer-based lead tracking system.

Previous Professional Positions

Assistant to the Corporate Vice President of Public Relations, XT-Systems, Inc.
Executive Assistant - International Department, Trammel Crow Company

EDUCATION

B.A., San Francisco College of Women
Graduate Study/Psychology, University of Geneva - Switzerland
Graduate Study/MIS, University of Washington

22

Security and Law Enforcement

Sample Job Titles

Corporate Security Manager
Corporate Security Officer
Crisis Response Manager
Detective
Director of Corporate Security
Director of Industrial Security
Director of Safety & Security
Emergency Planning and Preparedness Manager
Patrol Officer
Police Officer
Risk Management Specialist
Safety Officer
Security Manager
Security Officer
Supervisor of Detectives
Surveillance Technician
Undercover Officer

Vice President of Corporate Security

Vice President of Industrial Security

KeyWords and KeyWord Phrases

Asset Protection: Directed **asset protection** programs for U.S. embassies and consulates worldwide (total asset value in excess of $20 billion).

Community Outreach: Managed **community outreach** and community policing programs throughout the Detroit metro region as part of the Department's long-term commitment to cooperative community relations.

Corporate Fraud: Managed sensitive investigations of **corporate fraud** totaling in the millions of dollars and perpetrated over the past five years.

Corporate Security: Member of 6-person Senior Management Team and the most Senior **Corporate Security** Executive responsible for facilities, VIP protection, and intelligence.

Crisis Communications: Coordinated press relations and media interviews to expand **crisis communications** and outreach during LA riots.

Crisis Response: Manned and directed a 12-person **crisis response** team successful in resolving high-profile hostage situations.

Electronic Surveillance: Introduced **electronic surveillance** technology to improve physical security operations.

Emergency Planning and Response: Led the Department's annual **emergency planning and response** program in cooperation with local, state, and federal law enforcement agencies throughout California.

Emergency Preparedness: Developed monthly **emergency preparedness** training and field exercises.

Industrial Espionage: Directed covert **industrial espionage** intelligence gathering and reporting to high-ranking military officials.

Industrial Security: Created **industrial security** programs to protect company facilities, technologies, products, and other assets.

Interrogation: Directed **interrogation** in high-profile corporate fraud and espionage incidents.

Investigations Management: Coordinated worldwide **investigations management** team tracking the state's most wanted fugitives.

Law Enforcement: Advanced rapidly throughout 22-year **law enforcement** career, from initial field patrol through several investigative positions to final promotion to Chief of Police.

Media Relations: Appointed Departmental Spokesperson responsible for **media relations** and response to crisis situations.

Personal Protection: Provided **personal protection** services to top-ranking government, military, and industry officials.

Public Relations: Promoted positive community relations through a proactive **public relations** initiative.

Safety Training: Designed in-house **safety training** programs for all personnel within Digital Equipment Corporation.

Security Operations: Integrated in-house and contract personnel to create full-scale corporate **security operations** at all BanCorp facilities.

Surveillance: Conducted field **surveillance** and documentation for organized crime investigations.

Tactical Field Operations: Promoted to Police Lieutenant responsible for **tactical field operations** and deployment in both routine and emergency situations.

VIP Protection: Charged with planning, staffing, and all advance work for **VIP protection** programs worldwide.

White Collar Crime: Investigated alleged incidents of **white collar crime** throughout the emerging Internet and new media industries.

KeyWord Answers to Interview Questions

Tell me about yourself.

"Prior to September 11th, I looked at myself as someone who'd pursued a somewhat unique career path in **Corporate Security**. It wasn't a mainstream job, and my friends often remarked about why these companies invested so much in their security. Unfortunately, the answer to that question is now abundantly clear. In today's business world, companies like yourself need people like us ... like me ... with experience in **emergency planning and preparedness, crisis response, crisis communications, asset protection, industrial espionage**, and **VIP protection**. With more than 15 years' experience managing **security operations** for several Silicone Valley companies, I bring a wealth of knowledge to your organization and a guarantee of improved **security operations**."

What is the most valuable skill you bring to our company?

"My ability to respond effectively during a **crisis situation** has always been my strongest skill. I am level-headed, able to quickly assess a situation, determine what needs to be done and what resources are required, and initiate immediate action. I work collaboratively with local **police, fire**, and **rescue** crews as needed, and have personally managed **press briefings** on behalf of my employers. Under my leadership, there has NEVER been a work-related fatality, despite the fact that I've worked for companies using dangerous chemicals and laboratory processes."

What do you consider to be your most significant achievement or contribution?

"I'm most proud of my participation in the **design, development, installation**, and ongoing **management** of a state-of-the-art **electronic surveillance and security system** that we implemented at Phoenix Technologies. The design required a unique application of new **technology**, the integration of several different **electronic monitoring systems**, and a global **telecommunications** network. The results of the project exceeded the best of our expectations, and the project was honored by IEEE for **technology innovation and excellence**."

DONALD R. GRAYSON
drg@homestead.com

119 Mill Road
Greenspan, MO 58737
(414) 890-0080

November 19, 2003

Matthew Kimball
Director of Security Operations
AMX Security Systems & Technologies, Inc.
11 Main Boulevard, Suite 1190
Dallas, TX 78900

Dear Mr. Kimball:

As we are all working to reclaim our lives and move past the horrific events of September 11th, I find myself in the most unique of positions. Years ago, my career path was a bit unusual; today, it is one of the most critical professions in any corporation.

As the Security Manager for Dixie Metric Materials in Camden, NJ, I have been one of the driving forces in the creation of a comprehensive, plant-wide security program. With a staff of only 12, we have implemented systems to protect both our physical assets and intellectual property. Most impressive, all of this has been accomplished in just three short years (e.g., electronic surveillance systems, emergency preparedness and response systems, Internet security systems, personnel security systems).

Prior to my career with Dixie, I served with the NY Police Department for 12 years, first as a patrol officer and later as a detective in the Terrorism Prevention Division. As such, you can see that my experience is extremely relevant in today's unfortunate times.

Aware of the quality of your organization and its personnel, I would be delighted to have the opportunity for a personal interview. I am traveling this week to escort some visiting dignitaries, but will be back in my office at the end of next week and will follow up with you then.

I appreciate your consideration and can guarantee that the depth and scope of my experience will add measurable value and safety to your organization. Thank you.

Sincerely,

Donald R. Grayson

Donald R. Grayson

Enclosure

CHARLES E. FRANKLIN
cef@abc.com
1984 South Lincoln Avenue
Paramus, New Jersey 07665
(201) 654-9871

CAREER PROFILE:

LAW ENFORCEMENT OFFICER with 20+ years experience planning and managing Investigations, VIP Escort & Protection Service, Corporate & Industrial Site Security, Organized Crime, and Intelligence. Strong qualification in budgeting, personnel affairs, training, resource management, and emergency response. Excellent decision making and crisis management skills.

PROFESSIONAL EXPERIENCE:

MERCER CITY POLICE DEPARTMENT, Mercer, New Jersey   1975 to Present

Senior Staff Officer, Professional Standards Division (1994 to Present)
Commander, Special Investigations Unit (1990 to 1994)
Assistant Commander, Special Investigations Unit (1988 to 1990)
Sergeant, Detective Bureau (1985 to 1988)
Investigator/Detective (1980 to 1985)
Patrol Officer (1975 to 1980)

Promoted rapidly throughout law enforcement career, from early patrol assignments to most recent position directing high-profile special investigations. Supervised up to seven police officers and investigators. Directed case planning and management, personnel assignment, emergency preparedness and response, suspect interrogation, witness interviewing, and all reporting/documentation. Special assignments and position highlights have included:

Special Investigations

- As Commander of the Special Investigations Unit, responsible for discreet investigations and intelligence gathering activities concerning organized gangs, criminal activities within law enforcement agencies, VIP security operations for local and foreign dignitaries, bias crime investigations (e.g., ethnic, race, religion, sexual orientation), drug trafficking, extortion, counterfeiting, and other criminal activity.

- Deputized U.S. Marshall assigned to supervise federal DEA wiretap room during a sensitive investigation of alleged police officer participation in cocaine distribution.

- Managed investigative operations in the Violent Crimes Unit, Burglary Squad, Street Crimes Unit, and Robbery Squad.

VIP/Executive Security Operation

- Assigned to the Security Detail for the President of Greece. Worked in cooperation with the U.S. Secret Service and State Department to coordinate advance security, assess potential threats, and provide security escort services throughout the area.

- Assisted in directing protection and security operations for the Pope during his visits throughout New York and New Jersey. Coordinated site assessments, security advance work and on-site protection in cooperation with various local, state, and federal agencies.

CHARLES E. FRANKLIN - *Page Two*
cef@abc.com
(201) 654-9871

PROFESSIONAL EXPERIENCE:

MERCER CITY POLICE DEPARTMENT (Continued):

Industrial Security Operations

- Conducted extensive site threat assessment for the Fourth of July Sailing Event in New York City. Produced aerial photography to monitor site and planned emergency unit availability/response.

- Managed site surveillance, perimeter searches, investigations, and security planning efforts for corporate and industrial facilities throughout the New York/New Jersey metro region.

Hostage Negotiations

- Member of the Mercer City Police Department's Hostage Negotiating Team since 1989.

Professional Standards Division Operations

- Currently serve on the Deputy Chief's Staff with direct responsibility for coordinating operations between various units within the Division (e.g., Internal Affairs, Planning & Research, Inspectional Services, Medical Bureau, Police Academy, Pistol Range). Manage budget development/administration, officer assignment, recordkeeping, training coordination, and other critical functions to ensure cooperative internal operations.

EDUCATION & SPECIALIZED TRAINING *(partial listing)*:

- Emergency Management: Incident Command System Training, 1995
- Special Tactics & Security, 1995
- Corporate Executive Protection, Corporate & Economic Espionage, 1994
- Symposium on Terrorism, 1994
- Asian Organized Crime, 1993
- Hazardous Material Awareness, 1993
- Hostage Negotiations, 1990
- Advanced Criminal Investigation, 1980
- Graduate, New Jersey Police Academy, 1975

PROFESSIONAL PROFILE:

Honors & Awards: 50 Excellent Police Service Awards, 15 Commendations, Combined P.O.B.A. Valor Awards, Fraternal Order of Police Citation, Kiwanis Club Unit Citation, NAACP Certificate of Merit, Mayor's Certificate of Award for Civil Contribution

Public Speaking: Asian Organized Crime, Law Enforcement Intelligence, Executive Protection

Military: Corporal, Military Police, U.S. Army (1971 to 1975)

23

Teaching and Education

Sample Job Titles

Academic Administrator

Academic Counselor

Academic Advisor

Academic Dean

Adjunct Professor

Administrator

Admissions Counselor

Assistant Dean

Assistant Professor

Associate Dean

Associate Professor

Center Director

Chancellor

Counselor

Curriculum Developer

Dean

Director

Director of Special Education Services

Education Services Administrator
Educator
Executive Director
Financial Aid Director
Guidance Counselor
Instructional Specialist
Instructor
Librarian
Manager of Campus Disability Services
Media Specialist
Professor
Program Manager
Reference Librarian
Resource Librarian
Senior Instructor
Senior Vice President
Teacher
Trainer
Vice President of Academic Services
Vice President of Educational Services
Vice President of Fundraising

KeyWords and KeyWord Phrases

Academic Advisement: Established an **academic advisement** program for both degree and non-degree seeking students.

Accreditation: Led the university through a two-year successful **accreditation** process.

Admissions Management: Restructured the college's **admissions management** process to encourage enrollment by minority, handicapped, and other special populations.

Alumni Relations: Volunteered to build Catonsville Community College's first-ever formal **alumni relations** and giving program.

Campus Life: Introduced expanding educational, social, and recreational programs into the **Campus Life** Department to enhance students' experiences.

Capital Giving Campaign: Planned and directed the annual **capital giving campaign**, which raised $2.8 million (25% over goal).

Career Counseling: Created expanded **career counseling** programs targeted to non-degree seeking and continuing education students interested in professional, paraprofessional, and vocational opportunities.

Career Development: Negotiated cooperative education programs with local universities to introduce on-site **career development** and training programs.

Classroom Management: Demonstrated expertise in **classroom management**, student relations, and learner retention.

Conference Management: Directed annual planning, staffing, budgeting, and logistics for an 11-part **conference management** series.

Course Design: Led 12-person team in **course design** for Mathematics, Engineering, and Science.

Curriculum Development: Expanded **curriculum development** functions across all major academic disciplines to enhance the quality of education.

Education Administration: Appointed Program Director with full responsibility for budgeting, staffing, teacher training, **educational administration**, and Board of Regents reporting.

Enrollment: Forged strategic alliances with all public school systems to identify qualified applicants and drove a 16% increase in 1996 student **enrollment**.

Extension Program: Negotiated partnership with the University of Michigan for an off-campus **extension program** for hourly manufacturing workers.

Field Instruction: Designed and led **field instruction** programs in the Biological and Chemical Sciences.

Grant Administration: Responsible for **grant administration** of $2.2 million in funds.

Higher Education: Promoted programs and activities to promote high school students' appreciation for **higher education** opportunities.

Holistic Learning: Integrated Math, Science, Language, and the Arts to create a **holistic learning** and study center for senior adults.

Instructional Media: Acquired **instructional media** to develop alternative educational programs in foreign language instruction.

Instructional Programming: Led 6-person task force in **instructional programming** across all core academic disciplines.

Intercollegiate Athletics: Coached soccer team to #1 standing in the regional **intercollegiate athletics** division.

Leadership Training: Designed and instructed **leadership training** programs for newly appointed supervisors and team leaders.

Lifelong Learning: Lobbied before the state legislature for funds to promote **lifelong learning** within the community.

Management Development: Created innovative course offerings to strengthen **management development** opportunities for adult students seeking career promotion.

Peer Counseling: Identified need for immediate intervention and created a **peer counseling** program to link top performers with students in crisis.

Program Development: Championed innovative **program development** projects to gain a competitive lead over other area colleges and universities.

Public/Private Partnerships: Structured and negotiated **public/private partnerships** to fund alternative career and job skills training programs.

Public Speaking: Recognized for expertise in **public speaking** before regulatory, accrediting, and licensing boards.

Recruitment: Innovated strategies to accelerate **recruitment** and increase enrollment across all major academic disciplines.

Residential Life: Created a **residential life** program that rewarded students for peer counseling, student advisement, and tutorial assistance.

Scholastic Standards: Enhanced **scholastic standards**, enabling the college to compete with area universities.

Seminar Management: Directed staff responsible for **seminar management** at off-campus sites throughout the state of Michigan.

Student-Faculty Relations: Restored **student-faculty relations** following student unrest.

Student Retention: Increased **student retention** by 28% despite the addition of two new colleges within the local area.

Student Services: Expanded **student services** to include a monthly guest speakers program, biannual competitive sporting events, and one-on-one peer counseling.

Textbook Review: Led committee responsible for **textbook review**, selection, and acquisition.

Training and Development: Established Motorola's in-house **training and development** center for hourly, staff, professional, technical, supervisory, and executive personnel.

KeyWord Answers to Interview Questions

Tell me about yourself.

"I'm your typical **elementary school teacher** with a most atypical approach to **classroom management, curriculum development, student learning**, and, most importantly, **learner retention**. I pride myself on my ability to design innovative **educational programs** that spark my **students' interest** and encourage them to experience the world. What's more, I am active throughout the **school community**, working with the **PTSA**, the **media resources** committee, the annual **fundraising campaign**, and the **textbook review** committee. In addition, I coordinate **special events** programs, guest speakers, and field trips for the entire **elementary school.**"

What is the most valuable skill you bring to our company?

"My most valuable skill is my love for my children. Shouldn't that be at the heart of every teacher? I find tremendous personal and professional satisfaction in watching my children learn. It is this commitment to my students, along with my outstanding **teaching** skills that will make me a valuable and immediate contributor to your school's **community, students, teachers,** and **administrators.**"

What do you consider to be your most significant achievement or contribution?

"Nurturing **parental involvement** in the **classroom** is what I consider to be my most notable contribution. When I first came to Rodgers Elementary, there were no parents in my third-grade **classroom** who ever spent any time at school. So, I launched a plan to encourage my parents to participate in whatever way possible. Today I have, at minimum, two **parent volunteers** in the **classroom** each day, another group working on the end-of-year celebration, two parents that write and distribute a monthly **classroom newsletter**, and many other volunteers. It's created a truly **positive learning environment** for each and every one of my **students.**"

LYNN R. REYNOLDS, M.Ed., MBA
2110 Dover Dell Road
Reston, Virginia 24503

Phone: 804-388-9090   lynnreynolds@hotmail.com

February 8, 2003

Dr. Edward Louis, Director
Lincoln School
PO Box 2673
Rabi Bhawan
Kathmandu, Nepal

Dear Dr. Louis:

As per our previous email, let me again reiterate that I am quite interested in a teaching opportunity with the Lincoln School in Kathmandu, and have attached my resume (Word file) for your review.

The value and strength in performance that I bring to your school community includes:

- Success teaching across a broad range of learner abilities, customizing each program, course, and curriculum to the individual abilities of each student.

- A unique ability to build camaraderie between students, faculty, administrators, parents, and support personnel. It energizes me to work in an environment where spirit is strong, communication is open, and everyone is committed to success.

- A true, heartfelt commitment to student success, as evidenced not only in my teaching ability, but my active involvement in coaching youth sports and athletic programs.

- An extensive background in special events planning, logistics, public relations, and promotions.

When I read about your philosophy of the "optimal match" on your website, I was quite impressed. In fact, the entire educational concept of the Lincoln School is precisely the foundation upon which my career has flourished. We must nurture each student to academic and personal success. It is the commitment we have made as educators, coaches, and administrators.

I look forward to the opportunity to continue our discussions and thank you for your attention, support, and concern.

Sincerely,

Lynn R. Reynolds

Lynn R. Reynolds

Attachment

MARY B. WASHINGTON
152 Red House Drive
Summerville, South Carolina 28998
(816) 358-1324

EDUCATION SERVICES & PROGRAM ADMINISTRATOR

Talented Administrator with eight years of cross-functional experience in:

- Strategic Planning and Leadership
- Educational Programming and Services
- Teacher Training and Education
- Committee Leadership and Team Building
- Budgeting and Expense Control
- Curriculum Design and Development
- Student Placement and Advisement
- Community and Special Events

Excellent planning, analytical, and organizational skills. Effective project leader able to facilitate cooperation among administrators, faculty, students, and the community. MBA Degree.

PROFESSIONAL EXPERIENCE:

Coordinator of Curriculum & Instruction / Lead Instructor - Accounting   1990 to Present
BUSINESS & TECHNICAL INSTITUTE, Charleston, South Carolina

Senior Administrative Manager with this state/federally funded training center with 500+ students. Scope of management responsibility is diverse and includes strategic planning, budgeting, curriculum development, instruction, advisory affairs, faculty/staff development, accreditation, and operations management. Assist Vice President of Instruction in directing a staff of three administrative personnel with full management oversight for 30+ full-time professors and adjunct faculty.

Curriculum Innovation

- Developed certificate of completion program for specific courses to provide students with immediate employment credentials while completing long-term coursework.
- Evaluated current curriculum to expand course offerings and effectively prepare students for professional employment in business, professional, and technical fields.
- Led program development, textbook selection, instruction, and student evaluation for the Accounting Department, and all related courses and certification programs.

Staff Development & Instruction

- Managed the recruitment, selection, and training of nine new faculty members.
- Led a series of workshops, seminars, and continuing education programs for all faculty.
- Conducted periodic reviews of instructors to evaluate workload, teaching methods, student interaction, and overall performance. Coordinated workload scheduling for all faculty.

Articulation & Community Affairs

- Appointed representative for the Institute to promote programs and services, including participation in Career Day activities at high schools throughout the region. Achieved measurable increases in enrollment and community awareness.
- Launched innovative articulation program with several area high schools in a joint effort to provide technical training at the high school level.

MARY B. WASHINGTON – *Page Two*

Accreditation & Regulatory Compliance

- Led workshops for instructors and orchestrated the research, documentation, and presentation of materials for accreditation through the Council on Occupational Education.
- Implemented Institutional Effectiveness System (IES) into all core instructional programs to streamline planning, evaluation, and budgeting processes.
- Reviewed curriculum and programs to ensure compliance with state mandates. Facilitated integration and communication of changes/enhancements into existing programs.

Administration & Operations Management

- Designed, developed, and implemented improved business processes to streamline operations and reduce overhead costs.
- Assisted departments in the preparation and submission of annual operating budgets.
- Approved purchase requisitions for materials, equipment, and personnel.

COLLEGE OF CHARLESTON, Charleston, South Carolina   1989

Instructor - Business

Established program guidelines and taught a broad range of accounting and general business courses. Played a key role in expanding enrollment through personal commitment to curriculum development and quality instruction.

EARLY CORPORATE EXPERIENCE:

Advanced through increasingly responsible accounting, loan processing, and auditing positions. Gained extensive experience in general accounting, credit management, internal controls, regulatory compliance, executive presentations, and staff management. Career progression:

Senior Credit Auditor	**BANK SOUTH CORPORATION**	1984 to 1988
Supervisory Loan Specialist	**SMALL BUSINESS ADMINISTRATION**	1982 to 1984

EDUCATION:

MBA (Finance), Georgia State University, 1984
BA (German), Wake Forest University, 1982

Continuing Professional Education:
Completed more than 90 hours of professional education and training on subjects including Youth Apprenticeship, Distance Learning, Workkeys in Action and Computer Technology. Participated in several state and local Tech Prep conferences.

PROFESSIONAL AFFILIATIONS:

Board of Directors (Past), Habitat for Humanity
Board of Directors (Past), First United Methodist Church Pre-Kindergarten Program
Professional Member & Past Advisor, Phi Beta Lambda

24

Transportation, Warehousing, and Distribution

Sample Job Titles

Director of Dispatch Operations
Director of Distribution
Director of Logistics
Director of Operations
Director of Operations Support
Director of Transportation
Dispatch Manager
Distribution Manager
Driver
Export Manager
Fleet Administrator
General Manager
Import and Export Manager
Import Manager
Logistics Manager
Operations Manager
Operations Supervisor

Scheduler
Shipping Dock Worker
Terminal Manager
Terminal Operations Manager
Traffic Analyst
Transportation Manager
Vice President of Distribution
Vice President of Logistics
Vice President of Operations
Vice President of Transportation
Warehouse Manager
Warehouseman

KeyWords and KeyWord Phrases

Agency Operations: Transitioned from company-owned to **agency operations** at all major ports throughout North America, reducing net operating expenses by more than $15 million annually.

Asset Management: Directed **asset management** and allocation of more than $60 million in equipment.

Cargo Handling: Designed improved **cargo handling** procedures, reducing workers' compensation costs by 22% annually.

Carrier Management: Outsourced all transportation functions and designed operations for new **carrier management** program.

Common Carrier: Contracted with **common carrier** for the movement of freight from manufacturing to warehousing centers nationwide.

Container Transportation: Designed **container transportation** programs to optimize space utilization and provide small shippers with economical rates for international freight forwarding.

Contract Transportation Services: Replaced in-house freight management system with **contract transportation services**, significantly increasing customer satisfaction and retention while reducing costs approximately 10%.

Customer Delivery Operations: Revitalized **customer delivery operations** with a focus on staff training in customer service and communication skills.

Dedicated Logistics Operations: Recruited to Ryder's **dedicated logistics operations** to integrate traffic, dispatch, warehousing, shipping, and customer management operations.

Dispatch Operations: Consolidated **dispatch operations** for four centers into one facility, reduced staff 64%, and improved on-time delivery to a consistent 99%.

Distribution Management: Planned and directed **distribution management** across multiple channels throughout North America and Western Europe.

Driver Leasing: Introduced **driver leasing**, driver training, and equipment rental programs to expand market research and meet changing customer demands.

Equipment Control: Implemented **equipment control** processes and reduced damage costs by more than $2 million annually.

Export Operations: Senior Logistics Executive with full P&L, operating, staffing, and budgeting responsibility for all **export operations** to the Far East.

Facilities Management: Revitalized **facilities management** programs, reduced costs, improved staff competencies, and enhanced reliability of building management systems.

Fleet Management: Directed **fleet management** and fleet service for 2,000 company-owned vehicles.

Freight Consolidation: Established new **freight consolidation** center at the Port of Baltimore.

Freight Forwarding: Managed a 200-person **freight forwarding** operation managing freight movement for W.R. Grace, AlliedSignal, and Sears.

Import Operations: Assessed the profitability of existing **import operations**, eliminated non-profitable business lines, and transitioned organization from loss to sustained profitability.

Inbound Transportation: Built an $8 million facility to manage **inbound transportation** and freight forwarding.

Intermodal Transportation Network: Established an **intermodal transportation network** integrating rail, sea, air, and truck to service customers worldwide.

Line Management: Directed **line management** throughout the Far Eastern Maritime Service.

Load Analysis: Computerized **load analysis** and planning functions for all shipping operations.

Logistics Management: Senior Operating Executive with full P&L responsibility for a dedicated and fully integrated **logistics management** organization with 22 sites nationwide.

Maritime Operations: Launched a start-up venture servicing **maritime operations** worldwide with on-site stevedoring at ports in 62 countries.

Outbound Transportation: Assembled all commodities into a centralized **outbound transportation** center to reduce domestic and international freight forwarding and traffic costs.

Over-The-Road Transportation: Transitioned from **over-the-road transportation** to rail transportation to expedite customer delivery.

Port Operations: Directed staffing, budgeting, planning, asset management, and transportation planning for **port operations** in New York, Boston, Atlanta, and Miami.

Regulatory Compliance: Achieved/surpassed all **regulatory compliance** standards for both OSHA and DOT.

Route Management: Reconfigured **route management** programs to optimize personnel and equipment resources.

Route Planning/Analysis: Automated **route planning/analysis** functions, improved costing, and upgraded customer service.

Safety Management: Identified need and developed a six-part **safety management** and training program for all newly hired personnel.

Safety Training: Revitalized **safety training** program and reduced on-site work accidents by 89%.

Terminal Operations: Restructured high-volume **terminal operations** at the Port of Wilmington, reducing costs 20% and improving customer satisfaction ratings by 88%.

Traffic Management: Designed improved processes and systems to enhance **traffic management**, reduce reliance on paper documentation, and achieve all budgeted operating goals.

Traffic Planning: Introduced GPS and other technologies to improve **traffic planning** and routing capabilities.

Transportation Management: Redesigned Xerox's **transportation management** programs and saved the corporation over $10 million in annual traffic, warehousing, and distribution costs.

Transportation Planning: Directed **transportation planning** for all Caterpillar dealers and distributors nationwide.

Warehouse Management: Directed **warehouse management** operations for six facilities in the Northwestern U.S. distributing products throughout 16 states.

Workflow Optimization: Created performance-driven systems designed for **workflow optimization**, staff training, quality improvement, and cost reduction.

KeyWord Answers to Interview Questions

Tell me about yourself.

"Let's start with yesterday. I had 42 **truckloads** of merchandise delivered to my **warehouse** over a six-hour period, two supervisors who called in sick, a broken forklift, and **delivery drivers** who managed to get lost at least 20 times in one day. Well, before I left the **distribution facility** last night, all the merchandise had been **unloaded, barcoded,** and **warehoused.** Just another typical day at the Ryder distribution center! As a **dedicated logistics operator,** our **facility** is responsible for the **receipt** and subsequent **distribution** of over $100 million merchandise each year for Sears, Wal-

Mart, and Target. With a **workforce** of 58 and an annual **operating budget** of $2.8 million, I manage one of Ryder's largest and most profitable **distribution centers**. Combine that experience with my previous 12 years with Sears and you've found a candidate who can profitably and efficiently manage your **warehousing, distribution**, and **logistics operations**."

What is the most valuable skill you bring to our company?

"My **planning** and **organizational skills** are what allow me to perform so well within such chaotic environments. Whenever you're handling so much **cargo** with such a **quick turnaround**, there are bound to be problems that arise each day. I can minimize those problems through efficient **planning** and **scheduling**, and then manage those that do arise quickly and with minimum effort or further disruption."

What do you consider to be your most significant achievement or contribution?

"When I joined Ryder in 1998, the facility I was assigned to was overwhelmed with customer complaints. My first challenge was to fix the problems and be sure that we were able to retain our **key customers**. I started a **customer service improvement** initiative that impacted virtually every employee in the company, personally called on each **customer account**, and quickly diagnosed and eliminated a huge number of the problems. Over the next six months, we cleaned house and completely redesigned all **customer service processes** and **customer contact points**. Today, we provide the **quality standards for customer care** by which other Ryder facilities operate."

CHARLES T. MONROE, JR.

104 Maple Drive
Baltimore, Maryland 22412
(410) 949-0987
ctmjr@columbia.net

November 4, 2003

Claude R. Johnson
Vice President - Operations
Millview, Inc.
1644 Edmonds Street
Minneapolis, MN 55347

Dear Mr. Johnson:

For the past nine years, I have planned, staffed, and directed large-scale, fully integrated logistics, warehousing, distribution, and transportation operations for Ryder Dedicated Logistics throughout North America. The focus of my career has been divided between start-up operations and the aggressive turnaround/ repositioning of existing operations. To each, I have delivered strong and sustainable financial results:

- Built three independent logistics operations for one major customer, from start-up to over $5.5 million in annual revenues to Ryder.

- Led the successful and profitable turnaround of the Challenge Systems logistics operations, implemented training and productivity improvement programs, restored customer credibility, and improved financial performance.

Currently, I am orchestrating a complete revitalization of Ryder's operations in Baltimore, an organization fraught with customer dissatisfaction and poor financial performance. In less than nine months, my team and I have re-captured key accounts, improved revenues, and reduced operating costs. The organization is now positioned for strong growth and expansion.

Although my years with Ryder have been a wonderful experience, I am now ready to pursue new professional challenges. Thus my interest in interviewing as Millview's Director of Logistics. As requested, my salary has averaged $95,000 to $125,000 over the past five years.

Sincerely,

Charles T. Monroe

Charles T. Monroe, Jr.

Enclosure

LARRY P. DAWSON
65421 North Post Road
Virginia Beach, VA 23541
(757) 654-8971

PROFESSIONAL QUALIFICATIONS: TRAFFIC/TRANSPORTATION MANAGEMENT

Distinguished professional career directing the transportation of air and surface freight, personal property, parcels, and hazardous materials worldwide. Equally extensive experience in rates and tariffs, multimodal freight, and commercial airline load requirements.

Strong planning, organizational, logistics, TQM, human resources, training/ development, budgeting, facilities, technology management, and fleet management qualifications. Effective leader, decision-maker, and operations manager.

PROFESSIONAL EXPERIENCE:

TRAFFIC/TRANSPORTATION MANAGEMENT SPECIALIST   1987 to 2002

Fast-track promotion through several increasingly responsible positions in traffic/ transportation management with the U.S. Navy. Rank at discharge – Lieutenant Commander. Career highlights included:

Superintendent - Air/Sea Delivery Service (1993 to 2002)

Senior Operations Manager with direct responsibility for the strategic planning, staffing, budgeting, logistics, equipment resources, and daily operations of the air/sea delivery operation based in Japan. Scope of responsibility included the efficient transport of personnel, materials, equipment, supplies, and commodities throughout the Pacific Rim. Directed a staff of 182 personnel and administered a $750,000 annual operating budget.

Established policies and procedures to support transportation operations, developed/implemented safety training and support programs, and directly managed facilities and facility upgrades. Determined current and long-range equipment and technology requirements to support transportation operations.

Achievements:

- Directed the design and completion of a $200,000 facility construction project which now serves as the model for U.S. Navy operations worldwide.

- Resolved long-standing staffing issues through redesign of critical support positions and brought staffing from 60% to 100% to meet operational requirements.

- Reduced cargo processing delays by 75% through design and implementation of improved handling, staffing, and documentation procedures.

LARRY P. DAWSON – Page Two

Superintendent - Air Freight Operations (1987 to 1992)

Promoted through a series of increasingly responsible air freight operations management positions in the U.S., Korea, and Philippines. Served as Superintendent of Air Freight Operations, Air Terminal Manager, Passenger Services Manager, and Aircraft Warehouse Manager. Personally directed over 65% of the nation's strategic air/sea operations and moved the largest volume of cargo in the Department of the Navy.

Held significant decision-making responsibility for personnel, equipment, logistics, facilities, budgets, and operations planning/improvement. Trained/supervised up to 65 military and 30 civilian personnel. Controlled $8 million in fleet and technical resources for the movement of more than 45,000 tons of cargo and mail. Managed 66,000 square feet of warehousing, transportation, and support facilities. Demonstrated superior planning and organization skills.

Achievements:

- Improved aircraft/fleet departure reliability rates by 100% (unprecedented in such a large and diverse operation).

- Led a series of facility improvement projects, several of which now serve as flagships for other transportation operations worldwide.

- Designed and directed implementation of computerized transportation operational support and training programs (e.g., planning, staffing, documentation, analysis). Led to measurable improvements in operational efficiency, reliability, and quality while consistently reducing errors and time required for specific tasks.

- Planned and successfully managed massive freight operations initiated in response to crisis situations (e.g., Operations Desert Shield/Storm, Philippine earthquake).

EDUCATION:

B.A. in Transportation Management, 1987
OLD DOMINION UNIVERSITY, Norfolk, Virginia

Highlights of Continuing Professional Education:

- Air/Sea Transportation Management
- Operational Support
- Officer Candidate School

25

Winning Words That Give Your Resume Power, Punch, and Pizzazz

REVIEW THE FOLLOWING LISTS of Action Verbs, High-Impact Phrases, and Personality Descriptors, select those that accurately reflect you and your experience, and then integrate them into the text of your resume and cover letters.

Action Verbs

Accelerate	Assemble	Coach
Accomplish	Assess	Collect
Achieve	Assist	Command
Acquire	Author	Communicate
Adapt	Authorize	Compare
Address	Brief	Compel
Advance	Budget	Compile
Advise	Build	Complete
Advocate	Calculate	Compute
Analyze	Capture	Conceive
Apply	Catalog	Conclude
Appoint	Champion	Conduct
Arbitrate	Chart	Conserve
Architect	Clarify	Consolidate
Arrange	Classify	Construct
Ascertain	Close	Consult

Continue	Enforce	Initiate
Contract	Engineer	Innovate
Convert	Enhance	Inspect
Coordinate	Enlist	Inspire
Correct	Ensure	Install
Counsel	Establish	Institute
Craft	Estimate	Instruct
Create	Evaluate	Integrate
Critique	Examine	Intensify
Decrease	Exceed	Interpret
Define	Execute	Interview
Delegate	Exhibit	Introduce
Deliver	Expand	Invent
Demonstrate	Expedite	Inventory
Deploy	Experiment	Investigate
Design	Export	Judge
Detail	Facilitate	Justify
Detect	Finalize	Launch
Determine	Finance	Lead
Develop	Forge	Lecture
Devise	Form	License
Direct	Formalize	Listen
Discover	Formulate	Locate
Dispense	Found	Maintain
Display	Generate	Manage
Distribute	Govern	Manipulate
Diversify	Graduate	Manufacture
Divert	Guide	Map
Document	Halt	Market
Double	Head	Mastermind
Draft	Hire	Measure
Drive	Honor	Mediate
Earn	Hypothesize	Mentor
Edit	Identify	Model
Educate	Illustrate	Modify
Effect	Imagine	Monitor
Elect	Implement	Motivate
Eliminate	Import	Navigate
Emphasize	Improve	Negotiate
Enact	Improvise	Nominate
Encourage	Increase	Normalize
Endure	Influence	Observe
Energize	Inform	Obtain

Offer	Realign	Solidify
Officiate	Rebuild	Solve
Operate	Recapture	Speak
Orchestrate	Receive	Specify
Organize	Recognize	Standardize
Orient	Recommend	Stimulate
Originate	Reconcile	Streamline
Outsource	Record	Structure
Overcome	Recruit	Succeed
Oversee	Redesign	Suggest
Participate	Reduce	Summarize
Perceive	Reengineer	Supervise
Perfect	Regain	Supply
Perform	Regulate	Support
Persuade	Rehabilitate	Surpass
Pilot	Reinforce	Synthesize
Pinpoint	Rejuvenate	Systematize
Pioneer	Render	Tabulate
Plan	Renegotiate	Target
Position	Reorganize	Teach
Predict	Report	Terminate
Prepare	Reposition	Test
Prescribe	Represent	Thwart
Present	Research	Train
Preside	Resolve	Transcribe
Process	Respond	Transfer
Procure	Restore	Transform
Program	Restructure	Transition
Progress	Retrieve	Translate
Project	Review	Troubleshoot
Project manage	Revise	Unify
Promote	Revitalize	Unite
Propose	Satisfy	Update
Prospect	Schedule	Upgrade
Provide	Secure	Use
Publicize	Select	Utilize
Purchase	Separate	Verbalize
Qualify	Serve	Verify
Question	Simplify	Win
Rate	Sold	Write

High-Impact Phrases

Accelerated Career Track
Accelerating Revenue Growth
Aggressive Turnaround Leadership
Benchmarking
Best In Class
Business Process Redesign
Business Process Reengineering
Capturing Cost Reductions
Catalyst for Change
Change Agent
Change Management
Competitive Market Positioning
Competitive Wins
Competitively Positioning Products & Technologies
Contemporary Management Style
Core Competencies
Creative Business Leader
Creative Problem Solver
Cross-Culturally Sensitive
Cross-Functional Expertise
Cross-Functional Team Leadership
Decisive Management Style
Delivering Strong and Sustainable Gains
Direct & Decisive Organizational Leadership
Distinguished Performance
Driving Customer Loyalty Initiatives
Driving Innovation
Driving Performance Improvement
Driving Productivity Gains
Emerging Business Ventures
Emerging International Markets
Entrepreneurial Drive
Entrepreneurial Leadership
Entrepreneurial Vision
Executive Leadership
Executive Liaison
Fast-Track Promotion
Global Market Dominance
High-Caliber
High-Growth

High-Impact
High-Performance
High-Quality
Matrix Management
Multi-Discipline Industry Expertise
Organizational Driver
Organizational Leader
Outperforming Global Competition
Outperforming Market Competition
PC Proficient
Peak Performer
Performance Improvement
Performance Management
Performance Reengineering
Pioneering Technologies
Proactive Business Leader
Proactive Manager
Process Redesign
Process Reengineering
Productivity Improvement
Self-Starter
Start-Up, Turnaround, & High-Growth Organizations
Strategic & Tactical Operations
Strong & Sustainable Financial Gains
Strong & Sustainable Performance Gains
Strong & Sustainable Productivity Gains
Strong & Sustainable Profit Gains
Strong & Sustainable Quality Gains
Strong & Sustainable Technology Gains
Team Building
Team Leadership
Technologically Advanced Organization
Technologically Sophisticated Operations
Top Flight Leadership Competencies
Top Tier Executive
Visionary Leadership
World Class Leadership
World Class Operations
World Class Organization

Personality Descriptors

Abstract	Eager	Insightful
Accurate	Earnest	Intelligent
Action-Driven	Effective	Intense
Adaptable	Efficient	Intuitive
Adventurous	Eloquent	Judicious
Aggressive	Employee-Driven	Keen
Amenable	Empowered	Leader
Analytical	Encouraging	Loyal
Artful	Energetic	Managerial
Assertive	Energized	Market-Driven
Believable	Enterprising	Masterful
Bilingual	Enthusiastic	Mature
Bold	Entrepreneurial	Mechanical
Brave	Ethical	Methodical
Communicative	Experienced	Modern
Competent	Expert	Moral
Competitive	Expressive	Motivated
Conceptual	Forward-Thinking	Motivational
Confident	Global	Multilingual
Conscientious	Hardworking	Notable
Conservative	Healthy	Noteworthy
Cooperative	Helpful	Objective
Courageous	Heroic	Observant
Creative	High-Impact	Opportunistic
Credible	High-Potential	Oratorical
Cross-Cultural	Honest	Orderly
Culturally	Honorable	Organized
Customer-Driven	Humanistic	Outstanding
Dauntless	Humanitarian	Participative
Decisive	Humorous	Participatory
Dedicated	Immediate	Peerless
Dependable	Impactful	Perfectionist
Determined	Important	Performance-
Devoted	Impressive	Driven
Diligent	Incomparable	Persevering
Diplomatic	Independent	Persistent
Direct	Individualistic	Personable
Dramatic	Industrious	Persuasive
Driven	Ingenious	Philosophical
Dynamic	Innovative	Photogenic

Pioneering
Poised
Polished
Popular
Positive
Practical
Pragmatic
Precise
Preeminent
Prepared
Proactive
Problem Solver
Productive
Professional
Proficient
Progressive
Prominent
Prudent
Punctual
Quality-Driven
Reactive
Reliable
Reputable
Resilient
Resourceful
Results-Driven

Results-Oriented
Savvy
Sensitive
Sharp
Skilled
Skillful
Sophisticated
Spirited
Strategic
Strong
Subjective
Successful
Tactful
Talented
Teacher
Team Builder
Team Leader
Team Player
Technical
Tenacious
Thorough
Tolerant
Top Performer
Top Producer
Traditional
Trainer

Trilingual
Trouble Shooter
Trustworthy
Truthful
Unrelenting
Understanding
Upbeat
Valiant
Valuable
Venturesome
Veracious
Verbal
Victorious
Vigorous
Virtuous
Visionary
Vital
Vivacious
Well-Balanced
Well-Versed
Winning
Wise
Worldly
Youthful
Zealous
Zestful

Career Resources

THE FOLLOWING CAREER RESOURCES are available directly from Impact Publications. Full descriptions of each title as well as nine downloadable catalogs, videos, and software can be found on our website: www.impactpublications.com. Complete the following form or list the titles, include shipping (see formula at the end), enclose payment, and send your order to:

IMPACT PUBLICATIONS
9104 Manassas Drive, Suite N
Manassas Park, VA 20111-5211 USA
1-800-361-1055 (orders only)
Tel. 703-361-7300 or Fax 703-335-9486
Email address: info@impactpublications.com
Quick & easy online ordering: www.impactpublications.com

Orders from individuals must be prepaid by check, money order, or major credit card. We accept telephone, fax, and email orders.

Qty.	TITLES	Price	TOTAL

Books by Wendy S. Enelow

Qty.	TITLES	Price	TOTAL
_____	101 Ways to Recession-Proof Your Career	$14.95	_____
_____	Best KeyWords for Resumes, Cover Letters, Interview	$17.95	_____
_____	Best Cover Letters for $100,000+ Jobs	$24.95	_____
_____	Best Resumes and CVs for International Jobs	$24.95	_____
_____	Best Resumes for $100,000+ Jobs	$24.95	_____
_____	Best Resumes for People Without a Four-Year Degree	$19.95	_____
_____	Cover Letter Magic	$16.95	_____
_____	Expert Resumes for Computer and Web Jobs	$16.95	_____
_____	Expert Resumes for Managers and Executives	$16.95	_____
_____	Expert Resumes for Manufacturing Careers	$16.95	_____
_____	Expert Resumes for People Returning to Work	$16.95	_____
_____	Expert Resumes for Teachers and Educators	$16.95	_____
_____	Winning Interviews for $100,000+ Jobs	$17.95	_____

259

Interviews and Salary Negotiations

_____	101 Dynamite Questions to Ask At Your Job Interview	13.95 _____
_____	Dynamite Salary Negotiations	15.95 _____
_____	Haldane's Best Answers to Tough Interview Questions	15.95 _____
_____	Haldane's Best Salary Tips for Professionals	15.95 _____
_____	Interview for Success (8th Edition)	15.95 _____
_____	Job Interviews for Dummies	16.99 _____
_____	Nail the Job Interview!	13.95 _____
_____	The Savvy Interviewer	10.95 _____

Testing and Assessment

_____	Discover the Best Jobs for You	15.95 _____
_____	Discover What You're Best At	14.00 _____
_____	Do What You Are	18.95 _____
_____	What's Your Type of Career?	17.95 _____

Career Exploration and Job Strategies

_____	50 Cutting Edge Jobs	15.95 _____
_____	95 Mistakes Job Seekers Make & How to Avoid Them	13.95 _____
_____	100 Great Jobs and How to Get Them	17.95 _____
_____	America's Top Jobs for People Without a 4-Year Degree	15.95 _____
_____	Best Jobs for the 21st Century	19.95 _____
_____	Change Your Job, Change Your Life (8th Edition)	17.95 _____
_____	The Job Hunting Guide: College to Career	14.95 _____
_____	No One Will Hire Me!	13.95 _____
_____	Quit Your Job and Grow Some Hair	15.95 _____
_____	Rites of Passage at $100,000 to $1 Million+	29.95 _____
_____	What Color Is Your Parachute?	17.95 _____

Internet Job Search

_____	America's Top Internet Job Sites	19.95 _____
_____	CareerXroads (annual)	26.95 _____
_____	Directory of Websites for International Jobs	19.95 _____
_____	Haldane's Best Employment Websites for Professionals	15.95 _____
_____	Job Search Online for Dummies (with CD-ROM)	24.99 _____

Resumes and Letters

_____	101 Best Cover Letters	11.95 _____
_____	101 Best Resumes	12.95 _____
_____	101 Great Tips for a Dynamite Resume	13.95 _____
_____	201 Dynamite Job Search Letters	19.95 _____
_____	Cover Letter Magic	16.95 _____
_____	Cover Letters for Dummies	16.99 _____
_____	Damn Good Resume Guide	9.95 _____
_____	Dynamite Cover Letters	14.95 _____
_____	Dynamite Resumes	14.95 _____
_____	e-Resumes	11.95 _____
_____	Haldane's Best Cover Letters for Professionals	15.95 _____
_____	Haldane's Best Resumes for Professionals	15.95 _____
_____	High Impact Resumes and Letters (8th Edition)	19.95 _____
_____	Military Resumes and Cover Letters	19.95 _____

___	Resume Shortcuts	14.95	___
___	Resumes for Dummies	16.99	___
___	Resumes in Cyberspace	14.95	___
___	The Savvy Resume Writer	12.95	___
___	Sure-Hire Resumes	14.95	___

Networking

___	A Foot in the Door	14.95	___
___	How to Work a Room	14.00	___
___	Masters of Networking	16.95	___
___	The Savvy Networker	13.95	___

Dress, Image, and Etiquette

___	Dressing Smart for Men	14.95	___
___	Dressing Smart for Women	14.95	___
___	Power Etiquette	15.95	___

SUBTOTAL ___

Virginia residents add 4½% sales tax ___

POSTAGE/HANDLING ($5 for first
product and 8% of SUBTOTAL) $5.00

8% of SUBTOTAL -- ___

TOTAL ENCLOSED --------------------------- ___

SHIP TO:

NAME _____

ADDRESS _____

_____

_____

PAYMENT METHOD:

❑ I enclose check/money order for $ _____ made payable to
IMPACT PUBLICATIONS.

❑ Please charge $ _____ to my credit card:
❑ Visa   ❑ MasterCard   ❑ American Express   ❑ Discover

Card # _____ Expiration date: ___ / ___

Signature _____